Praise for "waiti

A message from Lisa

I started writing this memoir about the first ten years of my daughter's life mainly for my other children to have a piece of our family history readily at their fingertips. So, no, this wasn't *initially* intended for you. Ha! But after my first round of test readers, the response was overwhelming to say the least and I decided to publish this really private, super raw, kinda crazy book. Here is what some of them had to say:

"...ripped my heart out. Then kissed it, hugged it, and put it back filled with hope and appreciation and understanding and love. Your story is beautifully told and with two of my favorite attributes, brutal honesty and humor."

"Through your Isla my heart has changed in more ways than I ever thought possible and I have run through emotions in such a sequence I never knew was possible. This story is one that is so special and should be shared with the world."

"Isla has so much to teach us... not us always teaching her."

"I hope you decide to publish this story one day. I can only imagine how influential it will be to so many educators, mothers, therapists, and anyone who wishes to have their eyes opened to the mystery that is Isla."

"It is a story about love, faith, family and community and the power of one little girl to bring all those things together in a way that makes everyone better than they were before they knew her."

"This is so helpful for professionals/therapists as preparation for parents that are proactive and advocate for their children. It is a needed reminder to not take it personal when they meet or have to work with that "crazy" mom/dad. A parent's love for their child is not something that can be learned through a clinical text book."

"I will never look at or conduct ARD meetings the same again."

"I absolutely without a doubt loved every precious word in this book. I laughed, I cried, and I stopped to pray several times while reading. It was a blessing to me as a principal and a mother. Your honesty and sincerity is clear and refreshing. It is a book, that if published, I would have all my staff members read."

"Though it may seem that this story would be tailored to a parent with a daughter/son with unique needs, the message is universal. Every person placed on this earth has their own norm, and we all battle to be able to ensure those we love are successful. But, success is subjective."

"What you have done is opened the eyes of many parents, teachers, and doctors...I really hope you would think about making a movie about this for all those who prefer movie to books. You were meant to help children. Isla is the reason you should.

"It was eye opening... the energy that's needed by parents and all those involved with special needs children. A great read!"

"...it is the simplest, most insightful, and real look into what so many parents are going through. I love that you were candid about what was really going on in your mind through all of it. I want EVERYONE to read it! I laughed, I cried, I reflected and finally when I was done, I looked down at my babies and thanked God for them, imperfections and all."

"Thank you for being ballsy and allowing us to have insight on what truly happens. The full picture. It's not easy allowing others to see your "crazy side" or your "flaws", which I am learning is not crazy or flaws but just part of being a mother. To allow others to know things you are not proud of is what makes this so amazing and anyone who reads it will change the way they judge and assume... basically I am trying to say I ABSOLUTELY LOVED IT!"

My first ever book review from the most BIASED heart.

A letter from my dad:

My author,

You're a great mom. "Waiting for the Light Bulb" really impressed and touched me. It is overall very well written, funny, emotional, entertaining. You have a great command of the English language...I especially loved the ending of chapter nine.

Isla's story is our story but I can't help but feel that I could have done more to help you. Many of the incidents in the book I was aware of but really didn't know the depth of what you were going through. Just like you, I want to always be there for my children. Your story outlines how difficult it has been for you and it hurts knowing you had to walk those steps.

God has a plan and knew Isla needed you but it is obvious His plan is much bigger. Isla's story and her incredible mom will touch thousands of lives and truly help many people have a rich life with their special children.

I am very proud of you and honored to be called your father. I love you just as much as you love our precious little Isla.

Dad

waiting for the light bulb

the ramblings of a crazy, gritty mom

Dr. Lisa Peña

I have tried to recreate events, locales and conversations from my memories of them. In order to maintain their anonymity in some instances I have changed the names of individuals and places, I may have changed some identifying characteristics and details such as physical properties, occupations and places of residence.

This book is not intended as a substitute for the medical advice of physicians. The reader should regularly consult a physician in matters relating to his/her health and particularly with respect to any symptoms that may require diagnosis or medical attention.

ISBN 978-1-7901-1178-7

This book is dedicated to my daughter, June Olive, and my son, Greg Major. The idea of putting all that you are about to read in black and white was daunting. My motivation in every vulnerable word, honest sentence, and raw page was to give you a lasting piece of our family history. This book may be mainly about Isla, but it was written with only you in mind. I know that the life that lies before you may be different than most, but maybe as I share my heart and as you read how the story unfolds, you will understand why you have the kind of mom and sister that you do.

May you always live your life as though everything is a miracle.

I love you no matter what.

Mom

There is danger in a single story of anything or anyone.

Contents

Introduction

Hubby: "Hey babe, how did it go today?"

Wifey: "Eh, it was OK. She peed again."

Hubby: "Was it behavior again, or she just didn't make it in time?"

Wifey: "No, it was behavior. The therapist said she got frustrated during discrete trials, so she took off her clothes and peed on them."

Hubby: "Sorry."

Wifey: "It's OK. Hey, I'm gonna do a load of wash right now. Do you need me to throw anything of yours in there too?"

When the conversation above is completely normal and routine, when it causes no questions or alarm, no sadness or thought, that's how you know. That's how you know you are not a rookie anymore. That's how you know you are a bona fide, experienced parent of a special needs child.

Oh, and if you already know what discrete trials are, then you are way ahead of the game.

Chapter One: 0-1 year
Miss Love

Hubby: "Let's just build a big box. Just one open space with no walls."

Wifey: "You're crazy. What do you mean no walls? Not for bedrooms or bathrooms?"

Hubby: "Nah, we'll just keep it open. It would be cool."

It was a sunny Sunday in late December somewhere deep in the heart of Texas. Greg and I were making the ten-hour drive to our hometown. The same drive we'd been making ten to twelve times a year for the last four years.

We were high school sweethearts—the ultimate cliché. We'd been in love and together since we were sixteen years old, back when I was the nerdy valedictorian with coke-bottle glasses, and Greg was Mr. Popular, an athletic jock who also happened to be the class clown. During college, we floated around a bit, spending some semesters apart at different universities and others together at the same university.

After undergrad, I was accepted into the Doctorate of Pharmacy program at Texas Tech Health Sciences Center School of Pharmacy. Greg and I decided to make the move together, which meant a big move from our home in the Rio Grande Valley to Amarillo, Texas.

Literally one tip of Texas to the other. We got married after my first year of pharmacy school and Greg started his professional career as a coach and special education teacher.

But still, we headed back to the Valley frequently to visit family, and each time we traveled home and back we had plenty of time to "plan" our life. We planned houses, guest houses, pool houses, and beach houses. We planned our children and named them all. We planned our dream jobs, beach trips, vacations, and retirement. You name it, we planned it.

This particular ten-hour drive took place after my last Christmas break as a pharmacy student, when graduation was just one semester away. My parents and my two brothers were traveling close behind us with plans to join us in Angel Fire, New Mexico for a family snowboarding trip.

My husband and I arrived at our little rental home first, and I quickly hopped out of his big new Dodge Ram and rushed into the bathroom.

As was customary for this time of the month, I grabbed a dusty pregnancy test from way back in my bathroom cabinet. We'd been trying for a baby for the last two years with no luck. I had taken more than twenty pregnancy tests in that time, and I assumed this one would be like any other. Pee on the stick, try to preoccupy myself for those two infinite minutes, see the pink plus sign, throw it away, and go back to studying.

Wait. What? A pink PLUS sign?

I snatched the stick back out of the trashcan.

It couldn't be true. I wouldn't let myself believe it. The test was old; it was probably expired. This must be a false positive.

Not funny!

My family arrived shortly thereafter, and we all headed to a department store for last-minute gear before dinner. I secretly bought three more pregnancy tests, all different brands. I took one in the store bathroom while everyone checked out. *Plus sign.* I took another one at the restaurant. *Two pink lines.* At the end of dinner I looked down at my plate to realize I had just consumed an entire pot pie that was probably intended to be shared, along with a total of six jalapeños I don't even remember ordering. I took the third test back at home. *Pregnant.*

I felt great for the first few months, and my days were filled with pharmacy rotations, snacking, exams, studying, more snacking, and prepping for graduation and our move back home. In those days when I didn't have a belly yet, I remember feeling incredibly special, as if I had a secret inside me that only my baby boy and I knew about. Yes, my baby boy. I knew it was a boy, of course. There was never a question. I was going to give my husband three sons, all of whom we'd already named. We were going to have an awesome, crazy, busy life in sports, and I would remain the queen of my castle.

We made an appointment for 3D imaging to confirm the baby's gender, and in that room with dim lights, lullabies playing softly in the background, and cold blue jelly all over my growing tummy, the technician typed one little word on the big screen: G-I-R-L.

I turned my head and started to cry. I was mad. In that instant, her whole girly life flashed before me. Boys, periods, boobs, money, clothes, stress, heartbreak, bullies, weddings, worry, safety. My mind was racing. This was all wrong. I was supposed to have a rough and tough little boy who would hang out with his coach daddy all day and love his momma to death, and who I would never have to worry about.

Needless to say, Greg and our families were overjoyed. And after a few days, when the new reality set in and I recognized that what I was really feeling was fear, I was overjoyed, too. Even if I was terrified to fall so head-over-heels in love with someone I could not always protect.

Then the fantasies started.

Come on people, don't judge. Every expecting parent does it. So my fantasy baby girl was drop dead gorgeous, with legs like Gisele and hair like Julia Roberts in *Pretty Woman*. Not only was she gorgeous, but she was also a genius, and she would pick up reading at two years old. Obviously. More than likely she would be super athletic, and of course she'd be so naturally gifted she would never really have to try very hard. We would spend our days in Gifted and Talented programs looking for ways to challenge her and keep her involved in activities to provide her the most incredible opportunities in life. We would show her the world through travel and make her as well rounded as any big city kid. Meanwhile, she'd have the small-town values that came from living in the Valley.

She would have the biggest heart, and she'd be the most humble, beautiful spirit ever. She would probably go to an Ivy League school, start a non-profit in her early twenties, and contribute to the world in some tremendous way. She would more than likely also have some kind of mad talent, like Carrie Underwood's voice or something along those lines. You get the picture. Just small fantasies.

"DR. LISA PEÑA!"

Gosh, after eight years of falling asleep face down in books that weighed more than I did, that sounded so good. (But who am I kidding? No book in the world weighed more than me by that point.) I waddled my almost-seven-month pregnant self across the stage as my baby girl wriggled inside me. I was finally done with school and moving home to have my baby and put all of our plans in motion.

But there is a saying, "If you want to make God laugh, tell him your plans." Well I'll tell you what. God must have had roaring fits of side-splitting, knee-slapping laughter as He watched over me. I can picture Him laughing so hard He involuntarily snorts and then sighs at the end, a teary-faced, giddy mess.

The end of summer was coming fast, and I could barely walk. I could barely breathe. My face was so swollen I was hardly recognizable. Picture the Marshmallow Man from Ghostbusters as your visual. My feet belonged in a Flintstones cartoon. I take that back.

I hadn't seen my feet in two months, so who knows what they looked like in the end? But the last time I had seen them, they belonged in a Flintstones cartoon. My pregnancy was healthy overall. At thirty-six weeks I went into pre-term labor, but it was stopped quickly at the hospital, and I was sent home. So now, full-term and barely dilated, it was time for induction.

I will spare you too many details of that momentous occasion, mainly because one day I want my children to read this book. But here is the summary in one dramatic, exaggerated sentence: Dr. "Goliath Hands" had no mercy, ruined me for life, and now I had this crazy looking stranger baby in my arms, and I couldn't stop screaming in pain. OK, sorry kiddos, here is the summary in a normal sentence. A very rough doctor with a cold bedside manner delivered my first baby girl, and we were both very beat up from delivery. Better?

Here starts the mystery that is Isla.

It was my name jumbled up, and all the credit goes to my husband for choosing her beautiful name, inspired by her momma and our love for the island. Some call her "eye-la" and some call her "ee-sla". She gladly and happily responds to both.

I've already mentioned that my pregnancy was uncomplicated.

No health risks or factors, no gestational diabetes, no preeclampsia, nothing. I did not drink alcohol or smoke or do drugs or take any medication besides the occasional Claritin for my allergies. I had no fevers and no infections.

After two years of trying we did resort to Clomid, but we got pregnant with the lowest dose the very first time. Stress related to pharmacy school? Yes. Pre-term labor? Yes, but one dose of terbutaline did the trick. It was a vaginal delivery with an epidural, albeit a very ill-timed, ineffective epidural.

During the first minutes of Isla's life, her breathing seemed a little off. As I recovered and stared at her, lying in her little plastic see-through box on wheels, I remember thinking, *"Why is she breathing like that? Is that normal?"* Her breathing was heavy and loud whether she was asleep or awake. Almost like snoring. She cried a lot, and she was only calm when the nurse came to bathe her. That first bath was the first time I saw her eyes. Deep gray eyes. WOOHOO! That meant she was going to have some kind of color to her eyes right? Oh, and her hair! She had so much beautiful, dark brown, wavy hair. Throughout the course of those first twenty-four hours I fell hard for this beautiful little baby girl who breathed like an old man.

So I went home with what some would insensitively call a "bad baby." She *never* slept. She *always* cried. She *always* threw up. We tried breast milk, formula, gentle formulations of formula, prescription formula, and soy formula.

But she was only calm at bath time, so I have no shame in admitting that, with many, many baths per day, we had the squeaky-cleanest baby in town. I, on the other hand, smelled like vomit, armpit, and bad breath pretty much 24/7.

I am not sure if it's because I was relatively young or because it was my first baby, but man did I throw a huge pity party that first year. I never struggled with postpartum depression, and I never wanted to harm her or myself, but my body image and self-esteem were at an all-time low. I was a walking zombie, exhausted and saggy in places that should not be saggy. I lost my hair in globs and had many sob sessions in the shower with water up to my ankles as my hair clogged the drain. I was alone a lot. My parents and brothers had moved about five hours away while my brothers attended college, and my husband was a varsity football coach, so that left Isla and me alone.

Every night as I would rock Isla to sleep (which really means rock her *while* she slept, because that was the *only* way she would sleep), I would sing her the song I still sing to her to this day. This special song was a birthday gift I received during this lonely time. Isla was three months old, and I was back to work selling my soul slowly to the beast that is retail pharmacy. I got in my car, and there on the car dashboard was a CD titled "Miss Love." I already told you I was not in a great place mentally, so you won't be surprised to hear that the tears were already falling as I fumbled to put it in my car CD player.

Then there on my car speakers was my little brother's voice, accompanied by his acoustic guitar.

At nineteen years old, with no real world experience yet and no children of his own, my brother had written and recorded a song so true and so right that, to this day, I still wonder how those words came to him. After all these years, it's time to share his lyrics with the world:

You are my afternoon, and day and night too

I'll stay up with the moon singing you a tune

And I'm falling head over heels, again and again

My love for you is so real, it will never end

And I need you and you need me

And I'm holding on to all your love surrounds me

I can't replace holding your face to mine, there's nothing more to live for

And I can't conceive I can't believe you're mine, you're everything I live for

//And I love you and you love me yeah

Your love your love surrounds me //

We spend much time alone, me and my little girl

Come make my arms your home, you're my little girl

And the day will come when you'll see, you will understand

All the love that is shared between, you momma and dad

And I need you and you need me

And I'm holding on to all your love surrounds me

I can't replace holding your face to mine, there's nothing more to live for

And I can't conceive I can't believe you're mine, you're everything I live for

//And I love you and you love me yeah

Your love your love surrounds me //

In all my life, this has been, hands down, the best birthday gift I have ever received. And in case you're wondering, Isla's middle name is Love.

OK, wipe your eyes and let's get serious. Let's talk milestones. Don't you love how people obsess over milestones? Well, I didn't. I am in the medical field, remember? I knew that babies all develop differently, so when my baby didn't smile till around five months, I didn't worry. I cheered because she DID smile. When my baby was not sitting at six or seven or eight months, I didn't worry.

Instead, I waited patiently and cheered when she DID sit up at nine months. As her first birthday approached, she was barely crawling, and she wasn't cooing or babbling much at all. But I didn't worry about that, either. Her height and weight were always on target, and she handled all vaccines like a champ. She was never sick, and if I remember correctly she only needed one round of antibiotics in her whole first year. The baby spit up subsided around six to seven months, which was about the time she really started enjoying baby food. She was not a picky eater and ate whatever new food was put in front of her.

I did, however, worry about her sleeping habits, because she simply did not sleep more than an hour or two straight any given night. I did worry about her breathing, which remained loud and heavy, but her pediatrician kept insisting that it was a normal side effect of fluid from delivery and that it would go away.

Still, she was so darn beautiful with her big round hazel eyes and her messy curly mop of brown hair that to us, she was absolutely perfect.

Chapter Two: 1-2 years
Hi.

"Our Little Cupcake is Turning One!"

The sugary sweet theme—not to mention the adored child, herself—brought lots of family and friends to our home for Isla's first birthday party. Greg and I are the oldest in both of our families, so that made Isla the first and only grandchild on both sides. Need I say more? The kid got a lot of attention and love all around, as it should be.

For Isla's first two years, my aunt and Greg's mom, shared childcare responsibilities while I was at work. These two ladies were excellent at caring for babies so, needless to say, Isla was very well taken care of during this time.

In many ways, Isla's development was normal this year. Her teeth came in at appropriate times, and she handled teething really well, with no real pain or discomfort. She was a great eater and would try almost anything once. She continued to seem immune to illness. She was never sick and would only go to pediatrician visits for vaccines. Her colic and reflux had completely resolved, which meant her momma was starting to smell quite nice these days. Her body was developing normally, and she was growing taller and more beautiful with each passing week.

Looking back, many things were not "normal" per se, but when it's your first baby, you just don't notice. For example, go back to those teeth I just mentioned. Although her teeth came in on time and healthy, brushing them was a different story. Isla had a very strong gag reflex, and as soon as the toothbrush entered her mouth it would go off, sometimes so fiercely that she would end up dry heaving.

At first I tried to distract her by singing loud songs or making her laugh or brushing my teeth while she tried to brush her own. These efforts usually just resulted in both of us dissolving into all kinds of silly. I tried at least four different toothpastes, and none really helped. Against my better judgment, I spent almost $20 on one of them that proved to be helpful only as an emergency jewelry cleaner. I reverted back to that blue rubber finger brush that you use for infants, which did help with the gagging but also seemed to trigger lockjaw. This usually happened when my finger was inside Isla's mouth, so you can imagine we both began to really dread tooth-brushing time.

Her gag reflex was also evident when I would change her very robust-smelling diapers once all foods were on board. Poor Isla would gag with her own smell, making changing time twice as messy. I began washing small burp cloths with four or five dryer sheets so they would smell good, and then give her one of my DIY burp cloth sachets to hold to her nose while I changed her. That worked for a while…at least until we started to actively potty train.

While some of Isla's reflexes were extremely sensitive, others were lacking completely. She just didn't react to things the way you would expect. The best example I can think of happened at birthday parties. Picture the kids all standing in line waiting to hit the piñata. All the little kids would go first, and then the big kids, and then some pre-teen little leaguer would hit the thing hard enough for some candy to fly out. As you would expect, when the candy hit the floor, so did the kids. But not Isla. She would just stand and stare. We would scream encouragement with big smiles and loud clapping. We'd cheer, "Go Isla! Isla get the candy! Isla HURRY!" But she would just look at us like we were all crazy.

Someone would usually lift her up and place her right in the middle of the kids, with candy falling all around her. She would stand there and watch it hit the ground.

This was also the year that Isla started talking (kind of), and although she did say "momma" and "dada," most of her family and friends will tell you that they remember this year being the year of "Hi." Isla said "Hi" *all the time* and in response to *every* question and comment. At first it was adorable, but after a few months I noticed the inappropriateness of it all. Take, for instance, a typical conversation with a family member or friend:

Friend: "Hi, Isla!"

Isla: "Hi."

Friend: "How are you today, pretty girl?"

Isla: "Hi."

Friend: "Yum, your food looks so good! Do you like bananas?"

Isla: "Hi."

Friend: "Do you wanna go outside for a little bit? Do you wanna go play on the swings?"

Isla: "Hi."

As she got closer to two years old, it started to bother me more and more. I would try to guide her and explain that we only say "Hi" one time when we first see someone we know. I tried to teach her at least how to answer "Yes" and "No," but I was largely unsuccessful.

Another odd thing was she absolutely did not like or want to play with toys. In fact, the only things I remember her playing with at all were our remote control and our keys.

I know most kids want to play with remote controls and keys, but most kids like real toys, too. Not Isla.

She had countless books, toys, games, and dolls, but nothing sparked or kept her interest. Isla did not even watch TV—or anything on a screen, for that matter. At first, we thought she was just uninterested, but after a while it almost seemed like she purposefully tried to avoid it. We tried many kid-friendly shows and movies, but she wouldn't even glance.

Isla took her first steps around sixteen months, and I was relieved because even though she was a late walker, she mastered it quickly, and she was well balanced with appropriate gait and speed. But she still had problems with sleep.

Although the evening routine had improved, and she was now sleeping through the night in her crib, she did not take naps during the day. Even when she seemed sleepy, it required moving heaven and earth—or a very long car ride to nowhere—to put her to sleep. Of course, as soon as I would turn off the car, she would be wide awake. And on the extremely rare occasion she was down for a nap in her crib, if I so much as closed a cabinet in the bathroom on the other side of the house, softly, quietly, slowly, she would be wide awake. It was almost comical how much of a light sleeper she was.

But even though we noticed some of these odd things, we didn't *really notice*. For the first two years of her life, we did not think anything was wrong or abnormal, and neither did pediatricians, family, or friends.

That would all change very soon.

Chapter Three: 2-3 years
While You Weren't Sleeping

Now that Isla was two years old, it was time to start the great adventure that is daycare. We were excited about daycare. We thought it was good for socialization, and we hoped it would help Isla to communicate a little more. We had also heard that if you chose the right one, daycare could be a great reinforcement for potty training, which was already going well. In fact, the only issue we had with potty training was that Isla started to use it as an "out." So if we were somewhere that she didn't want to be, she would say "potty!" and hold herself and squirm like she just could not hold it another second. We would rush to the nearest bathroom, shamelessly pleading with anyone in line to let us cut, even if they were elderly or pregnant, and then Isla would take her time, peeking under stalls, splashing the water in the sink, and just having a grand old time, rather than actually using the bathroom. I assumed this was totally normal, so we would get after her quite a bit about this. Naturally, when we assumed she was faking it and decided to make her wait, she would have an accident.

When the search for daycares began, I visited and toured several daycares and preschools in our town, and one stood out by far.

It was a beautiful campus with kind staff and teachers, curriculum-based from the age of eighteen months, with daily chapel and excellent administration. Of course there was a waiting list. Isla would be able to start the following year when she turned three, but I was way too late for the current year. So I settled for daycare option two, which was not as impressive but still a great choice compared to the others.

I spent an entire afternoon with Isla in her new classroom so she and I would feel comfortable with the teacher and students. She was intrigued by each student, which made me hopeful that it was a good step for her. She was excited as we shopped for all her new supplies, including sleeping mats, lunch boxes, and a backpack. But the disappointment started on day one. Isla happily helped me carry all her supplies in, but as soon as we opened the door I saw that it was not the same teacher we'd met the week before. It was a substitute. She was friendly and nice, but I was uneasy pretending it was totally OK to leave the most precious thing I have with someone I had never met and didn't know at all. It was gut wrenching. Isla cried and screamed. I tried to be brief as I hugged and kissed her and left her on the substitute's lap. I closed the door behind me and stood in the hall trying to catch my breath and trying not to cry, myself, waiting until I heard her calm down. Luckily, she quieted as other kids started arriving.

Over the course of the next couple months that was the usual routine.

Once or twice per week there was a substitute, and my poor girl just could not handle these changes. She needed consistency and familiarity, but doesn't every kid?

After about three months I decided to look into daycare option three again. I scheduled an appointment to revisit the campus and ask more relevant questions regarding teacher attendance and turnover. The morning of the appointment, I dropped Isla off at daycare option two, and again there was a substitute I had never seen before. The substitute was a young girl, nice and friendly as all the others, but new to Isla. As I stood in the hallway waiting for the screaming to pass, I felt the guilt of looking elsewhere dissipate.

I headed to daycare option three hopeful.

I was waiting in the office for paperwork and to spend some time with the teacher when the substitute that was with my little girl that morning walked in the door. Not recognizing me, she started chatting with the office staff, taking out her cell phone to show pictures of the kids she'd been substituting that morning. All of her comments were kind, and she was trying to show how cute they all were, and Isla's name did not come up...but does anyone else see a problem here? Because I saw several.

No substitute of any kind had the right to have my child's picture on their phone without my permission.

Furthermore, I signed paperwork at that daycare declining all pictures of Isla being used for advertising or in school associated press.

How does anyone have time to take pictures of a bunch of two year olds when they're supposed to be taking care of them?

Why are you even on your phone when you are trying to take care of a bunch of two year olds?

And most importantly, if this lady wasn't at daycare number two, *who was taking care of my daughter?*

Before I could overwhelm this poor substitute with an interrogation, daycare number three's teacher came to get me, and we went to the classroom for our visit. Of course, I was mentally absent for the whole conversation because I was anxious to go back to daycare option two and have a little chat with the administration.

As soon as we were done with our visit, I did just that. As I explained what had happened, watching the administrator lean back in their chair, I knew the conversation would end badly by the tone of the first question.

Daycare Administrator: "Did you actually see the pictures?"

Totally doing the right thing Mom: "No, I did not, but she specifically said three names of little boys that I know are in that same class."

Daycare Administrator: "So she didn't have a picture of your daughter?"

Totally doing the right thing Mom, I think: "I don't know. Again, I am here because I don't think it is appropriate for the substitute to take pictures of any children on their personal cell phones, and I am not sure how that is even possible when she is busy taking care of a bunch of two year olds."

Daycare Administrator: "So you don't know if she had permission from those three boys' parents to take pictures?"

I really hope I am doing the right thing Mom: "Why would parents give her permission for that? Is there a form I missed?"

Daycare Administrator: "Their parents must have filled out the release form that allows us to take their pictures."

I *am* doing the right thing Mom: "I'm sorry, but I don't think you fully understand my concern. Can you just please talk with that substitute and check her phone?

I think it is appropriate to make sure the other parents are aware. Also, if the substitute was not here then who was watching Isla today?"

Daycare Administrator: "The teacher only had a half-day off and came back in the afternoon. And, no, I cannot check the substitute's phone."

Totally doing the right thing Mom: "Then I would like to withdraw Isla immediately. I will go to her classroom and get her things."

Daycare Administrator: "OK, but there are withdrawal fees that will be due immediately upon your decision to leave."

The whole conversation had me stunned.

I was a first-time daycare parent, and this was the first time I had *ever* had a concern and was totally dismissed. Worse, I got the distinct feeling the administrator thought I was lying or making something up.

This was the beginning of me learning how to be my child's advocate regardless of how uncomfortable it made me or anyone else. It was the first time I forged through awkward conversations and made myself look like the "crazy" mom in order to do what I felt was best to protect my daughter. It would serve as very good practice for what lay ahead for Isla and me.

Special needs children or not I learned that as a parent no one should ever make you feel like your concerns are not valid or true. An effective administrator will listen, empathize, and make parents feel comfortable. An effective administrator will get the details from both parties and make a fully informed decision on the proper way to handle a situation.

I encourage you to look for these administrators, because for me, excellent administrators were critical in setting my daughter and me on the right path.

So on we went to daycare option three. I soon realized I had put it at the bottom of the list for all the wrong reasons. This daycare was not as "pretty" as the others, it smelled a little "iffy," and it was not one of the "preferred" places to take kiddos in our town. However, the consistency was refreshing. The teacher was stern but kind, and she was actually present ninety-five percent of the time.

This daycare introduced the kids to many preschool basics through play and art, and overall I was happy. Isla was, too. She didn't cry or whine too much when I dropped her off, and most days when I picked her up she was clean and well kept, which I knew was tough to accomplish when caring for a room full of two year olds.

Isla did continue to have sleep issues and was still the only kid in the whole daycare that didn't nap regularly. Instead, the teachers took turns taking her for rides on a little red wagon through the hallways while everyone slept. Then one afternoon at pick-up time, I noticed something else. It wasn't an "aha moment", but it was one of those nagging moments. I couldn't put my finger on it, but something just didn't sit right.

I walked in the room, and all of the children were playing with toys, bouncing balls, or pretending to read books. These kiddos were all two years old, going on three, so they were not babies anymore and could play quite actively. I scanned the room for Isla and didn't spot her at first. When I found her, she was lying in the corner of the room the way an infant lies on her back and puts her feet and hands up to play. But she was not playing. She had lifted the corner of the carpeting and was chewing on it.

Whoa. This was a new feeling for me. As I rushed to go pick her up, I wasn't scared or even worried. I was…embarrassed? That was weird. Why did I feel embarrassed?

I picked her up and hugged her like nothing was wrong. She smiled, and we were happy to see each other.

Then the teacher said, "Not sure why she started doing that but she had an overall good day. Come look at the art work she made."

So I walked over to the other side of the room and saw five easels set up with a large white paper and a really big apple traced in black marker. The first four easels held a small jar of red paint and a brush, with messy marks of red in their apples. But on the fifth easel, Isla's, the paint had been used to the last drop.

The brush was covered down to the tip of the handle, and the red paint covered the easel legs and the plastic cloth covering the floor, with just a tiny bit on the very corner of the paper. The inside of the apple remained pristinely white. Again, that horrible new feeling washed over me.

Come on, Lisa. Get a hold of yourself! She is two. Everything is fine.

I smiled and told Isla what a lovely color red was, and I talked to her about all the things I could think of that were red, including the sweater I was putting on her. Isla smiled, and we left as if nothing happened.

Meanwhile, back at home, we decided to convert Isla's crib into a toddler bed. She loved the idea because it was new, and she loved scooting up and down the bed like a "big girl." By this point she was able to keep some stuffed animals and pillows on her bed, and she absolutely loved to snuggle in with all her bedding.

But the toddler bed wasn't a perfect setup, we would soon learn.

It began one night with a loud *thud!* I am a pretty light sleeper, so I was out of bed in a split second.

I rushed out of my room and saw Isla in her pajamas looking adorable and lost. Her hair was ridiculously cute when she slept—just a total curly mess. She had walked into a wall in the dark as she came to look for us and was not crying or fussing, but just standing there, waiting for someone to find her. I picked her up, took her back to her bed, and started to sing her special bedtime song. *"You are my afternoon, and day and night too, I'll stay up with the moon singing you a tune..."*

She fell asleep almost instantly, so I went back to bed, but about thirty minutes later, *thud!* There I went again: same scene, same song, and same instant return to sleep. But the pattern continued several times that night and for several days following.

She'd been sleeping through the night for about a year, and I'd gotten accustomed to doing the same, so I was definitely feeling the exhaustion. I convinced Greg to move her toddler bed into our room for a few days to see if I could figure out what was waking her (and, selfishly, so I wouldn't have to get out of bed so much).

The first night she slept in our room it was obvious. My kid was not breathing at night. Keep in mind that Isla's loud, heavy breathing had never gone away. And because her normal breathing was so obvious, so were the moments when she wasn't breathing. As I listened to her that first night, I could not believe how many times she just stopped breathing. I decided to pick her up and put her right next to me on my bed so that I could lightly shake her shoulder or leg when she stopped breathing. I was worried and confused.

Could it be that this had been happening every night? For how long? How many nights?

The pediatrician listened to her heart, lungs, took vitals, and asked me if there were any other issues. Besides not talking very much, there weren't. She was super healthy and happy, eating great and growing—overall, she was just perfect. So the pediatrician assured me that there was no real problem. Since Isla had no history of ear, nose, and throat (ENT)-type problems—no upper respiratory infections, no ear infections, no tonsillitis, nothing—he suggested that it may have just been congestion. I was instructed to use a humidifier or vaporizer and keep watching her.

I got less sleep the next week than I had when she was an infant. I would drift off for a brief minute, wake up in total panic to check her, and then instantly feel that hot wave of guilt come over me for falling asleep.

After that first week, I had to take action, so after a call to my insurance company, I made an appointment with a local ENT doctor. Of course the next available appointment was not for another two months so I tried to explain that my little girl was not breathing at night and that I really needed to be seen sooner. Can anyone guess what the response was? We've all heard it. "If it is an emergency please report to the nearest Emergency Center or call 911." OK, OK I know. I get it, fine. So instead, I asked to be placed on the call list in hopes there would be a cancellation. Good news: we got seen in just one month. Bad news: it was a very long, hard, scary, sleepless month.

I knew I needed evidence for the ENT. I needed them to hear what I was hearing at night, so I decided to record Isla while she slept the night before our visit. I used my nifty little Sony camcorder, and every time she would stop breathing I would whisper count the seconds in the background to measure how long each interval was.

The problem was that, of course, I didn't want her to stop breathing. I was used to waking her up as soon as she did. Just letting her lie there, not breathing, felt completely crazy. Well, let me tell you, when you are a parent, you do crazy things. I tried hard not to intervene. I allowed myself to count to fifteen seconds, but I could not handle going any further. I remember thinking, *"Am I just watching her die? What the heck is wrong with me?"* I needed proof, but even that proved almost too hard to get.

By the grace of God we got through that night. Actually, who knows how many nights Isla survived only by God's grace. With my video in hand, we waited for the ENT. Desperation. That's what I remember, just desperation. I could not go another night without sleep and neither could she.

So when the ENT entered the room and almost immediately asked, "Does she normally breathe like that?" I was instantly relieved. *Finally*, someone who understood what I had been trying to say!

Yes, Doctor! Yes! She has been breathing like that since birth, and now she isn't breathing at night. Please help us!

The ENT only briefly glanced at my video, which upset me at first because it was so painstaking to make. But he was quick to identify the problem, and he made it seem so obvious. Isla's tonsils and adenoids were abnormally large for her age and size, and they needed to come out. However, we would need an official sleep study for insurance purposes and to rule out central sleep apnea.

In my life with Isla I have been thrown many "uglies," which are what I call the—not so nice and/or sometimes scary—medical terms. "Central sleep apnea" was the first ugly.

My Googling skills were in desperate need of refinement, but I learned that the sleep study was to determine whether the size of the tonsils and adenoids were obstructing her airway *or* her brain was not alerting her to continue breathing. So ugly. I thought the nights leading up to the ENT visit were stressful, but nothing compared to watching her struggle at night and worrying that something might possibly be wrong with her brain.

Sleep study night. Isla and I walked the halls of the hospital toward the sleep study wing. She was dressed in colorful pajamas and was wearing fun, furry slippers I'd bought just for that night to make her feel special. We held hands while we walked, and as I looked down at her I started to rationalize.

Drama Queen Mom: Oh my God what are we doing here! How has it come to this?! *Cue dramatic sigh with back of hand to forehead*

Rational, Wise Mom: Calm down, crazy woman. It's a freakin' sleep study. Thousands of people get sleep studies done.

Drama Queen Mom: But why Isla? Why? Oh my God what if it is her brain?

Rational, Wise Mom: Seriously? The ENT said it was obvious that her tonsils and adenoids are extra-large. They will confirm that for insurance purposes, then they'll remove them, and it will be fine.

Drama Queen Mom: What if she freaks out, and what if they don't let me wake her up and she just…Oh my God! Why didn't I make her dad come instead?!

Rational, Wise Mom: Get a hold of yourself. You are in a hospital, which is the perfect place to be if she struggles during the test. And you didn't make your hubby come because you and I both know you are too controlling and you don't trust anyone else to help you or to give you all the details.

Drama Queen Mom: Oh yeah. OK. I hate that you are always right.

Rational, Wise Mom: I hate that you are always crazy.

So we got into our little sleep room, and Isla was just cute as can be, thinking that everything was so fun. The special bed with buttons and the special TV just for her made her giggle. Oh, and forget mommy's special furry slippers—she thought the hideous hospital socks were just all kinds of perfect because they matched the ones I wore at home. Yes, I still had the hospital socks from delivery two years before. Don't judge me. You and I both know they are comfortable and perfect for tile floors, so back off.

The sleep study technician was patient, and he slowly and methodically applied the leads to Isla's little scalp, chest, and neck. Isla handled it pretty well, with only a few minutes of fussiness as she tried to fall asleep on a very unfamiliar bed.

There was no cot or bed available for me, so I sat on a chair right next to her bed, preparing for a long night.

If you have ever done or witnessed a sleep study, you know that the machines really don't tell you much. Most of the monitoring is processed in another room entirely, and the only thing you can really see is the oxygen saturation of the patient, also called the SpO2. Oxygen is important, obviously, and 100% is always the goal. Between 90-94% is considered mild hypoxemia (abnormally low concentration of oxygen in the blood), 75-89% is moderate hypoxemia, and below 75% is severe hypoxemia. Typically below 70% there can be possible loss of consciousness and brain injury.

I spent the next few hours staring at that machine in awe and terror.

Every time Isla stopped breathing, I would start counting, staring at the oxygen saturation on the screen. 97%. 95%. 89%. 85%. *Oh my God. Oh my God I should have asked the technician at what point to call him in here.* 84%. *OK stay calm it's been 11 seconds, just wait, Lisa. Just wait. Whew, OK she is breathing.* 91%. *Oh my God how many more times is this going to happen?* 97%. *OK, OK, it's OK.*

Twice during the night, though, the percentage dipped so low that I nearly lost it. 97%. 95%. 89%. 85%. *Oh my God here we go again.* 84%. *OK stay calm it's been 10 seconds, just wait, Lisa. It will be over soon.* 81%. *What? Wait, how many seconds am I on?* 79%. *No, no I can't let this happen.* I stood up and looked out the window of the room, panicked. No one was around. *But they are watching, right? From some room? Are they on break?* 76%. *Oh God, what do I do?! Oh my God I am going to watch her die, oh my God.* 75%. *I think it has been more than 15 seconds.* I lightly started tapping the window so I didn't wake Isla.

The only rule the technician had given me was to make sure to not touch her or wake her during the study, and I wanted to follow the rules, because that is what I do best. *Wait, what? Screw the rules my baby is going to die, and I am watching her like an idiot!* 72%. *That's it—I am going to get someone.* I rushed to the door and turned the knob, and then I heard Isla take a deep, beautiful breath. After the second episode like this, I sat back down and, for the first time, I allowed myself to be sad. I put my head in my hands and cried and prayed. I remember asking God that, if my baby needed to die, that He please not take her here with me watching. I could not bear the guilt.

By the time 6 a.m. rolled around and the technician came in, I was a hot mess. He started taking off the leads, and Isla woke up and sleepily smiled at me as if the world was just right.

I smiled back at her and tried to forget everything that had just happened. Since I worked full time, I had brought her clothes for daycare and my clothes for work. We got dressed at the hospital, and I dropped her off at daycare with slimy goop in her hair and marks on her forehead and chest from the leads. After all that, I drove to work, exhausted but thankful to God that my little girl was alive.

Six long days and nights later, we had a follow-up with the ENT to go over the results of the sleep study.

They were detailed and confusing, but here was the summary I got: 0 central apneas, 32 obstructive apneas, and 27 moderate to severe hypoxemic episodes. Lowest oxygen saturation recorded was 70%. Isla had 25 events per hour during REM sleep and 5 events per hour during non-REM sleep. Diagnosis: severe obstructive sleep apnea.

The surgery to remove the "obstructions," which were the tonsils and adenoids, was scheduled for two days later. My husband and I were hopeful and relieved. A few minutes before the surgery, I was handed the official sleep study report. The first paragraph, titled "History," read:

This patient is a 2-year-old, 34", 26-lb female with complaints of "heavy breathing, sleep apnea, speech and behavior problems, slow learner, excessive drooling, mouth breathing" Other indications for study: snoring, waking gasping during the night, awakening at night with coughing, falling asleep during the day, trouble at school due to sleepiness, body jerks, and enlarged tonsils.

Ouch. Slow learner? I did not remember using those words, so why were there quotes on everything like I'd said it verbatim? *Drooling?* I remember saying that but, I'd also said I thought it was due to teething and congestion. As I looked up at Isla sitting on the bed in her miniature hospital gown, waiting for the surgeon, I started to get emotional. A nurse walked in to get vitals and noticed that I was starting to lose my composure. "This will help," she assured me. "We remove tonsils all the time, and for most kids it helps with learning issues because it improves hearing or speaking. Don't worry. You'll be so surprised when the light bulb just seems to turn on. "

My two year old had her first surgery that day. She was a trooper, and although recovery was painful, it was speedy.

That was when we started waiting.

We started waiting for that light bulb to turn on.

Chapter Four: 3-4 years
Olive to the Rescue

Nurse: "OK, Mrs. Peña, I am just going to leave this bag here for you to look through later, and I will go get the doctor."

Oblivious Mom: "Uh, bag for what?"

Nurse: "Well it just has some samples and coupons for you."

Oblivious Mom: "I'm sorry, I don't understand. I am here for…."

I peered down from my exam table into the pink bag on the floor and saw samples of pampers, lanolin ointment, diaper cream, formula, and a coupon book for many items I did not need because I was not pregnant. This lady had it so wrong.

Oblivious and now annoyed Mom: "Ma'am I'm here for my annual. You know, my pap smear. I'm not pregnant."

Nurse: "Oh my gosh I am so sorry. Let me go double check."

Oblivious and now annoyed Mom: "Yes, and please take this bag with you."

I sat there naked, annoyed, and cold in one of those ridiculous, paper-thin gowns thinking, *Man that lady almost made a huge HIPPA violation. I just saved her job and saved her from a fat fine. What an awesome, smart person I am.* (Insert eye rolling emoji here.)

Not that it would be a bad thing if I were pregnant. My husband and I had been trying for a second baby for many months with no luck, and I had taken a pregnancy test just a few days earlier. The mistake was really just a stinging reminder that we weren't successful again.

A few minutes later, the nurse very lightly knocked on my door and walked back into my room with the same bag in hand and a "please don't hit me" look on her face.

"Mrs. Peña, I am so sorry for the confusion, but you're the only Peña in the office this morning, and your urine was positive for…well, uh, you're pregnant." The poor lady lightly placed the bag next to me and rushed out before I could say another word.

I had really prayed hard for this baby. I thought that maybe it would have been better for Isla to have a sibling closer in age so she could play and talk and develop a little faster. Isla was already three years old, and I regretted waiting so long to give her a buddy. Maybe another sibling would help turn on the light bulb.

Meanwhile, the new school year had started, and Isla was at that amazing day school that I had been so anxiously waiting for. We were finally in! Though Isla turned three a few days after school started, we enrolled her in the two year old class knowing that she may be a little behind, particularly when it came to her speech. The teacher of the two's was the most nurturing, beautiful, Grandmother-like figure, and I loved the way she cared for and taught my baby all day. She was patient and kind, and she absolutely loved all of the children. Isla loved that day school.

She would skip in the parking lot most days and, though we had the occasional crying fit, drop-offs were usually seamless. There was chapel every morning, and it brought me to tears almost every time I attended. There was something so beautiful and innocent about a room filled with children of all nationalities, cultures, economic backgrounds, sizes, and shapes singing and praying together to start their day, every day.

The children would clap and join in on the motions for each song, and Isla loved it.

Oh, my girl loved to hum and clap and wave her arms high in the air without a care in the world. It was a wonderful time.

Isla was fully potty trained well before she turned three, and overall she did OK compared to the others in the class. She had some behavior problems—mostly trouble sitting still—but she was only three, and all the other kiddos had the same issues or worse. The only thing that really stood out was her speech. She just didn't have words. Her face was so expressive, and her body language was appropriate, but there were no words.

Fast forward to winter, time for Isla's first-ever class Christmas party. She looked so lovely in her red Christmas dress with white snowflake print, long curly hair, and big hazel eyes. Precious, that's what she was. She skipped, holding my hand, all the way into the classroom. She was so excited for me to be at school with her that day. We headed back to the classroom after chapel, and the party moms started setting up the tables with snacks and Christmas décor.

Then the teacher called on a little girl to say the prayer. She was petite with straight, jet-black hair and blunt cut bangs and just all kinds of adorable. She stood up obediently, clasped her little hands together, and sang the prayer in the most clear, precise way, with excellent pronunciation and tone, to the tune of the nursery rhyme, *"Are you sleeping?"*

"Thank you Father, Thank you Father for our snack, for our snack. We are saying Thank you, we are saying Thank you. Amen. Amen."

I had to step out. I hated that feeling. Every time I got that stupid feeling I worked very hard to try and figure out exactly what it was, and I usually ended up feeling guilty about the truth of what I felt. So I stood in the breezeway wiping my eyes, and arguing once more with my sane, rational self.

Emotionally unstable Mom: What a show off! How dare she sing that prayer so perfectly!

Sane Mom: You are ridiculous.

Emotionally unstable Mom: What's ridiculous is that she was probably held back and is secretly like four years old and it's not fair to have the most advanced kid in the class do the prayer. It does not reflect the whole class's abilities. I wonder how much she practices. Oh my God! I bet her mom drills her every night and doesn't let her go to bed until that prayer is perfect.

Sane Mom: Lisa. Wow. First, why do you keep wearing mascara that isn't waterproof? You are way too hormonal right now to pull that off. Second, it was one prayer and one kid. Have you done anything so far to help Isla?

Emotionally unstable Mom: What?! How dare you! I am creating life over here! A life that is supposed to help Isla! What do you mean have I tried to help her?! I read to her and talk to her and give her attention and love, and I try to teach her, and I pay for her to go to this school!

Sane Mom: It's time to get help. Professional help.

Emotionally unstable Mom: You are such a jerk. I do not need professional help.

Sane Mom: I meant for Isla, crazy lady. Make an appointment with the pediatrician. It's time.

Emotionally unstable Mom: Oh. Yeah, OK. Fine.

The answer was simple: speech therapy. We were referred by the pediatrician and started a week later.

The first visit was lengthy, with a series of questions for me about Isla's development and a brutal initial assessment for her. This would be the first of many times that I would have to sit and watch Isla being "tested." We sat in a therapy room filled with color and texture. There were hanging butterflies, suns, kites, and clouds coming down from the ceiling. There were toys in abundance neatly packed away in color-coordinated bins along the brightly painted walls. The alphabet rug was vibrant with corresponding words or objects for each letter.

Even the speech therapist's folder and notebook were colorful and bright. I felt so good as we sat down, and I thought, *gosh, what a beautiful place to learn.*

The assessment was one-sided and practically nonexistent. The therapist would ask Isla a question or use props to prompt her, and Isla would walk around, stare at things, and look out the window at whoever was passing by. I would convince her to sit, and after a few seconds she would get up again and go to the next toy bin or she'd stay seated but she'd pick at the rug and try to scratch off the letters. It was odd and disturbing, but the therapist didn't seem alarmed at all. Isla was highly distracted and got almost every question or prompt wrong if she responded at all. It was a very long hour, which ended with Isla frustrated and almost in tears because she wanted to leave the room so badly. The therapist was optimistic, and as we packed up to leave she told me that for the first session she would remove everything from the room to help Isla focus on her tasks. "Just wait," she said. "In six months you will be amazed."

These speech therapy sessions were twice a week, and they were supposed to be an hour in length, but that proved way too long for my girl. I stopped going into the actual therapy room, because we agreed I was a distraction for her, too.

So I would sit in the waiting room on a very hard, wooden bench and just hope that each hour was helping.

Unfortunately, these therapy sessions would also be the first time that Isla would use her "escape" mechanisms to avoid a learning activity that required attention or focus.

After a few minutes I would be called back because she had to use the bathroom or she was thirsty or hungry or she was crying because something "hurt" her. It was mainly the bathroom excuse, and it was amazing how convincing that little girl was at such a young age. She would not just say, "potty". She would hold herself and her private parts tight like she was going to explode, and she would hop around and squirm, and her facial expression would just look so desperate. She was stubborn and defiant and smart and determined. The therapist would say, "Well let's review these last two flash cards first, and then we can go to the potty," but that would only exacerbate Isla's fake desperation. The other issue with the speech therapy sessions was that, because I was a full-time working mom, I had to take her after school when, like most kids, she was mentally worn out. I tried to keep all this in mind, though I was beginning to feel that the sessions were not helping.

It was also around that time that Isla started to do things that were disturbing. I say that because some of her behaviors were common for kids, and others were not. For instance, Isla chewed her hair. I know a lot of kids that have a habit of chewing their braids or ponytails.

Isla chewed her clothes, too. I know a lot of kids that have a habit of nibbling the sleeve of a jacket at the wrist or a pull-string to a hooded pullover.

However, I didn't know any kids who took the habit quite as far as she did.

Isla's favorite pillow was about three feet long, with a beautiful print of the entire earth on the front.

It was colorful and detailed and showed each continent and all the bodies of water. Each continent had one or two common animals sewn on so they were raised and textured. Though she rarely paid attention to all that detail, Isla did like her pillow, and she would always place it back on her bed if it fell on the floor or wound up in another room. One day, I stepped away to wash dishes and left her playing on her bedroom floor with an old remote control. As I finished washing the last dish I realized that this was the first time I'd finished washing dishes without Isla interrupting me. She never played on her own for very long, so I knew something was up. When I peeked into her room, I saw her sitting on her bed with her back to me. Her head was moving so sharply up and down that it was disturbing so I quickly said, "Hey Isla what are you—" She turned fast, and her face was covered in polyester stuffing. It was on her eyelashes and eyebrows, in her nose and mouth. The look on her face was almost like she wasn't really aware of what was happening. It was a look of "help me stop what I am doing because I can't stop myself." It was the first time I would see that look on my daughter's face, and I wish I could tell you it was the last. Isla had bitten off each and every animal from the special pillow. The stitching was destroyed, and the stuffing was ripped out.

What remained of the animals was strewn all over her bed and carpet and in her hair. I remember letting out a gasp, and my first instinct was to do that mommy mouth sweep.

You know the one, when you grab your kids mouth so aggressively it looks like abuse and shove your fingers in there thinking that whatever is in there needs to come out now, and I don't care if I lose fingers in the meantime! Then I placed my hands on her shoulders and looked right into her eyes, and I just didn't know what to do. I hugged her, and I just whispered, "Oh my God what's wrong with you? What is this? No, no oh my God." I know that kids destroy stuff and tear stuff up and cut stuff up all the time, but that's not what this was really about. It was the *way* she was doing it. It was a violent, uncontrollable impulse, and on top of that I knew how special that pillow was to her. But most of all it was that look. That lost, confused, "what am I doing" look. And again, that feeling washed over me.

I would get mad at myself when I felt embarrassed about something Isla was doing. It felt wrong, and I was ashamed to be embarrassed of my baby. I went into super speed mode and picked up every single piece of stuffing and material. I wanted to throw everything away—fast and far. Fast enough so I could just forget it happened. Far enough so nobody else would see. I started thinking of lies I could tell if someone asked me where the pillow went. Maybe she peed at night and I couldn't clean it well enough? Maybe I tried to wash it and ruined it on accident?

As I was busy cleaning up and thinking of a lie, I noticed Isla again. She had a different look on her face now—one of sheer exhaustion. She was sitting up, but her eyes were extremely heavy, and her head was bobbing up and down. I laid her down, and she fell asleep instantly. That was weird. Why hadn't she just laid down? She was already sitting in bed. And why right then? It was still morning, and she hadn't been awake long.

I let my mind race again as I walked outside to the dumpster to throw everything that remained of the pillow away. When I came back inside, I tried to close the door softly, but Isla heard it and sprang up fast. It had not been more than eight minutes that she was asleep, and she woke up with bright eyes, like nothing had happened. Not a single sign of sleepiness or confusion. My girl was back. Back from where? That was the question I would give my life to find out, and since that day, I *have* dedicated most of my life to looking for the answer.

The movie *Little Miss Sunshine* totally rocks for so many reasons, but the absolute best scene is at the very end when Olive, the little girl, dances in the talent component of the Little Miss Sunshine pageant. The pageant is filled with thin-framed preteens with professional makeup, hair extensions, fake eyelashes, spray tans, and attitudes. Olive is not as thin, wears no makeup, keeps her straight hair down and natural, wears a simple dress, and is full of joy and innocence.

She is oblivious to everyone's judgment as she performs the dance her partially senile grandpa helped her choreograph to the song "Super Freak." The whole dance is awkwardly sexual and wildly inappropriate for a little girl, but Olive doesn't know or care, and she dances her heart out without a worry in the world. As the audience gasps and glares, Olive's whole family joins her on stage and starts dancing right along with her. It's a classic scene, and since watching that movie, Olive was my first choice for the name of my baby girl number two.

Unfortunately, my husband was not a huge fan, though he agreed it would be a pretty cool middle name. So in June, we welcomed Isla's sister, June Olive. (Unoriginal, maybe, but we love it.) When it was time for delivery, I dropped Isla off at my parent's house on the way to the hospital. I hugged her tight, crying on her little shoulder as I tried to soak in this last time that it would be just Isla. I was sad but hopeful— and after Isla's dramatic delivery, I was downright terrified.

June Olive's delivery was perfect. She was a one-push wonder. (Again, details spared for my darling children.) When I looked at that girl for the first time, I was in awe. Her face was perfect. Her head shape was perfect. Her skin was perfect. The delivery was perfect. Isla had a sister! How perfect! One of my most beautiful memories is of watching my Isla hold my June in her arms for the first time. Our family was growing and that bond would prove to be life changing for them both.

Chapter Five: 4–5 years
Whatever You Say Doc

A couple of days shy of her fourth birthday, Isla started a new school year in the three year old class. I had heard so much about the teacher of the three's from family, friends, and other parents at the school, Ms. Vela. She had been there for many years, and her love for teaching and the children was stronger than ever. She went above and beyond every year, and we were both thrilled to start Isla in her class. Ms. Vela had had her eye on Isla since the year before and had fallen in love with her because she was full of joy and energy—but also because she wasn't talking. This particular teacher loved a challenge, and helping Isla find her voice would be her challenge for the year. "I will get her to start talking," she assured me.

We had still not given up on speech therapy, even though I felt it was highly ineffective. Isla was still going twice per week while little June bug and I played and ate dinner in the waiting room and accompanied Isla to her three to four bathroom visits per hour. Instead of improving, Isla seemed to become increasingly distracted with each session. She simply could not focus, and every little sound or movement would throw the whole session into a mess.

She had also started to resist going in for sessions. As soon as they would call us back, she would wrap herself around me. She wouldn't cry or fuss, but she wouldn't budge, either.

June would be sitting on my lap whimpering for her dinner, and Isla would be stuck to me, sitting on my foot and holding on to my leg like a rope swing.

The therapist would be standing at the entrance waiting patiently, and I would become this crazy bag lady with one hand shushing June and the other hand trying to find the last remaining teething cookie for her in my gigantor purse or Isla's backpack or my enormous disaster of a diaper bag—all while trying to coax and bribe Isla with snacks or ice cream or a brand new car or anything, really—just to get her to cooperate. It would sometimes take almost half of the hour-long session to convince Isla to go in, and when things got desperate I would have to leave June on the floor crying while I carried Isla in myself, using my weak but improving peripheral vision to make sure June wasn't choking on whatever questionably edible item I'd found to give her. It was a struggle every time.

This started to happen at school, too. What had been seamless drop-offs a year ago were now sobbing, drama-filled mornings. Most days Ms. Vela would have to pick Isla up and carry her into the classroom. She would cry and call out to me. "Mommy!!! Peese I go you Mommy!!!" And the tears. Oh, the tears. They were unbearable.

It was a very hard way to start our day, but like so many of Isla's tendencies, it seemed very normal based on what I saw other parents go through.

The day school Isla attended had a standard way of evaluating students and conducted parent teacher conferences to update the parents on their child's academic and behavioral progress. Mid-fall of each school year, the teachers had to complete individual assessments of each child and then bring their findings to the parents.

In mid-spring the same assessment was repeated to check for retention and progress. So, when the time came for our mid-fall conference, I sat alone at a small table in the school library and listened as Ms. Vela described ten different assignments and tasks she used to assess the students.

"OK, for this assignment," Ms. Vela began, "we provide the students with a paper that has a big black circle on it. The only direction we give them is to draw a smiley face. Here is what Isla drew." Then she flipped over the paper and showed me. There was a small scribble of wavy lines in the lower right corner of the paper. No smiley face. Not even close. *Awesome.*

OK fine, I thought. *Big deal.* Maybe she didn't understand what a smiley face was. Maybe Ms. Vela should have worded it differently and instead asked her to draw eyes, a nose, and a mouth.

She turned to the next sheet in her stack. "For the next assignment we give the students a worksheet with different objects printed, and we tell them to circle the animals.

Here is what Isla circled." She flipped the paper over, and there were one to two random circles not necessarily drawn on or around any objects. *She probably heard Ms. Vela say "draw circles,"* I rationalized, starting to get annoyed.

"This assignment was three-fold," Ms. Vela said, moving on. "We told the students to draw a straight line going up and down, a straight line going side to side, and a wavy line. Here is what Isla drew."

Nothing. Scribbles.

Marvelous. OK, OK I get it. I started to fidget in my chair, and I could feel my face was flushed. Ms. Vela proceeded to show me the results of the remaining seven assessments, making it very clear to me that my kid didn't know anything and was not doing anything well.

Looking back, I believe it was important for me to see all of that to understand the severity of Isla's delays, but at the time it felt mean.

Ms. Vela was so experienced, and to this day she loves Isla so much that I truly believe she thought it was best to show me everything. But golly did it hurt. Do you remember that I mentioned I was valedictorian?

I mention that again here not to brag, but to make sure you understand that this was new to me. I worked hard at academics. I was an excellent reader, studied like a champ, and I made excellent grades and excelled at whatever I put my mind to.

I just assumed that every kid could do the same—and especially my kid, right?

I mean I know I had fantasies about her being a genius, but now the teacher was saying Isla was not even of average intelligence? What exactly was she telling me?

Ms. Vela asked for my permission to pass on the results of her assessment to the school's curriculum advisor. Isla would be headed to prekindergarten the next year, and she was concerned that Isla may not be ready. That seemed fair at the time, so I agreed. The whole time I kept thinking I was going to drill this kid every night with colors, shapes, numbers, and letters and teach her all I could to prove that she could learn.

Then came the first of three "aha moments" in Isla's story. Thanks to my dear friend Oprah Winfrey—well, she doesn't know she is my dear friend but nonetheless—thanks to Oprah, an "aha moment" actually has been added to the dictionary. It is defined as "a moment of sudden realization, inspiration, insight, recognition, or comprehension." People always ask me, "How did you know that something was wrong?" or "When did you realize something was off?" This was how, and this was when.

It was late October and time for the class Halloween party. Isla's day school had a really fun tradition where the younger children, dressed in their Halloween costumes of choice, would march around the school and into each classroom to show off their costumes while the older children handed them candy.

After the Halloween parade, we headed back to the classroom, where all of the kids went to their seats to get ready for snack time. I turned to put my purse down, and when I turned back I couldn't find Isla. I scanned all the desks, which were now filled with Elmo and Cinderella and Spiderman sitting patiently in place and waiting for yummy snacks, but where was my little genie? She was in a corner taking construction paper out of a bin. I patiently walked her back to her desk and got her all set up to enjoy the cute, creative Halloween snacks. But as I turned to talk to a parent, Isla decided to be creative too, taking her Oreo spider cookie and crumbling it in her hands. She was uber focused on her work, watching her hands and those crumbles intently.

I watched her for a while, just grabbing as much of the cookie as she could in each hand and then squeezing so the cookie and cream filling would seep through her fingers. Once each handful was sufficiently crumbled, she'd start again. I began to get that feeling again—you now the "e" word—so I intervened discreetly. "Hey, Isla, is that cookie yummy? Oh, let's try some juice. Here let me help you open it." We all know those darn juice pouches can be tricky, so I helped her put the straw in and tried to wipe some cookie crumbles from the table quickly before anyone noticed.

I turned to throw the crumbles in the trash and turned back around to find that Isla had squirted the juice on the plate with the cookie crumbles and was mixing it all together with her hands.

OK enough is enough. Just as I began trying to formulate a plan to stop this madness, the teacher broke in to announce it was time for a game.

Thank God. I tried to throw everything away quick. All the kids got up and walked over to the special circle-time rug. All the kids, of course, except Isla. She scrambled off to another corner, and I followed her quickly and pretended we were walking to the sink together to wash her hands.

"Good job Isla," I said, pretending it had been her idea. I quickly cleaned her up and sent her to the rug. The circle-time rug had individual squares on it for each student, but Isla plopped down almost on a kid's lap instead of on her own section. The kid, understandably annoyed, kind of squirmed, so Isla moved off his lap, but she was just so lost. *Why was she so lost?* I started to feel panicked. I am so ashamed to admit that I even considered picking up my cell phone and faking an "urgent" call from work just so I would not have to witness this anymore. Like everything else up to this point, I wanted to just pretend it wasn't happening. My mind knew the truth, but my heart hadn't caught up.

The game was hot potato, and the song was Monster Mash. Get it? Monster Mash, mashed potato, pass the potato... anyway, the kids were giggly and excited, and Isla started hopping up and down as the music started to play. The kids started passing the potato anxiously and nervously, shrieking occasionally if someone dropped it, but Isla was fascinated with everything and everyone *except* the potato.

She stared at each face intently. She watched everyone as if in a trance—the students, the parents, the teacher. She was so completely fascinated and distracted by everyone's reactions that she could not react, herself. "Pass it Isla! Isla, *pass it*! *Isla!!!*" Her friends screamed at her as she held the potato, completely unaware that something was in her hands.

It was right then, during a game of hot potato at a Halloween party that I knew. That's when I knew my daughter was different. She didn't act like everyone else. She didn't respond like everyone else. She didn't process instructions like everyone else. She didn't socialize like everyone else. She still didn't talk like everyone else. It was a moment of recognition that whatever "it" was, she was not just going to "grow out of it." If anything, "it" was getting worse.

It was a moment of comprehension that "it" was serious, and I needed to be aggressive and help my girl as fast as I could. I don't know how, but I knew then that I would never be the same. I just knew it. I could not begin to fathom all the challenges that lay ahead, but I did know they were coming.

By that time we had switched pediatricians. June and I had a bad experience at the first office we'd used, so I decided to get recommendations from friends and made a switch. I am so glad we did. The new pediatrician loved my kids—and still does to this day. He listened to me, however crazy I was, and never questioned my judgment as a mother or a pharmacist.

He referred us to one of the only available behavioral pediatricians in our area, but we were told it would be a five-month wait to see her.

I want to reiterate that Isla was not sick. She was not withdrawn or antisocial. She was full of joy, energy, love, and kindness. She had started incorporating a few more words by this point, mainly mimicking things I would say. She started saying "I wuv you," which, after three long years, was staggering to say the least. It was around this time that I noticed something special about my girl. Something that defines her, and I believe, will set her apart for her entire life.

One of the first times I noticed this special thing was on a routine trip to the grocery store, just Isla and me. Isla loved being out and about, but her attention span was so limited that I usually had to speed through stores like I was on a game show. I had a no-fail system. First, find a mini bag of Cheetos. Second, quickly head to the fresh produce and open the bag for her. I had until that mini bag of Cheetos was all eaten up to be in the checkout line, or I was in big trouble. I'd become such a champ at speed grocery shopping that, on this trip, I made it to the checkout line with a couple of Cheetos to spare. I started unloading my groceries onto the grocery conveyer belt when I noticed the cashier. Actually, I *smelled* the cashier. The line was filled with heavy smoke and cheap cologne. As the smell wrapped around me and lingered, I glanced up and saw an older gentleman, probably late 60s, behind the register. His hair was gray and not well kept.

He was wearing what looked like the entirety of his quite-eclectic jewelry collection, and his belly was sticking out of the bottom of his black shirt, which was worn so thin it was almost transparent. So after a couple of sneezes, I started hustling and loaded the conveyer belt as fast as I could, eager to get out of that line. Meanwhile my little girl was sitting in the front seat of the grocery basket, mesmerized, staring intently at all of him. I finished unloading and then moved my cart up toward the bagger, putting Isla almost directly in front of the cashier. She looked at him, giggled, smiled her big smile, and said, "You so cute!" I looked at her and then looked at him, and we were both equally shocked.

We awkwardly giggled, but before I could say anything, the cashier handed her a sticker and said, "Well if that is your way of asking for a sticker, then here you go." Isla grabbed it from him and put it right on her shirt. She was so happy she was completely lit up, inside and out. "I wuv you!" she blurted.

The cashier was quick and witty. "All the ladies do" he said.

I believe without a shadow of a doubt and with all my heart that Isla sees people through God's eyes. She sees people the way God sees people. She really sees them. She passes no judgment and no skepticism. She loves without needing a reason to love. She offers kindness without being asked. Isla's innocence is both terrifying and refreshing. That was one of the first "mommy lessons" that Isla has taught me.

I don't believe that special needs children are born to special parents. I believe that if you allow them to teach you, special needs children make parents special.

One week before our appointment with the behavioral pediatrician, I received a call from Isla's day school asking when I could come in to meet with Ms. Vela. I wasn't entirely surprised. Since our conference had been so rough, I'd had a feeling there would be a follow-up meeting.

But I was caught off guard when I walked into the office and the secretary said in a cheerful voice, "Oh hello! Let me tell the headmaster you are here."

What? The headmaster? I had never formally met the headmaster before. *Oh my God.* I just knew something was really wrong.

I walked into the conference room to find Ms. Vela, the curriculum director, and the headmaster all sitting at a table waiting for me. My heart was pounding so hard I could hear it and feel it in my head.

There in that room, I was told with more love, respect, and kindness than I could have asked for that my daughter could not continue at that school for the pre-K level. The headmaster and Ms. Vela were both quiet for most of the meeting as the curriculum director explained that, after further testing, it was apparent that they did not have the resources to help Isla to the extent that she needed.

I remember Ms. Vela staring at me the whole time with a caring smile and watery eyes, but all of us tried very hard to stay composed. I allowed my healthcare professional self to take over the meeting, because my mommy self was speechless for once. I asked what they recommended. I asked if she could come back if she improved. I thanked them for their time and attention and for being honest with me.

I told them I was already set to meet with a behavioral pediatrician in the coming week, and I was hopeful for answers. I could tell they were relieved by how I handled it, and I was relieved that I did not break—until I sat in my car.

The word that comes to mind was heartbroken. No more beautiful school? No more kind, compassionate teachers? No more Halloween parades? No more chapel? No more lessons about God's love? What now? Public school? I had worked so hard to have a career and finances that allowed me to pay for what I believed to be the best education money could buy, and she *couldn't* attend? Like I said, I was heartbroken.

One of the recommendations the day school gave me was to contact the local school district's special education department and have someone come out to observe Isla to see if she qualified for an early intervention program.

The very next day I went to meet with one of the local school district's diagnosticians in person because I have always felt that face to face interactions hold more value and can be much more impactful and memorable than phone calls or e-mails.

I had an appointment, so I was expecting an office visit of some kind, but when I arrived, the secretary wasn't quite sure where the diagnostician was and had to make a call to find her. After a few minutes, the diagnostician walked in with two other people, each with their hands full of Whataburger. I stood up to greet them, and she quickly apologized about the food. I sat in a conference room with the diagnostician and two speech therapists, one of whom worked with the autism team, and told them my story. Even though they were all chomping on lunch, they were attentive, and I could tell they wanted to help.

As soon as I was done explaining our situation, the diagnostician described some of their early intervention programs but mentioned that a therapist would have to go to the day school to meet and observe Isla first. I gave them my permission right then and there, and the speech therapist from the autism team, Miss. Sally was the first to volunteer. That would be one of the first times I would hear the word "autism" in relation to my daughter.

Miss. Sally seemed especially interested in Isla, which kind of bothered me, because I didn't know which part of my story or description of Isla made her curious about an autism diagnosis.

I didn't ask too many questions because I wanted all the help I could get. A couple of mornings later, Miss. Sally went to visit my Isla.

It was still early when my cell phone rang. "Well your baby is definitely not autistic," Miss. Sally said with certainty. I didn't think she'd had enough time for observation, but I didn't want to be rude, and I was far from an expert at the time. "When I walked into the classroom, Isla was the first one to come up to me," Miss. Sally continued. "She immediately said hi and held my hand." Yes, my sweet girl always noticed others and wanted everyone to feel welcomed. She then explained that Isla was too friendly and too outgoing to be autistic, and that children with autism are withdrawn and antisocial, especially with those they don't know. She explained that she would pass her observations along to the diagnostician and they would contact me with next steps if I wanted to move forward with that school district for the next school year.

It was time for our long-awaited visit with the behavioral pediatrician. Remember the one that was supposed to give me all the answers? It was the week before spring break, and I knew it was important for both my husband and me to be present for that visit.

We arrived on time, and like every visit that would follow, we spent a lot of time filling out reams of detailed, extensive paperwork. There were questions about my pregnancy, delivery, medications, my health, and Isla's health. They wanted specifics on when she first smiled, sat up, walked, rolled over, etc.

They wanted a detailed written explanation of why we were there and what we found to be abnormal with our child. There were questions about the family dynamic, siblings, parent marital status and household numbers. They even asked about our religious beliefs and our preferences about medication therapy.

A nurse finally called us in and proceeded to ask us all of the same questions that I had just taken so much time to answer on paper, but we were patient. The nurse took Isla's height and weight and then led us to a larger room filled with toys. There was a play kitchen with plastic food, laminated pictures on the walls, and bins of blocks. The doctor was the quiet type—reserved and dry, but attentive. She asked us almost every single question that I had just answered on paper and for the nurse, and as I recited the details for the third time, I started to think, *man, this had better be worth it.* The doctor spent about twenty minutes with Isla. She asked her questions, asked her to complete stacking and counting tasks with blocks, asked her to find certain items from the kitchen and place them in specific containers, and asked her to sing a song of her choice. For the most part, Isla seemed to either ignore her or not understand the requests, though if I remember correctly, she was able to mumble some words to *"Twinkle Twinkle Little Star"* and the alphabet song.

When the doctor stepped out to complete her assessment, we praised Isla and told her she did a great job. Honestly, we were just happy she hadn't fussed too much about wanting to leave the room, so to us she had done a great job.

After what seemed like eternity, the doctor returned with a stack of papers and sat down across from us. Isla continued to play with the toy kitchen as the doctor explained to us that Isla was too young to diagnose anything right now.

What? Then why the heck are we here?! Pissed-off Mom reared her head immediately at the thought that we'd wasted our time and would be leaving without any answers.

The behavioral pediatrician told us she tested Isla using a physical scale, adaptive behavior scale, social emotional scale, and a communication scale, all of which showed she was equivalent to a two year old. She went on to say that part of the assessment was to get a baseline IQ and that Isla's was very low.

Greg totally sensed that Pissed-off Mom needed him to step in at this point. "OK. You can just tell us. What are you saying?" he asked.

"Well, IQs are not formal or final until after the age of seven," the doctor said. "But IQs lower than 70 indicate a diagnosis of MR."

"What?" Super pissed-off Mom chimed in now. "MR? Wait, what?"

"Right now Isla is testing as mentally retarded", the doctor said coolly.

"WHAT?!" I yelped.

Oh my God. Gosh that was such a humongous "ugly". My head started to spin, and I started to cry. Greg rubbed my back, and I couldn't believe he was so calm and collected. He asked the doctor what her recommendation was.

Yes, of course, OK, fine. What is your recommendation now that you have ruined my life, doctor? Fortunately, super pissed-off Mom was too stunned to speak.

"If I were you I would withdraw her from private school immediately," the doctor said. "She needs to be enrolled in public school as soon as possible to start receiving special education services. Do not waste time."

Did you just tell me not to waste time? After you made me wait five freaking months to see you? I'm the one wasting time?! Oooh no you didn't!

She then mentioned that she thought Isla would benefit from occupational therapy in addition to speech therapy because her fine and gross motor skills appeared delayed. We had noticed that, too, so it was not surprising.

In fact, on top of lacking motor skills, we'd also noticed that she continued to lack normal reflexes or responses. For example, if someone dropped a full cup, they'd rush to pick it up to hopefully prevent a big spill. Not Isla. She would just stare at the cup on the ground as all the liquid seeped out. The same happened with toys or other objects. If they fell, she would just stare. We weren't sure if occupational therapy would help with that, but we were hopeful. According to the behavioral pediatrician, Isla was considered delayed in all areas—about two years behind her biological age.

As the doctor left the room, Greg thanked her for her time because he was amazing and composed. Meanwhile, I allowed my world to crumble around me.

I looked at Isla as she played and smiled back at us. *That doctor was dead wrong. MR? Give me a break. She doesn't know my kid and all she can do.* No, I was not accepting that. I did not accept it. I told Greg that we were not going to tell anyone about what had just happened. It would not be official until she was seven, so nobody needed to know, not even family. He smiled at me patiently, agreeing only because I was so distraught and dramatic.

During our forty-five-minute drive back home, we decided to take the doctor's recommendation, withdraw Isla, and see if a local elementary school would accommodate her. Greg headed back to work, and I headed to Isla's day school to update them on the sad news.

It was on that drive that I decided to throw myself a marvelous pity party. Oh, and it was marvelous. There were streamers of anger, balloons of frustration, confetti of fear, cocktails of sadness, and gifts upon gifts of loss.

Right there, right then was the moment I started to feel loss. Where was the daughter I'd dreamed of? If she was that lost and "MR," did she even know what was going on around her? Did she know how desperately I loved her? Was this going to be forever? Would she live with me forever?

My heart was hurting, and my head was hurting, and I was now in the parking lot of that absolutely amazing day school about to withdraw her.

Feeling completely sorry for myself, and even more exponentially sorry for my baby girl, I dragged myself out of my car and gently placed Isla on the sidewalk. We held hands as she skipped into the front office.

With no expression I asked to speak to the curriculum director. She quickly came out of the office, took one look at my face, and knew something was wrong. I explained what had happened in the shortest, most unemotional way I could, and she hugged me and said she was sorry to see Isla go but wanted the best for her. I agreed, and I was just about to leave and rejoin my pity party when the headmaster came out of her office.

"Lisa, come in here."

We stepped into her office while the secretary kept Isla occupied.

"What happened?" she asked.

I answered dryly and unemotional, "The doctor said she needs to be in public school. She said not to waste time and to start services as soon as possible."

"Did she test her IQ?" When I nodded, she asked, "What was it?"

At first I was indignant. My daughter's IQ was none of this lady's business. Plus, I had just told my husband we wouldn't share that detail. But I was in a daze, and something about her forwardness compelled me to answer.

"Under 70. The doctor said it is not final until seven years old but right now she is MR."

I closed my eyes and began to cry, right there in her office.

Then that lady, that headmaster, whom I hardly knew and who later became a great friend, took a chance. She didn't know me either, but experience and conviction told her she needed to step in. She placed her hands firmly on my shoulders and looked me square in the face. "Lisa, you are a parent of a special needs child. You need to educate yourself as much as you can in the next few days and weeks. Nobody else will advocate for Isla if you don't."

Right then and there, something shifted in me. Almost immediately I packed up the streamers of anger, popped the balloons of frustration, swept up the confetti of fear, and tossed those cocktails of sadness down the sink. The gifts of loss stayed unopened in the corner of my mind. My pity party was over, thanks to a brave, excellent administrator.

That same day I got my hands on a "Special Education in the Public School Law" book. I read it front to back. Most things I didn't understand yet, but I wanted to know where to find information in the future.

I contacted a local elementary and convinced the principal to accept Isla as a transfer. It was a tough sell to take a new student after spring break, almost at the end of the school year when we all know everyone is mentally checked out—not to mention a student who would need to be tested and who would need special education services.

She agreed, but she made sure I knew she was doing me a huge favor.

Again, humbled and grateful, I had no choice but to swallow my pride and thank her profusely as I prepared myself mentally for what the next few weeks would bring.

So here is my small request for any and all principals reading this book. When a parent calls you with a request like mine, please, please don't say, "Well OK, but I want you to know that I am doing you a huge favor." Really? Even if you are doing them a huge favor, just say yes or no and be as kind as you can.

The biggest challenge with transferring Isla to public school was that she had never been to public school, and Texas law required her to be in a regular education classroom for six weeks so the teacher could evaluate her to be sure she qualified for special services and testing. I knew those six weeks would be very difficult for both Isla and the teacher, but we had to follow the rules.

Meanwhile we started occupational therapy twice a week, which meant we were in a therapy of some kind four times per week. Isla seemed to enjoy occupational therapy at first, seeing as there were so many sensory-friendly toys to play with. However, she eventually started having the same problem as she was having in speech therapy sessions. Her distraction was overwhelming, and she started resisting the sessions.

It took only two weeks for the school to contact me. The teacher simply could not accommodate Isla in her classroom anymore. We had to set up an emergency meeting so that I could sign the consent forms that would allow the school to move her to the PPCD classroom.

PPCD stands for Preschool Program for Children with Disabilities.

"Disability" was another one of those "uglies" for me, not because I don't believe in true disabilities but because the image that brought to my mind didn't match up with my image of my girl. By that point there were only six weeks left of school, so all formal testing would have to wait until the following year.

So we continued taking Isla to speech and occupational therapy, and we waited patiently for the next full year to start.

It was very important to me during that time to protect Isla. I didn't want to share too many "uglies" with too many people, because what if things changed? So we avoided discussing all but the bare minimum about Isla, and because we remained positive, so did our family and friends. I specifically remember a dinner date with some good friends whose children were the same age as ours. We sat around their dinner table with delicious pork lettuce wraps and homemade kimchi, and I told them how the doctor said we should consider Isla about two years delayed in every way. Our good friend looked over at me and said, "So when she is 26 it will be like she is 24?" He smiled, and we all laughed. Great point.

I was hopeful. Who knows? Maybe private school was too advanced. Maybe public school or the PPCD classroom or the new teacher would help turn on the light bulb once and for all.

Chapter Six: 5-6 years
Welcome to the Spectrum

The week that Isla turned five years old, she started her first full year of public school. She spent her days in a PPCD class that was co-taught by two special education teachers. One of these teachers, already an acquaintance of mine, came highly recommended, so I was happy and felt comfortable with her placement. To my knowledge, Isla had to be formally tested by the school's diagnostician, speech therapist, occupational therapist, and special education teachers in a process that would take several weeks. Meanwhile, I was asked to fill out evaluations of what I'd noticed at home regarding her challenging behaviors and academic strengths and weaknesses. This would all determine the "labels" that would be placed on Isla to qualify her for special education services within the public school system.

Once the testing was complete, it was time for our first official ARD meeting. During Admission, Review, and Dismissal (ARD) meetings, a group of people come together to make an Individualized Education Plan (IEP) for a special needs student. For parents like me, these meetings are critical.

Each professional that had taught or tested the child and really gotten a sense of their academic delays, challenging behaviors, progress etc. presents his or her findings to the parents and the school administration, usually the assistant principal.

But this was more than an opportunity to hear from the experts—it was a formal opportunity for parents to advocate for their children. If something needed to be changed or improved in the education plan, or a child needed particular equipment or resources, this is where the parents could ask.

Perhaps with the exception of the diagnostician (because this is their main job), it is rumored that the other parties in the room don't look forward to these meetings very much. For the therapists and special education teachers, they require a crap load of paperwork that may or may not even be read and they can really take away time from their day and their class. For the administrators, although these are routine, they also take away tremendous amounts of time and attention seeing as they have to run an entire school in the background. And for the random teacher walking the hall at the exact moment everyone realizes they need one more teacher present to legally start the ARD meeting, they are just plain bad luck.

In preparation for our first ARD meeting, we received a large packet in the mail about one week prior. It included an agenda, some of the findings from the speech and occupational therapists, and instructions to review all the documents before the meeting.

I put the packet aside and waited until the evening before the meeting to review it with Greg so we could discuss the results and think about what we wanted to include in Isla's IEP. The first document was the agenda, and on the very top it read, "Isla has reached the age of 16 and is no longer eligible for services." *Uh, what?* Then further down it read, "Isla Peña, 1st grade." *Hum, wrong again.* I busted out my highlighter—well two different color highlighters to be exact.

With the yellow highlighter, I highlighted everything that was just blatantly wrong, and with the pink highlighter I highlighted every spelling error and grammar error. Then I realized that there were many duplicated sentences, so I just circled those with my pen. I know I sound like a nut job, and I know that therapists, teachers, and diagnosticians are human and make mistakes, too.

But when I went back to count everything I'd highlighted and circled, I counted almost thirty mistakes. I was looking at perhaps the worst copy-and-paste job possible.

On top of all that, after all the testing, all the waiting, and withdrawing Isla from private school, the packet showed she was approved for just thirty minutes per week of speech therapy and thirty minutes per week of occupational therapy. THIRTY MINUTES A WEEK! I could elaborate here but what's the point. In the famous words of my hands down favorite writer of all time, all I have to say is…horsecrappery.

This is what I took Isla out of private school for? Did they even test her for real? Does their software allow them to copy and paste to every student's report? Was this even Isla's report?

Now, if you'll remember, my husband had a minor in special education and knew first-hand about ARD meetings, documentation, and paperwork. He also served as an excellent balance for my crazy self in any situation, so he was a good barometer for whether I was overreacting. But he agreed that the copy and paste job was bad enough that I needed to address it at the meeting. *Address it? Oh man, was I going to address it.*

I want to direct this part to anyone who is a special education teacher, public school speech or occupational therapist, public school diagnostician, and/or administrator. I want you to know that I don't pretend to know your job. I have always been mindful that we cannot judge others if we don't walk in their shoes. I do know your days are crazy busy. I do know that you deal with behavior issues, restraining students, emotional disturbance, abuse and neglect. I know you see it all, and I know that sometimes, like all of us, you hate and love your job at the same time. I want you to know that I know you have the best intentions for every child. I also know that you may not have the time, resources, or training to deal with all of the special education students in your school effectively or to the extent that you'd like. On the flip side, when I got pregnant and had this little baby inside me, I dreamed of Gifted and Talented meetings, not ARD meetings.

As a parent, I don't want to attend these meetings any more than you do. I did not plan on having children to watch them struggle, to be so intellectually, academically, and developmentally delayed that they couldn't be in a regular classroom. It is sad and hard and lonely, and the feeling of loss is great. So since we all have to attend these meetings, let's do our best and give our best each time. I am only asking you to take a quick second to do a spell check and grammar review, and maybe just to read your reports out loud to yourself before you submit them. These students may be just names on a roster, but for us parents, they're our most precious gifts.

But back to the ARD meeting.

The first meeting served two purposes: to label my kiddo with a specific disability and to determine how much of which services she qualified for. Labels are also "uglies," and the very first label that Isla was given at her new school was OHI: Other Health Impairment. The sarcastic translation is, we have no idea what is wrong with your kid but she *definitely* needs to be in special education so we'll use this one.

The official translation is, your kid is not presenting with hallmark characteristics of any specific disorder or label, so we will place her where all the mystery students go—in the OHI pile—until she gets older and can be more "testable." In Texas this is also known as "NCEC" or "Non-Categorical Early Childhood" and is used for students aged three to five who have delays that necessitate special education services.

It is very difficult to diagnose these young children, and sometimes with early intervention they will "graduate" from special education services by the first grade. So the state uses NCEC temporarily to ensure the special education or disability label will not follow them through each grade.

Needless to say we had to continue speech and occupational therapy in the evenings because 30 minutes a week at school was not sufficient, which was a total bummer. During the fall of her first year in public school, attention deficit disorder became more apparent. Isla was all over the place. She required constant redirection in the classroom and really began to exhibit behavior problems. She would act out and then become destructive and aggressive when disciplined. She was highly inattentive and was still not showing any academic progress.

That was about the time I decided to branch out and get a second opinion. I mention "branching out" several times in the next few chapters, so I want to make something clear. I love my home. The Rio Grande Valley (RGV) has been my home since I was in the fifth grade, and it will always be my home. Most of our family lives in the RGV, and it is a great place to raise children, offering an idyllic small-town environment with large cities close by. However, one of the biggest drawbacks of living here is the insufficient number of healthcare facilities and professionals. The RGV is extremely underserved in terms of almost every single medical professional you can think of, so imagine you are one of the only specialists in the RGV.

You are bombarded daily with more patients than you can safely or effectively manage. Do you think you have time to read up on the most recent advances in medical care? Do you think you want to read articles on the latest research in pediatric neurological disorders when you go home each night? Or review all the clinical trials that were incorporated into the new DSM V criteria? Or review the new evidence-based therapies for special needs of all kinds? Probably not. Most physicians and specialists barely have time to "fight the fires," much less dig into all of the latest and greatest for your kid. So I branched out.

I made an appointment with a pediatric neurologist at a prominent children's hospital in the next big city, which was two hours away from us, Corpus Christi. The night before we left, I prepared a timeline for the pediatric neurologist so he could get a good picture of Isla as a patient and see how everything had progressed over time.

As I drove I watched Isla through my rearview mirror, and I was hopeful. We had bought her a portable DVD screen—the kind that Velcros to the head rests—to play movies. It lasted about twenty minutes before Isla kicked it, broke it in half, pushed all the buttons and then started chewing on the wires. I should have known better. But she was carefree and happy, with her big curls bouncing up and down to the music.

This new doctor was nice and friendly. He asked me what seemed like a hundred questions as he reviewed the timeline I'd provided.

He also asked Isla many questions and observed her for a while as she interacted with me and some toys, and he listened carefully to her responses to his questions.

Suddenly he swiveled his little doctor stool around and looked right at me.

"Your daughter is on the spectrum."

My head immediately felt like it weighed fifty pounds, and I got a little faint. "I'm sorry, I'm not understanding. What, what spectrum?"

He smiled. "Your daughter is autistic. She has PDD."

OK now I was really lost, and also panicking a little.

"OK. Hold on. Wait. Can we start from the beginning? So the sleep apnea did not cause these delays?"

"Oh no," said the neurologist. "If she had brain damage from the sleep apnea it would already be apparent in her physical development, and there would be other medical complications, as well."

"So you are telling me my daughter has autism and also just happened to have sleep apnea when she was a toddler?"

"Yes."

By now I was in full-on panic mode.

"What does that mean? I mean, what does PDD stand for?" I asked.

Meanwhile, my sweet Isla Love had come over to me because she heard my shaky voice and knew—she just sensed something was not right. That was my beautiful Isla's spirit, so in touch with others feelings and emotions.

She sat on my lap and studied my face intently, desperately trying to be reassured that I was OK. Her eyes were darting, scanning every single quiver of my lip, every flare of my nostrils and the tears welling up in my eyes, and when she confirmed that everything was not OK, she put her head on my chest and wrapped her little arms around me.

"Pervasive Developmental Disorder," the neurologist said. "It is on the high functioning side of autism."

I could hardly get my head around what he was saying. High functioning? What did that mean? She didn't even know her colors or shapes or numbers. How high functioning could she be? *What is happening?*

"So I want to make sure I understand. This is not going to go away, right? I mean, is she going to be with me forever? What is the prognosis?" My tongue was numb and I remember feeling like I was slurring every word.

The doctor's knowing smile said it all. This was the first time I can remember getting a pity smile. And let me tell you, those do not feel good.

Right then and there, everything that was *not* going to happen over the next twenty years flashed before my eyes. No organized sports? No regular classrooms? No college? No job? No boyfriends? No wedding? No children? No retirement for Greg and me? Would we have to get her a caregiver?

I started to feel her as she sat there hugging me. I started caressing her legs and arms and hair and tummy.

This can't be true. Not my perfect girl! My sadness for Isla was all encompassing. How would her life be fulfilling if she would never experience all of the wonders it has to offer? She would never know the way it feels to win the big game or get an A+ on a paper she worked hard for. She would never know what it feels like to go to college, be independent, make friends, and make a ton of fun mistakes. She would never have a first kiss or know the love of a husband. She would never feel a baby kicking inside her or know the love of a child.

The doctor finally interrupted my endless loop of no's and never's. "I know this is hard and unfair, but all of her future depends on you. There are a lot of parents that send their children to school each day and just try to keep them safe and happy.

There are others that go above and beyond to get them the best support and look for something they love or are good at to build on and help them become independent. It all depends on you."

"What do I do?" was all I could manage. "What would you do if you were me?"

"You need to give her aggressive ABA therapy for as many hours as you can afford. Every brain can be trained."

Every brain can be trained. ABA therapy. Aggressive. Wait. What is ABA? Who cares, Lisa! She needs it.

I was trying to make mental notes as fast as I could.

He handed me a pamphlet for the one ABA program in town and encouraged me to visit.

We were two hours from home, but of course as I skimmed the pamphlet I made a mental note to stop by and at least see what it was all about.

"I also recommend that she gets an MRI and a chromosome analysis," said the neurologist.

How many times could I get caught off guard in one conversation? "An MRI? For what?" I asked.

"To rule out brain tumors, brain damage, etc." he replied.

That was too many "uglies" to process.

I signed a consent form for the MRI and chromosome testing, and we headed to another wing of the hospital for the blood work. The chromosome testing would be done that same day with a simple blood sample, but Isla would need to be under general anesthesia for the MRI (staying still was not her strong suit), so we'd have to schedule that for another day.

As we waited to be called in for the blood work, everything started to get mixed up in my head. *Wait a minute—the school district said she was not autistic. So who is wrong?* Our local school district had declined to test Isla for autism because the neighboring district had already "ruled that out." I rubbed my eyes and tried to focus on the task at hand.

As I scanned the room for something to take in with us to distract Isla while they took her blood, I noticed the people around us for the first time. There was a woman sitting in the corner, crying while she rocked a car seat with a newborn inside.

There was an older woman holding a toddler, both in pajamas and both nodding off. There was a middle-aged man sitting alone with his hands clutched together, head down, and feet fidgeting. I remember wondering what everyone's story was.

How did we all end up here, and what were the others waiting to learn? I seriously wanted a group hug. Don't worry, the nurse called us back before I could ask a room of total strangers for a group hug, and Isla did amazing.

On the way home I called Isla's school and told them that the pediatric neurologist had just given us an official diagnosis of ASD (Autism Spectrum Disorder)—specifically PDD (Pervasive Developmental Disorder)-NOS (Not Otherwise Specified). I requested that the school test Isla for autism as soon as possible. I also specified that I wanted a particular administrator from the special education services department to conduct the testing to ensure a thorough evaluation by the most experienced professional. Yes, parents, you have the right to ask for your preference when it comes to testing. Find the most experienced person on the team, and request that person.

It wasn't five minutes after we got home that I put Isla to sleep and got on my laptop. My Googling that night was aggressive and intense. I searched everything I could think of, every which way I could think of, so I wouldn't miss anything. On that day I learned about Applied Behavioral Analysis (ABA therapy the neurologist had suggested).

It turns out ABA is an evidence-based therapy treatment for autism, and the United States Surgeon General recommends two years of aggressive ABA therapy for forty hours per week upon initial diagnosis. But the recommendation alone wasn't enough. I am a studies girl. I wanted to read the data. I wanted proof, and I wanted *valid* proof. I read articles, clinical trials, studies, ongoing research updates, and the actual document from the US Surgeon General.

I read the entire "The First 100 Days" packet from Autism Speaks. Once I was convinced that Isla needed ABA, I began a new search. *Where are these programs?*

The closest was the one the pediatric neurologist had mentioned in Corpus Christi, but the website specified that it was not full day and was not covered by my insurance because it involved music therapy. *Hmm.* We were going back for the MRI in a week, so I knew I still had to visit to rule it out. What about options in the Valley? Everything I Googled pulled up the name of just one professor at a local university, whom I e-mailed immediately. But still, I'd found no evidence of a school, a program, or a facility. So again, I branched out.

I extended my search to all of Texas, and lo and behold, the options were endless. There were schools and programs all around the state, with the closest reputable one about four hours from where we lived. I read reviews and newsletters from each. I joined e-mail groups for updates. I e-mailed several that looked promising to inquire whether they'd accept my insurance.

I was on a mission, and I am totally embarrassed to admit how many times I clicked refresh on my e-mail waiting for responses…at midnight.

I fell asleep that night thinking that we could not move. *We can't move, right?* I had my dream job already, and so did my husband, and although it would be easy for him to find work anywhere, it wouldn't for me. I had to stay within a certain area of Texas in order to continue receiving my salary, which I knew would be important to afford the therapy. And of course, all the ABA schools or programs I liked were outside that area.

The first contact I made was with a therapy center in my town that mentioned "ABA principles" on its website. It was really a speech and occupational therapy center, but a particular lead therapist who worked there had great interest in ABA therapy and incorporated that model into her practice. I made an appointment with her right away for a face-to-face visit. Annie was warm, inviting, and genuinely passionate. She was not a Board Certified Behavioral Analyst (BCBA) or certified to give ABA therapy, but she had worked for clinics in other parts of the country that incorporated the same ABA models and methods in speech and occupational therapy for children with autism and had found it to be very successful compared to conventional models.

Was that why "conventional" speech and occupational therapy had not worked for Isla?

She also told me that there was free ABA training available online for parents and teachers.

These courses were not licensed or official, but she vouched for their effectiveness in helping parents and teachers incorporate ABA principles in the home and classroom.

Annie had also started a small parent support group that met monthly at her clinic, and she invited me to attend. I agreed, and as chance would have it, the next meeting was that same week. In hindsight, I was totally not ready to attend one of these. In total there were four parents, one researcher, one vendor, and Annie. First on the agenda was a discussion on wandering. I sat there, dumbstruck, as parents told horror stories of their kids wandering out of their homes, going missing for hours, and sometimes being found near bodies of water.

I heard stories of parents getting calls from the school staff when their kids had wandered off during recess and were nowhere to be found. I heard stories of children following certain vehicles or people that interested them with zero sense of danger.

The lump in my throat grew larger and larger, and I quickly realized that I was not ready for all of this. I didn't know enough and hadn't experienced enough to share or to even really understand that this was what our future looked like. My mind was just racing with thoughts of tracking devices. I could certainly give Isla a cell phone, but should I also buy a harness or leash for public places? Good God, it was too much.

Next on the meeting's agenda was the researcher who was from a local university who spoke to us about a project they were working on called "The Tooth Fairy Study."

The study specifically targeted Hispanic children with autism because this population had not yet been researched at a national level. Their theory postulated the possibility of neurotoxins in the environment affecting children in ways that trigger autism. It was proposed that the teeth of these children could be tested to measure what substances the children were exposed to in utero. All I could think of was the excessive amount of Taco Bell I'd consumed during my pregnancy. *Surely there aren't neurotoxins in the nachos bell grande?*

When the meeting finally ended, I was out the door quick, a mess of new neuroses and worries and guilt. If you are a parent whose child recently got a diagnosis like this, it is hard for me to advise you to go to a parent support group as quickly as I did.

I would highly suggest that you look for a group that focuses on issues for *new* diagnoses. The particular group I went to was too much too fast, and it was too scary for me that soon after diagnosis.

The last resource that Annie gave me was the name of a retired BCBA in the area who was involved in research regarding testing for autism. The professional was offering free autism assessments to test diagnostic methods and provided one free hour of consultation in return. I was all in, so I set up a meeting.

The door to the office indicated that the retired BCBA was a behavioral consultant, and she had many, many letters after her name.

Isla and I walked into a dim office full of incense and what sounded like soft tribal music. The walls were painted deep, warm colors, the floor was lined with animal skins, and there were small and large artifacts on every wall and table. It was kind of creepy but kind of cool at the same time. I felt Isla tense up a little bit as she scanned the walls and smelled the incense, but the soothing music kept her from totally freaking out. The test Isla took that day was called the ADOS-2 assessment, which stands for Autism Diagnostic Observation Schedule-Module 2. It was a standardized assessment of communication, social interaction, and play or imaginative use of materials in order to diagnose autism or other pervasive developmental disorders within the autism spectrum. This test was totally weird. I'll give you two examples that I remember. First, the dolls. The consultant placed three dolls in front of Isla—a mom, a dad, and a baby—and she left them there for a bit to see what Isla would do.

Isla hadn't really started playing with dolls yet, so she just stared at the consultant. The consultant didn't say a word—no prompt, no instruction, only silence. It was seriously awkward.

After bouts of staring, she wrote something in her notebook and then placed a toy sofa and a toy truck next to the dolls. Again no prompts or instructions. Isla smiled at me, and I smiled back with an "I am so sorry this is so weird" smile. Finally the consultant said, "Isla you can play with the dolls if you want to." After a few more moments of staring around the room, Isla finally picked up the mom doll and placed her on the sofa.

She didn't bend the doll's body to sit her down, but just laid her prone on the sofa. The consultant jotted down more notes and moved on to the next task. The other example I remember involved a bar of soap and a small washcloth. The consultant sat Isla at a small desk and placed both the bar of soap and the washcloth in front of her, then asked, "Isla, can you show me how you wash your face?" As soon as she finished her question, my frustration started to build, and as usual the crazy mommy thoughts started once again.

Getting frustrated Mom: Ugh! NOT FAIR! Shouldn't the consultant have asked me first how we wash her face? Isla doesn't wash her own face, and we don't use a bar. In fact, I don't think Isla has ever seen a bar of soap in her life!

Calm, Educated Mom: It has to be part of the evaluation. Trust the process.

Isla just sat there, staring at the soap and then the washcloth and then me.

I struggled to contain myself, and when the consultant asked "Isla can you show me how you wash your hands?" I silently begged Isla to *do something* to indicate she noticed the soap—pick it up, touch it, or even just point to it—so the consultant would finally move on.

Finally, after a gauntlet of puzzles and flashcards and "seek and find" tasks—none of which Isla responded to— it was over, and the consultant thanked us for our time.

I made a follow-up appointment for the next week to get the results and my free hour of parent training/consultation.

I went to that appointment alone and sat a little nervously as the consultant slid the results across the table.

Results: "The total score for Isla on the ADOS-2, Module 2 is 5. The cut-off score for autism spectrum, for a child who is 5 years or older, is 8. Based on this ADOS-2 administration, Isla does not meet the criteria for the autism spectrum disorder."

WHAT. THE. HECK.

By this point I was confused and upset and frustrated. Was she autistic or not? Was the school going to do the same test and say the same thing? Why didn't the pediatric neurologist mention the ADOS-2 test for diagnosis? He told me he used the DSM-V for diagnosis—the *Diagnostic and Statistical Manual of Mental Disorders, 5th Edition* was the gold standard for everything mental health. I knew I was going to have to go home and reread the portion of DSM-V pertaining to autism. At the end of the consultant's findings was a disclaimer:

"The results for this ADOS-2 assessment are not a component of a multi-disciplinary team assessment. If these results are used to obtain services through the public school system, it is recommended that a multi-disciplinary team assessment be completed to obtain more complete information about Isla."

No kidding.

I composed myself because now I had to sit through a parent training, and I needed to focus. The consultant was incredibly knowledgeable and genuinely wanted to help me.

We discussed certain behaviors that concerned me, and she encouraged me to use the Questions About Behavioral Function (QABF) form to track each behavior. You are supposed to list the problem behavior on top of the form and then answer questions like when it occurred, how it occurred, what triggered it, how the child responded or acted, etc. Each answer comes with a point value, and at the end, your point total identifies the probable source of the behavior—for example, whether the child was seeking attention or showing non-social cues. The idea is that, if you know why the child is doing something, you can help eliminate the triggers and use positive reinforcement and praise in moments when the child does not exhibit the behavior.

This consultation was also the first time I heard of visual structure, which involves actual pictures of tasks placed on a board or wall. These pictures should be of activities like a child making a bed or brushing her teeth and of objects like an iPad or a swing set. The idea is to arrange the activity pictures on the board or wall each day in the order you want them completed. The object picture represents the reward or positive reinforcement for completing the tasks.

Next, I asked how I could help Isla develop her social skills, and the consultant recommended frequent, brief, supervised play dates that were structured with games and music. After a few more questions and answers, I gathered all of the paperwork and thanked the consultant for her time and attention. She wished me luck.

Yes, I thought, *good luck to me.*

As I stepped out of the building my cell phone rang. I saw the number from the children's hospital on the screen, and my hand literally trembled as I fumbled with my phone, afraid of what I was about to hear.

As I expected, it was the pediatric neurology nurse calling with the results of the genetic testing. I put on my very best calm voice to cover the panic as I told her to go ahead and give me the report. It was mercifully short.

"Everything was normal." Just like that, I scratched ~~genetic abnormality~~ off the list.

Now it was time for the MRI.

Again we made the drive a couple of hours back to the children's hospital and prepared for Isla to be put under general anesthesia for the second time. She had tolerated the anesthesia very well when she had her tonsils and adenoids removed, so that was not my worry.

My worries were a thousand other things. If it wasn't genetic then it had to be some kind of damage, right? Or worse, some kind of growth? Your mind can play dirty tricks on you in these situations, and I had to keep reminding myself that my girl was super healthy. I had absolutely no reason to believe that she was gravely ill.

As I knew she would, Isla did great with the anesthesia and the MRI, and we were out in time to stop by the ABA clinic the pediatric neurologist had recommended. Isla was still groggy and stayed with my parents in the car while I went inside by myself.

There were two chairs and a small desk in the waiting room, and one of the chairs was occupied by a young man wearing a padded helmet and tapping his head backwards against the wall, arms crossed on his chest. The friendly lady behind the desk gave me some brochures and information to read while I waited for one of the main behavioral therapists to begin my tour.

My guide showed me each room/activity center and explained that the ABA program here consisted of four hours per day of one-on-one therapy. She told me that several local school districts were incorporating ABA into their special education classrooms but that it was hit or miss depending on the teacher, training, and skill level. Right away I knew that particular place wasn't for Isla because half day was not what I was looking for, and it would also require us to move. However, as I toured I noticed many of the recommendations the consultant had given me, including a variety of visual structures on the walls and individualized token boards for rewards and positive reinforcement. I was reassured, and I knew then that I had to make finding a full-time ABA program for Isla a priority.

Shortly after that visit the professor I mentioned earlier, who worked at a university in the Valley, got back to me. She was a BCBA and had worked many years as a diagnostician in the public school districts. She was sorry she couldn't help me more, but she did take time to educate me on BCBAs. Board Certified Behavioral Analysts are licensed professionals who can bill insurance for ABA therapy.

I found out that, while ABA was a method that could be incorporated into a lot of daily activities, a BCBA was the only licensed healthcare professional who worked solely with the ABA model. She told me there was only one BCBA in the RGV— her name was Eileen and she was her protégé, but Eileen was already helping four to five children privately in their homes. She told me that insurance was the biggest obstacle in Eileen's case. Since there was no program or facility or school, parents had to pay out of pocket.

Either way, due to the intense one-on-one attention ABA required, Eileen was booked with just the few patients she had at the time. The professor provided me with Eileen's contact information just in case and encouraged me to contact our health insurance companies to ask about what ABA services and providers they covered. Lastly, as kindly and as sweetly as she possibly could, she recommended I go to the Tropical Texas Behavioral Health as soon as possible.

I held it together just long enough to thank her very much for her time and information. But the second that call ended, oh how I cried. It was the "ugly cry," my friends. (That's another term coined by my dear pretend friend Oprah Winfrey). I wept with anger, sadness, and disbelief. There were tears falling and boogers flying and saliva dripping, and there was dry heaving, and, well, it was not pretty.

Let me tell you a little bit about Tropical Texas Behavioral Health. In the late '60s the Texas legislature passed House Bill 3, which created the community mental health and intellectual and developmental disability system.

Basically, if you qualified for these services you no longer had to go to a state hospital to receive care. You could stay near your home, and services would be brought to you. The Rio Grande Valley was one of the first areas to initiate that system in the state of Texas, and when the local facility first opened it was called "Tropical Texas Center for Mental Health and Mental Retardation Center." *Mental retardation center.* Really? That was the place you went to put your child on "the list." Still is, though they've updated the name a bit. Have you ever heard about families who receive disability checks for their children's special needs? This is where they go to sign up.

Have you ever heard that some states have programs to provide financial assistance to certain patients if they are not able to maintain a job or secure income when they turn eighteen? This is where they go to sign up.

"Crazy people," "psychos," "retards," and Spanish terms like "malitos" and "mensos"—those were the words used to describe the people that needed those services—who "belong" in the "mental hospital." These are the completely unfair, untrue, overwhelmingly hurtful, and offensive things that people say about that place and the people who go there. The world is cruel. I have always known that, and I have always known that lack of education and lack of understanding of the unfamiliar is a common problem in our society.

But the reality of my daughter now carrying that stigma—that unfair, disgusting stigma— well, it broke me for a while. As a mother, I knew I would not always be able to protect Isla.

I knew I would not always be able to keep her safe from danger. I knew I would not be able to stop someone from breaking her heart. I knew I would not be able to prevent her from feeling disappointment, rejection, low self-esteem, and all the crap that comes with being a woman. What I was not prepared for, and what I did not know, was that one of the things I would have to shield her from was the world's incompetence regarding her mental health. It had never crossed my mind. And so continued my internal dialogue, with determined, on-a-mission Mom stepping in while the rest of me sat, bitter and speechless: *Lisa!* Stop it! Just stop. You are a planner. You are going to march your butt to Tropical Texas and put Isla on the list, and no one has to know. You do not know what the next few years will bring, and she may never need these services, and maybe she will never even know you put her on the list to begin with. Suck it up, girlfriend! Isla needs you, and if the light bulb turns on soon we will forget this ever happened but if it doesn't, and she turns eighteen with no services, you will hate yourself for not doing what was best for Isla right now. You have never been a prideful person, and you will not start being prideful now!

With tears still running down my face, I called Tropical Texas Behavioral Health and made an intake appointment. In summary, Isla was added to the list. We did not qualify for any services or financial help due to our income, but Isla would have some financial assistance when she turned eighteen if she was not able to support herself.

Shortly after that, I made contact with the only BCBA in our area, Eileen. She was beyond knowledgeable and, just like the professor, sorry she couldn't help me more.

Eileen confirmed that she currently provided in-home therapy to five children, whom she saw two to three times per week for four to six hours each. Again she mentioned litigation and insurance being a huge obstacle for ABA therapy-based clinics and programs in our area. She told me that reimbursement rates were low for insurance, and private pay patients were paying $80 per hour for the in-home therapy. I quickly did the math in my head. $80 x 40 hours = $3200 *per week*, so that was $12,800.00 per month. Everyone, say it with me: O. M. G. Looking back now, I never could have imagined that Eileen and I would cross paths later in life, in what was nothing short of a miracle.

But for now, I was still waiting anxiously for the results of that MRI. So when my phone rang a few days later and the number for the children's hospital popped up on the screen, I put on my best calm act, as I waited to hear what the pediatric neurology nurse had to say.

"Isla's MRI was completely normal."

~~Brain tumor. Brain damage. Brain cancer.~~

Next step, call the insurance companies. Mine was straightforward: ABA therapy was not covered at all. *Fine, jerks.* Next was my hubby's insurance, which did cover ABA therapy. After doing some more math in my head, I figured the therapy would cost somewhere between $700 and $1000 per month out of pocket. Whew, OK, we could manage that. But we still had a big problem.

Even if Eileen became available in the future she was not listed as a provider and would have to register as a provider, which would be . difficult seeing as she practiced independently. Either way, Isla was only on my insurance plan and could not be added to Greg's insurance until the next school year.

I maintained e-mail contact with the professor and Eileen, who assured me they would at least try to work with Greg's insurance company to become providers but could not promise me a time frame.

Now it was time to focus on getting Isla into an elementary in a bigger school district that offered more services. I started at the top with the Regional Director of Special Education, because that is how I roll. She gladly took time for me, and we had a good telephone conversation during which she informed me about newsletters, conferences, and trainings but reiterated that litigation was holding up ABA therapy. She recommended that I reach out to the school district in which I wanted to place Isla and specifically meet with the special education administration involved with the elementary level schools.

I showed up for my appointment with one of the elementary administrators for the special education department with my questions, notes, and colored highlighters in hand. (Don't judge.)

I wanted to be sure to ask everything I needed to know to make an informed decision. But as soon as I sat down, the administrator's body language and facial expressions made it very clear she was annoyed that I would want to meet. This was surprising.

It was a very prominent school district, and I had many family and friends that worked within the district or sent their children there, and they all had positive things to say. But I guess my expectation of a warm reception was too high. But I wasn't deterred. I started by giving a brief description of Isla, the school she was at now, and why I needed to switch districts. I specifically asked about the PPCD classrooms and whether there was any particular one she could recommend, perhaps with a teacher who had more experience with autism. Her reply was simply, "All of our teachers are good." OK, but that was not what I asked.

"Plus, not all of our elementary schools have PPCD classrooms," she added.

I knew that already, but I also knew I needed to change the tone of this meeting, so I decided to play dummy mom and let her feel superior. I reminded myself to put my pride aside and do what was best for Isla.

"Oh, I didn't know that. Can you provide me a list of the schools that have PPCD classrooms?" I asked.

"I don't know that off the top of my head but I can get you a list" she replied, still highly annoyed.

"Awesome," I said. "That would be helpful. Do you know if any of the PPCD classrooms use the ABA model?"

"What?"

"Does the district provide ABA training to the special education teachers that have students with autism?"

"No schools south of San Antonio offer ABA in public school," she assured me.

That wasn't true. I already had researched ABA in public schools, and the ABA center in Corpus Christi told me it was being used in that area which was two hours south of San Antonio.

"OK so the district does not provide ABA training for teachers?" I asked.

"Our teachers do a fine job and get the training they need."

I could feel my face flushing. Why was this person being so defensive? Was it me? Was I being a jerk? How else could I ask these questions without sounding rude or like a know it all? But then I realized, so what if I knew a lot? Isn't that what school districts want? Engaged, educated parents? Especially for special education students? What was I doing wrong?

I knew I needed to wrap up the meeting pronto.

"OK, I am sorry I've taken up so much of your time already, but I have one more question. When Isla transfers to this district, will they consider the new diagnosis of autism that we just received?"

"She will be transferred under the same label she has at the school she is at now until we are able to test her," the administrator said. "You do know that the principal does not have to accept the transfer, right?"

Wow. Looking back now, I wish I'd had more of a spine at the time. I wish I had put my notebook aside, looked her right in the eye, and explained that I needed help.

I wish I had shared that I was scared and felt very much alone and I just wanted to do the right thing. I wish I had told her to her face that I felt she was being defensive and there was no need to feel threatened in any way.

I wish I had explained that I was just a mom who wanted nothing but the best for my daughter and I wouldn't apologize for being educated and advocating for my little girl. I wish I had said that the district came so highly recommended that I expected more from its representatives.

I never got that list, so I resorted to calling every single elementary school myself and asking the receptionists if they had a PPCD classroom. I found out that there were several elementary schools near my work that did have them, so I decided to choose one and meet with the principal.

The principal was exceptional. The real deal. She was incredibly engaging, concerned, welcoming, kind, warm, and understanding. She gave me her full attention and put it simply, "If you want us, we want Isla." I could have bear hugged her. I was instructed where to go to fill out the appropriate forms, and Isla would be set for the fall.

It was now nearing the end of the school year, and it was time to review the results of the semester-long testing that the requested administrator of the special education services department had conducted. I sat down in a conference room and he placed in front of me a thirty-five-page document that contained a very thorough and professionally presented evaluation of my daughter.

The details were exhausting, so I will try my best to summarize the highlights. Isla was given the following assessments: physical, sociological, language, intellectual/cognitive, adaptive behavior, academic achievement, emotional/behavioral, assistive technology, and six different autism evaluations. Here are some direct quotes from the summary provided to me:

"Item analysis of the quantitative measures and the classroom observations support the presence of Attention Deficit Hyperactivity Disorder (ADHD) and an Oppositional Defiant Disorder (ODD)."

"Many of the behaviors endorsed by the raters that Isla displays categorized as 'strange and odd' seem to represent the ADHD traits. She does sit and stare for extended time periods. She does intrude on other's personal space, but this intrusion is related to the ADHD and not ASD."

"It is not unusual that approximately 30% of ADHD children exhibit ODD. This type of child is easily frustrated, has difficulty with working memory, and enjoys 'testing the boundaries.' The difficulty with working memory may eventually impact academic progress and display specific learning disabilities."

So far I was OK. I had always kind of assumed she had ADD or ADHD, so that was no surprise. But I did not fully agree with the autism evaluations. Here are some quotes from that portion.

"It is the consensus of the Autism Team that Isla *does not* meet eligibility for an Autism Spectrum Disorder. She does not display deficits in social communication nor does she display repetitive behaviors."

"Isla's conversational skills are age appropriate."

No way. Isla didn't have friends her age because all she could say was, "Wha ah you doin?" over and over again. The kids her age would get annoyed with answering so much, make a face, and walk away. Was that age appropriate conversational skills?

"Although Isla does have difficulty establishing and maintaining social relationships appropriate to her developmental level, this difficulty seems best explained by the ADHD. She is friendly toward everyone but does have difficulty reading social cues, following social routines, and understanding personal space."

OK, but children with ASD also have difficulty reading social cues and following social routines. So couldn't she have both? ASD and ADHD?

"Isla does not display a hyper- or hypoactive reaction to sensory input or unusual interest in sensory aspects of the environment. Isla does not display any sensitivity to loud noises, textures, or her surroundings."

Wrong again. We had been to many birthday parties where my little girl had just shut down.

At first she would be excited about being somewhere new, but as kids ran in and screamed and shouted and played and ran and people talked and hit piñatas, she would hit the proverbial wall.

It would start with a signature scowl on her face and then she would sit close to me. All of a sudden she would become nonverbal and start to mumble and groan like she was uncomfortable.

But because she did not physically cover her ears to show the special education team that she was obviously bothered, that means she was not sensitive to loud noise or her surroundings?

He told me that the ADHD was so prominent it made it very difficult to test Isla. He told me that all of this was according to Texas Education Agency (TEA) guidelines and should not replace any medical diagnosis. He also recommended that Isla not be tested again anywhere unless she was medicated for ADHD and added that some students with the first trial of medication at even the lowest dose show huge improvement from day one.

"It is like the light bulb just turns on," he said. Yes, the light bulb. I was very sure to let him know that I would take all of the recommendations into serious consideration. I was grateful for all of the time and attention given to Isla to provide us with the best evaluation possible. Although I did not agree with everything, I understood that it is difficult to test or evaluate a child in *all* situations. This man did not see Isla at birthday parties or at home or with her family. So, I understood. He gave me his best that semester and that day, and I was grateful.

I went home that night and had a long talk with my husband. We talked about all the results and discussed what we had been dreading all along: medication. Despite sharing the decision with him, I still felt all the pressure. I was the pharmacist, remember? My husband trusts me 100%, and that can be empowering and overwhelming at the same time. So I called to make an appointment with our pediatrician, and then I called my brother, who is also a pharmacist.

Together we tried to narrow down which medication we thought was best for Isla based on the fact that she could not swallow a tablet, a patch would be too distracting for her, and she needed something long-acting to last the entire school day on just one dose. Together with our pediatrician, we decided on a medication that came in a long-acting capsule that could be opened and sprinkled into Isla's applesauce or yogurt each morning.

I requested a thorough exam of her heart to make sure she could tolerate a stimulant, and then I headed to the nearest pharmacy to fill the first-ever controlled substance prescription for my little five-year-old.

As I handed over the prescription I wondered how we'd gotten to this point—how had it come to this? I had no idea what to expect, but here was what I did know: My daughter needed help, and I did not want to have regrets.

I had to try everything at least once, and this was a perfect time for a medication trial, because with one month left of school, these teachers who had been working with Isla all year would be the best to give me insight as to whether the medication was helpful and what changes they noticed, if any. The teacher gladly gave me her cell phone so we could text each other throughout the day as we started the trial. As a pharmacist I also knew that a trial of this particular medication would not hurt her long term, so even if there were side effects they would go away when I stopped the medication. So anyone who is judging my decision or me, go hate on someone else. There is nobody that loves my daughter the way I do and nobody that would lay down their life to see the world through her eyes for five minutes the way I would. We made a hard decision that day, not to make it easy on the teachers or easy on us at home, but because it might—just might— help our daughter learn, and nobody can blame us for that.

Day one the first text came in around 10 am, saying that Isla was complaining of her stomach hurting. Yes, that was normal and expected. Abdominal pain was a common side effect and may take one to two weeks to subside. I didn't panic. At the end of day one I asked the teacher for some details of the day, and she told me that Isla was the most still she had ever been but mainly because her stomach hurt.

OK, so we would be patient. By the time I got home from work, the medication had worn off and Isla was her usual self. This was good. The timing was working the way I wanted it to.

For now, I would just continue to pray and be patient. The rest of the week went about the same, and I was relieved that, by Friday, there were no more complaints of stomach pain. I was happy to give her the weekend off medication and hopeful the next week would show signs of focus and attention in the classroom. No such luck. On Monday, stomach pain was back—and worse. I was so mad at myself. I shouldn't have stopped it over the weekend because now she had to adjust all over again. I tried not to beat myself up too much, and I decided to continue the medication each weekend until her body had had more time to adjust. But at the end of that second week I started noticing the weight loss. Isla was already a very long, lanky girl, so just a pound or two made a big difference. It was during the second week I cried as I bathed her, using the washcloth to clean her sunken in tummy and her delicate ribs and collar bones. She wasn't eating, and I was getting pissed. It was one of the first times that I remember having angry conversations with God. *How could He allow this?* I thought. *Forget about me—how could He allow Isla to suffer? Was God just going to let her waste away? Not cool.* I am not proud of those thoughts, but I want to be as honest as I can. She was so innocent, and I was trying something in faith, but she was in pain and not eating and still not learning. I decided right then and there, as I hugged her skinny body in the bath towel, that I was going to show God that I was serious.

If Isla was not going to eat, I was not going to eat.

I was raised in a household where we learned to trust and serve God. I grew up believing in the power of prayer even though it had never really been real in my life.

I was blessed that I had not had a life-threatening event that dropped me to my knees in desperate prayer. So I did the only thing I knew to do when I have no control over a situation: pray. The very next day I started my "lunch" routine. On my lunch break I would drive to Isla's school, park as close to her classroom as I could, and pray. I did not eat lunch. I sat there with my arms stretched out to her classroom and I cried and prayed. I prayed for her stomach pain to go away. I prayed for God to use the medication for a great, positive outcome. I prayed for Isla's appetite to come back. I prayed for her body and her mind and her spirit not to be broken in the process. I prayed for God to make it obvious and clear if I should stop the medication. I did that for two weeks straight until the last day of school. Isla's stomach pain did subside, but the teachers agreed that although Isla was more focused and could hold attention for longer spans of time, she had not shown any academic improvement.

During the summer months that year, Isla attended a private-pay daycare that cared for children with special needs. There was no curriculum or therapy, but it was a safe place for her to be taken care of until she started the next school year in the new district. It was during these summer months, when she was still on medication, that we noticed freezing spells. It would happen randomly and never at expected times. Isla would just freeze.

Sometimes she would have her arms and hands suspended in front of her, frozen. She would scowl her little face and look sad and lost. It did not happen every day, but when it did it was heartbreaking.

We also started to notice more pronounced, irregular sleep episodes. These are hard to explain, but for a couple years already, Isla had displayed some weird sleep episodes during the day. It was not narcolepsy, but almost. Isla would be at a table eating or playing, or at school during circle time, and she would start to show signs of sleepiness. Her head would bob dramatically and her eyes would be super heavy, but she wouldn't actually fall asleep until someone helped her lie down all the way. Then in five to ten minutes Isla would wake up startled, happy, and ready to go as if nothing happened. As these episodes became more frequent and pronounced, we attributed this to her ADHD and the medication, and we didn't worry because she slept so soundly for ten to twelve hours every night without waking. But the medication was changing her. She was losing the joy that defined her.

It was almost the end of summer and she had lost seven pounds by that point. So we decided to put her on a medication vacation for the week we attempted our first-ever family vacation. My parents, two brothers, two daughters, and my hubby and I stayed at a family-friendly resort hotel in central Texas, where there were daily activities for the kids, a lazy river, and everything we needed or wanted on site. It was a beautiful place, but my girl just could not handle the activity. It drove her crazy to know that we were in a hotel room and all her family was just a few doors away. She was restless and relentless.

She would wake up at 6 am with nonstop requests to go to my parents' room, but when she got there, she would ask to come back to my room, etc. That would go on and on all day.

We would go to dinner, and something would trigger her and she'd want a different chair or different food or different drink. Whenever one of us went to the bathroom, all of a sudden her world was not right, and she would want to go to the bathroom or want everyone to go with her to the bathroom.

I was tired and already dreading going back to work, because my "vacation" had been a lot of work already. But I reached a breaking point on the night of the outdoor movie. There was a spacious lawn with a large, inflatable movie screen, and all the guests were invited to watch a movie outdoors and make s'mores over an open fire. Isla loved to be outside, and I thought maybe—just maybe—it was late enough that she would lie on a blanket and rest. Oh no. The girl was up and down the hill, getting blankets for everyone from a bin the hotel provided. She dropped the blankets and picked them up again, and tried to fold them, and brought them to us, then took them back, then wanted popcorn, then dropped the popcorn, then asked to go back to the room, then asked to come back outside, it was exhausting. Finally on her 287th trip back to the blanket bin, she tripped over a young couple lying down close to us and fell on them. I was in a fury. I didn't even spit out an apology to the poor lovebirds because I knew I would sound like a barking, rabid dog.

I grabbed her by the arm and literally almost ran into the hotel and back to our room with her. I was frustrated, angry, and bitter. Crazy mom voice was screaming in my head, telling me I'd never be able to take a vacation and railing against my family for making me come here with them even though they knew this kind of thing was nearly impossible and almost always embarrassing. I sat Isla on the hotel bed, locked the front door with the dead bolt, and then locked myself in the bathroom and raged.

I was screaming and crying and yelling and sobbing, and my poor Isla panicked. She started banging on the bathroom door, crying and yelling too, because I was scaring her. My husband came in the back sliding door of the hotel room with his key, and Isla immediately started screaming at him. "Daddy help Mommy! Help Mommy! What wrong, Mom?! Help!"

It was during moments like these in my life with Isla that her panic would startle me. Here she was banging and screaming and begging someone to help *me* while completely ignoring the fact that she was the cause of my outburst. She didn't have to understand *why* someone was hurting, all she knew was that someone was in need. This is because Isla loves people. More than she loves people, she loves helping people. She is naturally drawn to anyone in need. She can't help it. She has no control over it. She is so interesting because, in certain situations, she is so incredibly observant.

She loses her shoes and toys constantly, and she can't learn or retain colors, numbers, or shapes, but if you so much as sniffle in her vicinity, there will be a Kleenex in your face in an instant. If you are sitting down on a sofa or at a restaurant and so much as turn your head as if you are looking for something, she will bring you your phone. If you stumble over a toy in a dark room, she will turn on the lights immediately. If I so much as touch my forehead and frown as if my head hurts, our blue polka dot medicine bag will be on my lap in five seconds flat.

I have a grandfather who was diagnosed with Parkinson's years ago and now is wheelchair bound. Most children avoid the elderly and are scared by anyone in a wheelchair or anyone who looks different or sick. Not my Isla. She is powerfully drawn to them. She hugs and kisses my grandfather and pushes his wheelchair no matter how heavy it is for her scrawny body.

She stares with concern when my family is transferring him to a chair or when he looks uncomfortable. It is like she senses their need and their inability to help themselves, and she wants to be that help. No. She *has* to be that help.

When Isla uses the iPad to watch kids YouTube, she always seems to find the videos of special needs children loading buses or playing or learning how to buckle up their special equipment. Without actually saying it, it's as if she knows she is different, too. She knows she is not quite like everyone else, so when she sees others who don't quite "fit in" either, she wants to be a part of them.

She wants to help them. She wants to love on them. What a powerful humbling lesson my daughter continues to teach me. I have never in my life met another child with such an incredible gift of unconditional love for all, and I don't think I ever will.

You have probably heard the phrase, "It takes a village to raise a child." That could not be truer for my Isla. Greg and I are the oldest of both of our families. Together we were the first to graduate college, first to get married, and first to have a child. We made everyone grandparents, aunts and uncles for the first time, and they had fantasies, too. I assume they fantasized about what Isla would be like and act like and how they would spend their time with her. I assume they fantasized about babysitting and building a relationship with her. They were not expecting this, either. But you know what? We have many people in both of our families who love my Isla. They have patience with Isla—the kind of patience that only is possible when you truly love. They embrace every single oddity and behavior with kindness and understanding. They love her even when it's not easy, even when it's inconvenient, even when it's messy.

And oh how Isla loves them all. She craves their attention and time. She is her most true self with her family because they allow her to be. So yes, it takes a village to raise a child and an even more exceptional village to raise a child with special needs.

I know that our family members would agree with me when I say that Isla was not given to us because we are a special family. Isla was given to us, and Isla made our family special.

Chapter Seven: 6-7 years

One little Prayer

I held June's little two-year-old hand as we walked into the chapel. It was my June's turn to attend the day school that I'd had to withdraw Isla from, and I was overjoyed as we sat in the chapel for "Welcome Day." I know I am biased, but June was just the cutest thing ever with her new little dress and super straight, shoulder length hair. I thought June was a genius. Really. My mommy brain was so skewed with all of Isla's delays that even though June was right on target for all milestones and development, she was my genius. It was fascinating watching her learn. I would stare at her sometimes as we read or as she watched TV or played with toys, and I would focus in on her eyes, amazed at the way she would take it all in. We sat together in that chapel and listened to the headmaster give her official welcome followed by directions about visiting each classroom and teacher. June would be starting the two-year-old program, so we got up and headed to that area of the building to meet the teacher and to see her new classroom. "Lisa!" I heard someone call me and turned to see another mother of a child who had been in Isla's class. We hugged, happy to see each other, and then I noticed her daughter behind her. Her daughter had been Isla's desk partner when they were in the same class.

She stood there next to her mom, so mature and grown and composed. It was the first time I had seen a student from Isla's day school class in almost two years. I could barely look at her because I was so overcome with sadness. My voice got a little shaky as I asked her mother what grade she was going to. Since Isla had been in a PPCD class for a couple years now, I had totally lost track of what grade she was in or should have been in.

When the mother told me Isla's former desk partner was going into first grade, I didn't know what else to say, so I just blurted out, "Oh awesome. How did kindergarten go?" *Wrong question, Lisa. Wrong question.* The mother started raving about the day school program and talked about how easily her daughter learned to read and write. She went on and on, saying all the awesome, appropriate mommy stuff you say about your kids. I wanted to go home. I wanted to go home and lie down with my own personal bag of Little Caesars crazy bread and cry and feel sorry for myself and Isla. *I* wanted to rave about Isla and what a great reader she was. *I* wanted to brag about Isla and how fast she picked up on the curriculum. *I* wanted Isla to experience the world like her old friends. I realized then that, anytime I entered the school, I'd have to make a conscious effort to focus on June. It was hard enough to split my time between children, and even more so when one naturally required so much more attention.

I have always been very careful about how I praise them and discipline them—always fair and equal, regardless.

But it was this year, walking into that day school and sitting at chapel services where Isla's old friends read scripture and acted out plays and sang songs that I allowed the feeling of loss to settle in deep. Where was my Isla? Where was my strong, smart girl? Where was the daughter I'd dreamed of for so long?

Just a few days after Isla started at her new school, we celebrated her sixth birthday with family and friends at a popular pizza party restaurant. I decided not to give her medication that day because I wanted her to enjoy herself and be herself, no matter how difficult that would be. The party proved to be too much for my little girl. She was all over the place. She jumped from game machine to game machine with no sign of stopping.

As family and friends arrived, she became so excited with each new guest that I thought she was going to pass out. She would jump and shake and laugh, but it was all uncontrollable and somehow inappropriate. After the first few people arrived, I noticed she had urine running down her leg. I don't even know if she felt it. I quickly picked her up and rushed her into the restroom before anyone saw. I started to scold her, but then I stopped. It was her day.

It was her birthday, so I had to let it go and hope the rest of the evening went OK. I did not have extra panties for her, but I had changed her from her school clothes into a dress for the party, so I put the loose shorts she'd had on earlier in the day under her dress.

And off she went. Like a twister or a pinball, she bounced off everyone and everything. She was happy and carefree but unmanageable and defiant all at the same time. I started to regret not giving her the medication, but there was nothing I could do now.

I was at the party tables mingling with some party guests when all of a sudden my dad came up behind me and whispered for me to follow him quickly. I played it cool and left the table, noticing that my dad picked up a big stack of napkins on the way back to Isla, who was in the game area.

When I got to Isla, she was standing on a kiddie ride that had stopped. She was staring at me with a hand in her mouth. She was lost. Scared. Confused. My dad bent over and, with the napkins, picked up a piece of her feces from the floor.

No. NO. NO! Please no. I bear hugged her, lifted her up, and rushed into the bathroom. I wanted to spank her. I wanted to hug her. I wanted to cry with her. I wanted to yell at her. I wanted to tell her it was OK and make her feel loved. I wanted to scream. I wanted her to be able to tell me what she was feeling and why that happened.

Instead I just knelt down in that bathroom stall, and as she stared at me with her big hazel eyes, I placed my hands on her shoulders and I said these words: "Oh my Isla. I am so sorry. I am sorry, my love. No more. We are done. No more."

I made two big decisions that night. 1. No more medication. 2. God would have to do the rest.

The very next morning we did something as a family that we had never done before. Before we left our house for work and school, we laid hands on Isla and prayed. There on Isla's head and shoulders were my husband's hands, callused and tough; my hands, dried out but soft; and June's little hands that smelled like cheerios. I asked God for help. Plain and simple. I told Him I was tired and that we were not going to give Isla medication anymore because we trusted that there was another answer. I asked God to show us what to do, and I promised to be still as we waited for Him to show us the next step. I told Him that whatever His will was, it was good with us. We accepted Isla the way she was, now and forever.

I told Him that whatever plans He had for our family, for Isla, we were ready for Him to put them in motion.

Three days later I got an e-mail: "New ABA Clinic Location Coming Soon!" This was one of the many ABA clinics whose e-mail lists I'd subscribed to when we first got the autism diagnosis. This clinic offered 40 hours of ABA therapy per week for children with autism. It had locations around the country, but the majority of them, including their headquarters, were in Texas. I quickly went to the website and saw that the new location was coming to Corpus Christi, the same city where we'd visited the children's hospital and gotten the diagnosis—the city that was two hours away.

For just a few seconds I got excited, but then the reality set in.

Moving would require selling our house, finding new jobs for my husband and me, finding a new school for June, and leaving all of our family and friends. No way. It was out of the question.

The week I decided to stop the ADHD medication I made an appointment with our pediatrician to update him and to get Isla's required physical for her new school. Our pediatrician was understanding and kind and recommended food allergy testing. Seeing as we were stopping the medication, he thought I should look into gluten free diets as an alternative. As I discussed with him some of Isla's persisting delays, we also decided to double check her hearing and test for color blindness just to be sure. The allergy testing and hearing test were done that day, and both came back normal. ~~Gluten allergy. Hearing impairment.~~ The color blindness evaluation was completed on a later date and was also normal.

~~Color blindness.~~

It was one week after we had laid hands on Isla—a few days after I learned about the new ABA clinic opening—when my boss called me into his office. He noticed I had been requesting leave to travel to Corpus Christi frequently over the last couple months. He told me that he was expecting an opening at our facility in that city in the near future and asked me if I wanted to be considered for the transfer.

In the words of my other pretend bestie, JLo, I got "goosies." I was caught off guard for a bit. At the time I had my dream job.

I had an awesome work partner whom I had grown to love as a dear friend and colleague, and I was in the nicest, newest facility that my job had to offer. I had a flexible schedule and was respected and had grown close to my team and co-workers.

But still, I said yes. I mean, it wasn't for sure right? He had said he *may* have an opening, so I at least wanted to have the chance to turn it down if it actually happened.

Meanwhile, Isla was transitioning to the new school, but there was a problem. There was no actual "transition." I remember taking Isla to meet the teacher a couple days before school, and although I did fill out paperwork I remember wondering why the teacher didn't need more information about Isla and all her diagnoses. I hadn't seen any evidence of an education plan, and I wanted to be sure the teacher was ready to help Isla learn. The paperwork asked about drop-off details, who could pick her up, emergency contacts, pediatrician information, and insurance information, but what about everything else? I asked the teacher if she had received information about Isla from the other school. The teacher said that she thought they had received a file, but she had not seen or read Isla's folder yet. I was alarmed, to say the least.

Did she plan to read the file, brush up on all of Isla's diagnoses, research all the best teaching methods for these diagnoses and then make materials and lesson plans for Isla in just two nights. Because surely, surely I could not convince myself that the opposite was true.

I mean there is no way that the file is not important because in PPCD the goal is just to babysit, right? Or maybe every child regardless of their unique special needs was made no accommodation and had to just learn like everyone else? No, no, no. I refused to believe that. I believed in teachers, and I believed they cared about my child and wanted the best for her, so I knew this new teacher would read Isla's file that night, then research and plan and give Isla her best.

You will not be surprised to know that Isla did not do well in that new school. Drop offs became difficult, with Isla crying and making me force her through the doors each day. The classroom she was in had some students with severe delays, which limited the amount of interaction Isla had with other children who could play and talk to her. The after-school care didn't help, either. School was out at 3:30 pm, but I got off work at 4:30 pm, so I paid a small fee for after-school care. The problem was that there was no specific supervision for special needs students during that hour, so Isla sat in a cafeteria with a huge group of rowdy kiddos for an hour. She was stressed and frustrated, and it was obvious when I dropped her off and picked her up each day.

Then the injuries started. The nurse called one day and told me a child hit Isla in the face with a tennis racquet because Isla walked right in front of the tennis match during PE without paying attention. Then, she starting coming home with bruises and scratches, but because she was not fully verbal she could not tell me what was happening.

When I asked the teachers, they said it must have been happening at PE. One of Isla's sensory issues involved hyposensitivity to pain. To this day, she has an unusual pain tolerance, and it takes a lot to make her react or cry when she is injured. So the teachers would tell me that she hadn't complained of pain all day. *Well, yeah.*

Then came the behavior reports. The teacher gave each child a binder to take home each day that included the "daily behavior" report. I was supposed to read and sign each day's report and return the binder to school with Isla each morning. But the more reports I read and signed, the more annoyed and, frankly, offended I became. The document was coded by numbers and letters, so for example:

1. Circle time behavior:
   a. Spoke without being called on
   b. Disruptive to others
   c. Aggressive – hitting or kicking students or teachers
2. Lunch behavior:
   a. Did not wait turn in line
   b. Did not throw trash away
   c. Disruptive to others

So I would get a report like 1b, 2c, etc.

OK. Problem #1: There was nothing positive on that dumb form. Problem #2: No kidding. My child had special needs directly related to autism and ADHD, which are usually characterized by these behaviors. So every day that these numbers and letters were circled on that ridiculous form was an unnecessary reminder of all that was "wrong" with my child. Problem #3: Where was the behavior plan? If Isla was causing so many problems in the classroom, had the district behavioral interventionist been contacted to implement a behavior intervention plan?

Needless to say, when ARD meeting number one came around with that new school, I was ready. I had kept all of the daily behavior reports and notes of all the times Isla was injured and all the times and dates of the nurse phone calls. The principal had never seen these daily behavior reports and agreed they were not appropriate. The whole group stared at me when I asked to see Isla's behavior intervention plan. Just stared. I requested a shadow or supervision for Isla during PE. I requested a behavior intervention plan. I requested supervision during the after-school program. I got two out of the three. They were not able to help me with the after-school program supervision due to legalities and funding.

I want to repeat myself here and make a very important statement and observation. I have a lot of friends and family who are educators, administrators, district therapists, and counselors, including my husband.

I have a tremendous amount of respect and gratitude for this group of people for choosing this career. I know for certain that every single teacher, administrator, counselor, and therapist that Isla and I have come in contact with has had nothing but the best intentions for Isla.

I know they want nothing more than to do their best. The truth is they can't. They don't have nearly the amount of resources they need to do their job well. Sometimes they lack training. Sometimes they lack education. Sometimes they lack assistants or paraprofessionals. Sometimes they lack funding. Sometimes they're just plain burned out. They always lack time because they are up to their eyeballs in forms and paperwork and documentation. The problem is that when you are a parent with a special needs child, you still have to fight to get all you can out of a broken and overwhelmed system. It's not personal. It's just our daily reality.

One week after my boss called me into his office, he sent me an e-mail informing me that the transfer position was open and I had one week to give him my decision.

Was this really happening? Was I really going to sit down with my husband and have a serious conversation about moving? Keep in mind that Greg was a football coach and it was early fall, which meant football season was in full swing. It was horrible timing. *Maybe I should go alone? Just me and Isla?* No, no, no we had to stay together as a family. I knew that was critical—not just for my sanity but for all of us.

The first conversation with Greg was very short. He asked me two questions that I couldn't answer. First he asked when the school was opening. Second he asked if insurance would cover the full forty-hour week. Clearly, I was getting way ahead of myself, so the next day I started with the ABA clinic. I was in contact with the site manager in charge of securing the new location and an intake specialist.

The site manager told me that there was already a BCBA hired to run the clinic, but the hold-up was securing an actual building to work out of. He expected the clinic to be up and running in one month. Next, the intake specialist encouraged me to fill out the application packet to verify insurance benefits and to see if Isla was a candidate for the program based on her medical history and diagnosis. My insurance was government funded and therefore did not cover ABA therapy at all at that time. So we would have to rely solely on my husband's insurance. That was the problem.

We could verify coverage based on the job he had *now*, not based on the job he would have to secure in Corpus. OK, time for the second conversation with Greg. He was quiet as I explained all of the insurance mess, and then he walked outside to call his brother, one of the very few family members who did not live in our town at that time.

He was also a coach and teacher in Corpus where the new location was coming, and we stayed with him when we visited the children's hospital for appointments.

I didn't hear the conversation, but when my husband walked back in the house he was smiling that same "you've got to be kidding me" smile I had when my boss told me about the job transfer. My husband's brother had told him that that same week a coach at his school had quit suddenly, leaving a coaching position open. And the coach that quit also happened to be a special education teacher, so the special education department was in a hurry to fill the position as soon as possible.

That's when we knew.

All of this was falling into place about one month after we had laid hands on Isla, asking for help. How could we ignore this? We couldn't.

Before my husband scheduled an interview I called the ABA clinic back and asked them to look into the insurance that the new job for my husband would offer. ABA was covered. No prior authorization required. O.M.G.

But we had one more big hurdle. Our house. There was no way we were going to afford that huge monthly co-pay for the ABA therapy, my enormous student loan payment, *and* a second mortgage. We did not have the 20% equity in our home that was required to rent it, so we would have to put it up for sale. It was a Thursday night. I cleaned our house and took pictures of each room and of the exterior. Friday morning I walked into my boss's office and accepted the transfer on the condition that I could wait until Isla's new school opened to make the move.

Friday I printed flyers with the pictures I took of our house and bought a sign for the yard that said, "FOR SALE BY OWNER." There was a home football game that night, so I knew it was a good night to post the sign because there would be traffic that evening that our little town wasn't used to seeing. I sighed a big sigh, literally said out loud, "In the name of Jesus," and shoved the sign in the ground. Then I loaded up my girls and headed to the football game. Saturday morning I had a garage sale, and at about 10 am I got my first call from a family that wanted to see the house. We agreed they could come by at 3 pm when my husband would be home. At 8 pm, that same family made an offer. We'd sold our house in 24 hours.

Within four weeks from the time of Isla's birthday and our family prayer, we found an affordable, 40 hour per week ABA program for Isla, I had a new job, my husband had a new job, and our house was sold.

OK, everybody, just calm down. I know that while half of you are bawling your eyes out right now and thanking Jesus, the other half are rolling your eyes and thinking that, even if I haven't exaggerated that timeline, it's all purely coincidence. That is the great thing about our story. It doesn't matter what you think. It happened, and it happened just the way I described. You can call it God's will and our family prayer answered, or you can call it fate, karma, or coincidence. But no one can deny that doors opened for us. Doors opened for Isla. As for me and my house, we knew who was in charge.

But still, moving was bittersweet. And to say the next month was very hard on all of us would be a massive understatement.

I was consumed with sadness at work. My work partner was sad. My other co-workers were sad. I was also scared. I knew that jobs and partners like that didn't come often, and I knew exactly what I was leaving behind. I knew the reputation of the clinic I was moving to, and it was not positive. On top of that, I would be alone. No team, no friends, no camaraderie, just me. I would be the only person doing my type of job at that clinic. On my last day of work, I couldn't face my partner. This is not flattering to admit at all, but I was a total coward. I left a few minutes early and sent her an e-mail asking forgiveness for being such a coward.

The day I had to tell June's school I was withdrawing her was even more heartbreaking. I couldn't speak as I hugged her teacher and tried to sputter my words. She probably thought someone was on the verge of death by the way I was acting, so I had to totally explain myself through an ugly cry.

We just stood there and hugged and cried.

The guilt was overwhelming. How was any of this fair to June? She was in the best school with amazing curriculum and compassionate teachers, and after just two short months I was going to whisk her away to a city we don't know, and I hadn't even found a daycare or school for her yet. Was I doing the right thing, making the whole family sacrifice for one?

Then there was Greg. The only way you can truly and fully appreciate my husband in this part of the story is if you are a coach or coach's wife or maybe even a coach's kiddo. My husband had been a coach and teacher at the same school for seven years. In fact, it was the same school where we had attended high school and where we first met. There was history, family, relationships, and bonds. The community was invested in our family, and we were invested in the community. Football season was just taking off, and Greg knew that for insurance purposes he would have to leave as soon as possible so that Isla would be ready to start when the new ABA clinic opened. I know that there was probably a lot that Greg experienced those last few weeks and days that I will never know. But I do know he had to stand up in a locker room with an entire football team—JV and Varsity—and an entire coaching staff right in the middle of football season and say goodbye. After seven years, these coaches weren't just co-workers. If you ask Greg he would tell you they were friends, family, and brothers.

I know that that day he had to share his heart through many tears. He had to allow himself to be vulnerable and explain why it was necessary. I would like to think that all of the tears the coaches and players shed that day were not just of sadness but also of admiration.

I have always been so grateful to my husband's coaching staff and our alma mater for the way they treated him.

The head coach did not make him feel guilty or wrong. Instead he gave my husband wonderful recommendations and encouraged him. The coaches loved him, and they were sad, but they understood that family comes first. I know the emotional toll I was feeling leaving my job was nothing compared to what he felt. I remember he called me on his last day as he walked the football field for the last time alone. We cried together, we laughed together, and we hoped we were doing the right thing.

There are many reasons I love my husband, and there have been several times in our marriage when I've found a new appreciation for him. That was one of those times. I was proud of us. Maybe the move was crazy. Maybe the move was a horrible idea. Maybe it wouldn't help Isla at all, and we would be left broke with ramen noodle as our main food staple forever. It didn't matter. We were in it together. We both went in faith, and we both knew we would have more regrets if we didn't try. He never complained. He never made me feel guilty. He never questioned my judgment.

Within eight weeks of Isla's birthday, eight weeks after stopping medication, and eight weeks after our family prayer, we had Isla enrolled in the new ABA clinic for a forty-hour week. We had each started a new job. June had been enrolled in a new day school. We had sold our home and moved into a small rental home in Corpus Christi.

Isla was the very first student to be enrolled in the new ABA clinic location, and we were quickly scheduled for the initial evaluation that the BCBA would conduct.

I was a little alarmed as I pulled up to what seemed to be an older home. The yard looked like ours did during football season, and the only thing that made me feel safe to enter was the fact that it was located directly in front of the children's hospital.

Isla and I knocked on the door, hand in hand, and a very young and bubbly BCBA greeted us. She explained that none of the furniture had arrived, and that the ABA clinic had just recently signed a lease for the building and had not had time to maintenance it. So we sat on the floor, and the BCBA started the evaluation. It was the first time I'd seen the ABA model in action.

The BCBA had a stack of flashcards with very basic pictures on them—apple, banana, dog, etc. She would show the cards to Isla to see if Isla could verbalize what the pictures were or lay them down and make Isla pick the correct item by pointing. As was typical for Isla, the activity interested her for about five seconds before she got up, curious to see all the rooms. The BCBA did not say a word. She got up followed Isla, then stood in the doorway Isla was trying to get through. Isla kind of stared and then looked at me, smiling like, "is this a game?"

Isla scooted to try to get by, and the BCBA smiled and scooted too, telling Isla that as soon as she finished the flashcards they could move to another room. The standoff was long and drawn out, but after about ten minutes, Isla went back to the cards, sat down, and handed the stack to the BCBA. She got through all of the flashcards by pointing, and then she got to visit the other rooms to explore.

Seemed basic enough, right? But what school teacher would be able to be with Isla one on one all day and have time to stare at her for ten minutes until she finished a task? Exactly. We were in the right place.

The idea of ABA therapy is to use only positive reinforcement so there is never a "no" or "don't do that." Instead they use phrases like, "let's do this instead," and, "as soon as you are done with this task, we can do something else." The ABA model was very difficult to mimic as a parent because it went against everything I knew parenting to be.

As a parent you have to put a stop to a problem behavior immediately so it doesn't escalate. As a parent you say "no" a lot, and if you don't, well you a rare species. ABA principles require you to ignore problem behaviors, which encourages the children to stop the behavior because they are not getting the response they expect. Basically, when they see that they aren't getting a rise out of you, they stop the behavior.

When I dropped Isla off for her first eight-hour day of ABA therapy, I felt like a real-life dancing Beyoncé GIF. It was the culmination of such a stressful time, and to leave her with a therapist that I knew would give her one-on-one attention and not send home reports of all that she did wrong was such a relief.

Regardless of whether the program worked for Isla, I knew she was in a place where she would be understood, where she would be shown patience, where she would not feel lost.

Isla was the only student enrolled at the clinic, and that was great because it meant she could receive all the attention and training in the beginning, and then as others trickled in she would already be established and comfortable.

Two weeks after Isla started at the ABA clinic we were called in for our first parent training. Yes, we had to attend monthly parent trainings. I was thrilled.

The BCBA sat us down and presented us with an overwhelming amount of data. I had never seen so many graphs revolving around one human being in my life. There were pie charts and line graphs and scatter plots.

The BCBA had tracked every single behavior, initiated interventions, and then tracked the interventions and how they affected Isla's behavior. She was sputtering out all kinds of words like "elopement" and "discrete trials" and the terms for all kinds of reinforcements. She talked about targets and goals and the specialized program she was creating for Isla. Holy Moly. This smart momma was blown away.

I'd thought my Googling days were over, but that night I Googled so many words I felt like I was in pharmacy school all over again. I lay in bed that night reviewing all of the printouts she gave us of the charts and graphs and Isla's program goals. I remember thinking how unfair it was that we had to pick up our comfortable, awesome life to move hours away just to get this kind of time and attention.

I started thinking back to all the ARD meetings and how ridiculous they seemed compared to this. I started thinking of some specific friends and family members who are educators and would have been salivating over this kind of information. They would have loved to be trained to track behavior this way. As I closed my eyes that night, I began to create a new mission for myself. I was going to get this ABA clinic to open a location back home. No matter what.

It was now late fall, and we had only been in Corpus for one month when I started the "Get us Back Home!" e-mail chain. I had noticed weeks before that the ABA clinic website had an area where you could "Request a Location".

What would happen if I got all of my friends and family and co-workers to request our city back home?

I e-mailed every person I could think of and told them to forward the e-mail to whoever they thought of, too. I told them to go online and request our city for the next location. Then, I waited.

Meanwhile the intensity of the eight-hour days was a big challenge for Isla, and some disturbing problem behaviors began to show up.

For the first time, Isla was being held accountable for completing every task, and it was exhausting for her. I loved that she was being challenged, but at the same time I could see her changing as she escalated her behaviors to escape any task that required too much focus.

It started with defiance and quickly moved to aggression.

The therapist would describe meltdowns that included throwing objects across the room, hitting, kicking, and flipping over learning games or stacks of cards. Some of these meltdowns were long and drawn out, exhausting Isla so much that she would need to nap afterwards. Keep in mind that these meltdowns started as a result of Isla not wanting to complete a task that could be as simple as putting blocks away. I also have to specify that we did not see these behaviors at home—ever. Isla was not easy, to say the least, but she was manageable. We disciplined her the same way we disciplined June. She was not exempt from house rules or chores, and I felt that when she did act out it was just like any other six year old would act out.

The big difference was that, with ABA you don't respond to the behavior, so it has a chance to escalate. At home that escalation was not allowed.

Isla was able to work through all of her wildest fits and meltdowns during the day with the supervision of a one-on-one BCBA and a registered behavior therapist. It was necessary for her. But then a disturbing behavior started to emerge. At the time it was far from funny, but now I jokingly call it "escape by urination."

Isla was pushing the limits and testing boundaries big time. It started with defiance, then aggression, then screaming and crying, and then when she realized that she was not going to be able to leave the therapy room until she finished a task that she *really* did not want to do, she would urinate on herself...on purpose.

For sanitary reasons the therapists could not leave her or the room soaked in urine, so they would have to remove her from the room and change her. Isla had been potty trained since she was two, so except for the rare excitement-induced accident, that was something we absolutely never saw at home, or anywhere else for that matter.

The first day it happened, one of the two therapists that were now working with Isla, had to make a trip during the day to buy clothes for her. The BCBA kindly asked me to start sending extra clothes in case that happened again. She explained the context in which it happened so I would know that it wasn't that she couldn't hold it. She purposefully and knowingly urinated on herself as an escape mechanism.

I promised myself that I would be honest while telling my story even if it made me look bad, so here I go. *Cue deep breath.*

I sped home that day literally, almost 100 miles per hour. I was so angry that, for a few seconds, I thought I could breathe fire. *How dare she think she can get away with that for one second?* I called my husband and basically yelled the story through the phone. It was simple. She would be spanked. Now don't get all feisty on me, people—we don't spank our kids often. I believe in getting a child's attention quickly when they engage in a dangerous behavior, and that was usually when I would use spankings. Example one: I catch the girls playing with the stove, they get a spanking right then and there so they know that feeling and remember it is off limits.

Example two: the girls are running around a parking lot, playing and jumping when a car almost hits them, they get a spanking right then and there so they know that feeling and remember to not play in parking lots.

This would be one of the first times I would spank Isla for something that had happened hours before and that didn't technically endanger her life.

I was not sure if I could do it until I actually closed the door to our guest room and spanked her once. She looked at me, confused and not really understanding.

So I told her why I was spanking her, and as I spoke images started pouring into my head of my beautiful, tall girl urinating on herself everywhere because she didn't get her way. I pictured her as an adult trying to maintain a small job and urinating herself because she wanted to get out of doing something the job required. I spanked her again. She just said, "Mom." I spanked her again. She started to cry.

I sat her on the bed and told her not to come out until I came to get her. I closed the door behind me and headed to the laundry room. I stuffed her urine-soaked clothes into the washer forcefully and, as if it would help, slammed the washer door shut. I just kept telling myself I was doing the right thing. I didn't care if Isla never learned her ABCs or colors or shapes or could never be in a regular education classroom or didn't ever leave my home, but I'd be damned if she grew up urinating on herself for attention or to get out of something.

The next day it happened again. Isla was so happy driving home that day with her bag of peed clothes on her lap. She was oblivious, and I was furious. When we got home, we headed to the guest room again. But the third day, when it happened again, Isla was different as we drove home. She knew what was coming.

How long should I do this? I wondered. *A week? A month? Does she even understand? How long do I do this until I am convinced that it is ineffective?*

On the fourth day, that stupid bag of peed clothes was waiting for me again, and I cried all the way home, arguing with myself as I so often did these days.

I didn't want to spank her, but I couldn't allow her to grow up with this type of behavior. I had to be consistent. But the thought of spanking her every day made my stomach churn. Where was the line between tough love and abuse?

By the time we got to the guest room, I was crying too much to spank her.

We sat on the bed next to each other as I cried, and Isla started crying too. Then I started yelling. "Why are you doing this?! Isla, why are you peeing yourself? Tell me what is happening! You know how to use the toilet, Isla! You are a big, beautiful girl! *Why*?!"

Through tears Isla yelled back at me. "I NOT KNOW!" She threw her arms around me and hugged me tight.

She was right. She didn't know, and that's why I had to stop spanking her.

At our next parent training, the BCBA was on point. She smiled as I explained that this was harder than expected, and it never crossed my mind that I would have to deal with behaviors like this. The solution was simple: Ignore it. Pretend those peed clothes don't exist. The more attention we brought to the behavior, the more it would continue. She would move on to another behavior and another and another until she realized that it was all ineffective for getting her way or for reaching the outcome she wanted. Sounds easy enough, huh?

Around that time I received a call from a representative from the ABA clinic. Their inbox was flooded with requests for a location in our hometown. I literally laughed out loud. He was kind and explained to me that it wasn't that easy. He told me that the corporation required at least five families that were interested and that could get through the application process before they would consider a location in our hometown. Why hadn't he just told me that in the beginning?! I went right back to my e-mail, and this time I was specific.

I told all of my friends and family and co-workers and acquaintances to give my cell phone number to anyone and everyone who might be interested. I knew that I would be most effective if I could share my story with them and be honest about insurance and cost.

I kid you not when I say that, within ten minutes of sending that e-mail I got my first call. Ten minutes. I spoke to a mom I had never met before. I shared my story, and she shared hers.

We had been to the same doctors, gotten the same runaround, experienced the same frustration with lack of resources and the public school special education programs, we had the same worries, and we felt the same sadness. We cried together and laughed together. The first family was on board.

I received several calls and e-mails over the next couple days, and some people just called the ABA clinic headquarters directly. One incredible story I have to share includes Greg's grandmother. She doesn't have e-mail, but she knew that I was working on getting the ABA clinic to open a location near our home. One day she was at a shopping mall and noticed a mother having a hard time with her daughter. My hubby's grandmother started talking to the mother and found out that the little girl had been diagnosed with autism and the mother was struggling to find services and resources for her. Greg's grandmother asked her if it was OK that I call her to give her information about the ABA clinic. The second family was on board.

There were so many inquiries that the clinic decided to hold an open house in our hometown to gauge true interest and scout the area for location sites. With the help of a local pediatrician I'd contacted, who also had a child with autism, the event was a success.

Crowds of people showed up to a local bouncy house with standing room only. There were people from surrounding cities up to forty-five minutes away. It was confirmed. The interest was overwhelming, and the ABA clinic would move forward with a location in our hometown.

We were now going on three months of ABA therapy, and we were starting to notice changes. Let's start with what improved almost immediately. Isla's vocabulary.

Isla started using words that I never knew she was capable of saying or understanding—and using them in the correct context. One day we were in the car, and she sneezed, and let's just say she needed a tissue pronto. "Oh Isla I hope you aren't getting sick," I said.

"No, no, no, Mom. It allergies," she replied.

Allergies? Wow. I had chronic allergies, so Isla had heard that word for years and observed what I was doing when I said it. Could it be that she was putting complicated things like that together in her head? Was that a light bulb flicker? Isla was also now able to handle one-step tasks without forgetting or needing further direction. For example, I could ask her to please bring me a tissue from the box in her bathroom. I could ask her to bring me the keys that were on the front door hooks. She was learning, but she was learning very selectively. Colors, shapes, and numbers were still a no go. She was still very defiant and stubborn at times. She was not able to process or accept a "no." She would fixate on something she wanted to do or somewhere she wanted to go, and she could not drop it no matter how hard I tried to distract her. Example:

"Mom, I go outside?" she'd say.

"Not now Isla," I'd reply. "Come look out the window with me. See how it is getting dark? See how it is starting to rain?"

"Mom I go outside?"

"Isla, let's go outside tomorrow when it's sunny."

"Mom peese? Peese mom! Mom I go outside?"

"Hey, I know! Let's get the play dough out!"

Isla would rush to the door and start to walk outside. I would pull her back inside and say, "Isla no. I said no."

"Mom wittle bit," she'd persist. "Pease! Mom, I go outside?"

This would go on and on and on, sometimes for hours. Usually it would last longer when she was sleepy, so as I would bathe her and tuck her in she would still be asking to go outside, even with sleepy, half-opened eyes.

The other issue we were dealing with was that, after three months, Isla was still the only student attending the ABA clinic. Keep in mind that Isla was outgoing and friendly, and she craved friends and interaction even though she could not handle it well at times. I also felt that maybe she was getting a little too much attention, seeing as she had the full, undivided attention of two adults who adored her. These two ladies loved Isla, and she loved them. Their compassion and kindness were obvious from day one. They were both young and just starting their careers, and for both of them Isla was their first patient. They were learning, and so was Isla, and the relationship they all shared comes only a few times in a lifetime. But it was about that time that I had to really think about what was best for Isla.

Should I keep her there for consistency with the BCBA and therapist? Should we move back home when the new location opened if there were more children her age attending?

Would that cause regression? Is it best to be around family or away from them during her therapy? It was tough, and I wrestled with that for a while, until God intervened again.

I had stayed in contact with the representative from the ABA clinic as they worked to set up the location in our hometown. I provided them with realtor recommendations and leads for potential employees.

So I eventually found out that the clinic would be opening around spring break, and there would be seven patients, all within the ages of six to eight years old.

Guess who they hired as the BCBA to run the clinic? Yes, Eileen. I knew then that we had to move back home for Isla.

We were in a rental home, so even though we would have to pay a couple thousand dollars to break the lease, we wouldn't be tied down by a mortgage. June's day school back home was overjoyed to have her back, so now the only thing left was our jobs. In less than one year I was asking for another transfer. In less than one year my husband was looking for a new coaching job, again. My boss was accommodating and kind. He told me that there was a position opening up back home, but it would be in a different area of pharmacy than I currently practiced. I would have to be willing to be the program manager in charge of a very big project to centralize services across four clinics. I would have a lot of work ahead of me, but I would be able to choose my team of five. *I'll take it.*

Now, for Greg. Most importantly, he would have to choose a school district with an insurance policy that covered ABA therapy.

He had his top picks of course, and he started with his first choice. He had one contact at that particular school—a college buddy who was originally from Oklahoma. Get this: the two of them had met in college in Iowa, and this buddy happened to meet and marry a girl from a neighboring town close to ours! What are the odds? So they had lived near us for years and had daughters who were Isla and June's age and happened to go to the same daycare as June had when she was a baby!

I would pass them almost every morning in the hallway as I dropped off June oblivious to how our paths had crossed in the past or how they would cross in the future.

I had known the buddy's wife from cheerleading in high school, and the way God used them and continues to use them in our story is pretty incredible.

Also, remember Annie? She was the therapist I mentioned earlier in chapter six who promoted ABA principles in her clinic and ran the parent support group. Her hubby had been a coach at the same school Greg was applying to, and they had recently moved out of state along with another coach, leaving two positions open. Greg killed the interview, as he always does, and he was hired on the spot. To this day, my husband is the only coach I know who has been employed with three different school districts in one school year.

The BCBA and therapist were sad to see Isla go, but they knew it was for the best. The ABA clinic headquarters sent a therapist, Michelle, who would be working with Isla at our hometown location to help with the transition.

During that last week they were able to share notes and complete a warm handoff, which was necessary and much appreciated. Isla and I finally got a real transition.

We'd been in Corpus Christi for eight months, and I had dealt with some mild depression from missing my family, my home, my job, and, well, myself. Greg had been a trooper, happy and content anywhere and everywhere. He was able to coach alongside his brother for half a football season, and together we met some incredible people whom we are happy to consider lifelong friends.

But during these months, something else really important started happening. The bond between Isla and June really started to grow.

They were four years apart in age, but with Isla's delays and June's accelerated mind, they were more or less on the same page. They loved each other, looked after each other, cared for each other, worried about each other, played together, and slept together.

They were polar opposites.

Isla was always happy, joyful, carefree, and fearless. June was skeptical, cautious, a worrier, and shy. But they helped bring out the best in each other since then, and it all started in that little rental house. It was because of June that Isla learned how to "pretend" play. For the first time in Isla's six years of life, she played. They played house and school and grocery store, and Isla was using her imagination and pretending. That sounds so natural for most, but for Isla it was groundbreaking.

I look forward to the day when my June will realize that she was one of the best things to happen to Isla and the best therapist Isla ever had.

By that point both of my brothers had moved out of my parents' home, which left room for us to live for a couple months as we planned our next move. The events of the last year had wiped out our savings completely, and we were back to square one. But when I pulled up to the new clinic location in our hometown for the first time, I knew it was worth every penny. The new location was walking distance from my work, and it was beautiful inside.

Not because of the décor or the building, but because of the people. To see and hug Eileen was a full circle moment. I found out that both of her children went to the same day school June was in, and it was just meant to be that our lives had crossed. And there were so many therapists! Remember that each child was guaranteed one-on-one therapy.

And they were all young, happy, excited, and motivated. I saw Michelle who had traveled to help transition Isla, and she was beaming as I hugged her. I remember thinking that day that they'd be amazed if they only knew all that happened to open these doors and the role they were playing in Isla's incredible story.

Then there were the children. Remember family one? Family two? They were there. Many of the families I'd spoken to were there. I was humbled, and I just felt so blessed.

I was overjoyed once more on the day I held June's hand and proudly walked her right back into the classroom she'd left in the fall.

I would later find out that there was a little boy in June's class who'd had a mad crush on her. When she left suddenly, he was heartbroken, and his mom told me that every night during dinner and bedtime he would pray for June to come back. The day the teacher told the class that June was coming back, he was thrilled to tell his momma that Jesus had listened to his prayer. So if it was our one little family prayer that helped us move to Corpus, then we like to think it was that little boy's prayers that helped bring us back.

Of course being back at June's school and seeing old friends was also a brutal reminder of the reality of Isla's delays. Here I was, so proud that Isla could now "pretend play," and the kids her age were competing in academic competitions, reading, writing, and doing complicated math.

By that point I had read many articles and books about special needs children and their families and talked to many people with special needs children, and I was getting upset that no one was being honest about that horrible gut wrenching feeling of loss.

Why did nobody talk about that? Why did nobody say that parenting a special needs child often feels like you are grieving someone you lost?

I know that I am very blessed to have a healthy daughter, and I also know some families suffer horribly with severe disabilities and medical emergencies.

Let me share with you how I started to cope with the loss of my pretend, fantasy Isla.

The month we moved back home there was a news story that I will never forget. Three children were playing in their front yard when one of the little girls, almost exactly Isla's age, walked into the street and was run over. Her brother and friend witnessed the whole thing. She did not survive. I did not know the family personally, but because we live in a small town our paths crossed many times. Their family loved the beach and went often as mine did. The terrible tragedy of it all just broke my heart. The family was in pain. Agony. Unbelievable, suffocating sadness.

That night, I slept with Isla. All night long I held her. I cried in her hair. I rubbed her legs and arms and back. I smelled her and watched her breathe in and out. I sang our special song over and over even though she was asleep. *"You are my afternoon, and day and night too, I'll stay up with the moon singing you a tune…"* I prayed and thanked God for her life. It was "aha moment" number two. You see, I had not lost my Isla. I had my Isla. I could see her, hug her, laugh with her, cry with her, and enjoy her company. I could watch her grow and learn, regardless of how fast or slow that may happen. I could watch her run and play and be silly. I could see her love on her sister and her family.

I remember seeing a short video that the family posted of the little girl's father at her grave. As he lay in the grass next to her grave, he wept and cried out over and over again, "Where is my sweetheart? Where are you?"

That is loss.

From that day on, every single time I would feel a second of loss or sadness, I would think about that daddy.

I see her mother from time to time around town, and there is nothing like seeing a mom who has lost a child. It is against nature for parents to have to bury their children.

There is a sadness to their faces, even when they smile. There is a sense that something is missing that exudes through their body language. That family's story changed my outlook on my daughter's life forever. Rarely does a day go by that I do not think about that family and how they taught me the true meaning of loss.

That summer was our second attempt at an annual family vacation, and my dad chose a cruise. Like the last family vacation, it proved to be way too much for Isla. With all the people and activity, it was just too much stimulation for her. The cruise line offered a daily kid's camp at the rear of the boat where you could drop off your child for daily activities, crafts, games, etc. We were told they had extra help for special needs children, so we tried it out. Each family was given a pager in case of emergency.

June loved it and was always upset when we would go pick her up after a few hours. Then there was Isla.

Right about the time I ramped up enough guts to unveil my "I-have-birthed-two-giant-babies" bod to all the cruise goers and the open ocean, convinced Greg to finish lathering sunscreen on my back, and adjusted my laying down position just right to hide my stretch marks, create a faux thigh gap and make my stomach pooch look that much smaller…we would get paged.

For me, that trip was all about acceptance. When Isla was inside my belly I promised to show her the world. But if Isla wasn't ready to see the world, maybe that was OK, too. If we never got a "normal" vacation again, maybe that was OK too. It was definitely a summer of reflection for me, not just about Isla but also about our life as a family, our finances, and our future.

Chapter Eight: 7-8 years

The Missing Link

Isla's seventh birthday party felt triumphant. Yes, I am aware of how cheesy that sounds, but it's true. For me it was nothing short of a victory celebration. We did it. We had moved and come back and brought the school with us. Now, surrounded by all of our family and new friends, we were back home for good. I wanted to chest bump every single person that walked in the door. Instead, I was totally awkward and gave an emotional little speech about how I could not help but think what a difference one year had made.

Around this time we started a family project. Since we had been married, my husband and I had bought and sold two homes, rented three homes, and rented one duplex and one apartment. We had experienced living on the poor side of town and on a country club golf course, and now it was time to decide again where to put our family. By this point in our marriage, I guess you could say we had a different perspective than most. Our life experiences so far had really taught us more about the value of family, health, happiness, humility, and love than about money or status.

For years, my parents had offered us a piece of family land to build on, but it never really fit into our financial plan or family plan.

But now we had the chance to decide again. We could shop for a big, beautiful home in a great neighborhood that was close to our approved mortgage limit, or we could start building a home on our gifted land.

We decided to build a barn house. That's right. We decided to build one big box of metal— completely open, cozy, and unconventional. It was Greg's original dream. We literally drew it up on a napkin on my parent's kitchen table and decided to subcontract the whole project to save money.

We tried to do as much of the project ourselves as we realistically could, and the girls made for some excellent helpers. Isla was especially helpful, and it was amazing watching her become so independent and functional.

I want to focus this chapter a little more on why Isla was such a mystery. The only way I can do that is to try to remember and describe some of the things she could and could not do in relation to preschool basics and speech.

Let's start with colors. I had purchased three large educational charts for Isla, which I laminated and put up in her bedroom. One had numbers with corresponding pictures, one had shapes, and the other had colors with pictures of objects that were each color. Every once in a while I tried to engage Isla with these charts in a moment when she was happy, not sleepy, and not prepared for a lesson (if she caught on to the fact that she was learning, she'd be resistant).

For example, randomly I asked her one day, "Hey Isla can you show me where brown is on this chart?" She pointed to red. "Can you show me where pink is?" She could usually identify pink, but this time she pointed to white. "Can you show me where white is?" She pointed to red again. She clearly knew the names of the colors, even if she could not identify them. The incorrect answers were disconcerting, but the grin on her face made me wonder if she knew all along, and was just playing games with me. I would have to be much more creative in these secret tests. I looked through her collection of pretend play food, and I made three ice cream cones. One was brown, one was pink, and one was white. "Hey Isla, let's play ice cream shop, yeah?" Isla was happy to play, and she sat behind the little play grocery display we had in her room.

I placed all three cones in front of her. "Hello, ma'am! I would like to order an ice cream cone with chocolate ice cream, please." Isla giggled and handed me the brown ice cream.

"Hello, ma'am! I would like to order an ice cream cone with vanilla ice cream, please." Isla giggled again and handed me the white ice cream.

"Hello, ma'am! I would like to order an ice cream cone with strawberry ice cream, please." Isla giggled and said, "Mom! That lot of I-cream!" Then she handed me the pink ice cream.

Though she could almost never identify colors by name, Isla could certainly identify ice cream flavors by their colors.

No matter how many times we played that game, and no matter what order I requested the flavors in, Isla got it right, every time.

Isla had also always been able to remember and identify all of the vehicles that belonged to her family members and friends. We would be driving and all of a sudden Isla would say, "Mom, look! You friend." I would look around and see a vehicle with one of my buddies inside. Even if Isla had only met the person once, she'd recognize the car. But if I asked her what color the car was, she would get it wrong every time.

All of Isla's therapists had tried different methods to teach colors, but they resulted in temporary memorization at best. She would master one color and be able to identify it in a group of other colors, but as soon as a new color was introduced, the first color was out the window.

So at home I had to say things like, "Isla go get your black jacket—the one that is the color of the marker Mommy uses to write your name on your stuff for school." Or "Isla can you bring me my towel? It's yellow like a banana and a school bus." Does Isla know colors? In a way, yes.

But unfortunately, the world doesn't talk in associations, and neither do IQ tests.

Next up, numbers. Isla loved gadgets, but she could not use them correctly because she could not identify numbers. She had memorized her phone number verbally but could not identify it on a keypad.

She had learned to hand the remote control to June so June could put in the right numbers for the Disney channel or Nick Jr.

She knew how to turn on the TV, because the button was red like an apple, but how do you associate numbers? Isla was extremely independent and wanted so badly to do everything herself. She could get her own plate from the pantry, get the bag of frozen chicken nuggets from the freezer, open and close the bag correctly, and place nuggets on the plate. However, she could not count out how many nuggets she had, and she could not find the right numbers on the microwave. She would get frustrated when I tried to help, saying, "No, no, Mom! I do it!" So I would sit back down and try to explain to her from my spot. "OK Isla, first push number 1. It is a straight line that goes from the top to the bottom. No not that one—that is 5. Look for a button on top that is a straight line." She would point to the top where the power options and quick starts for popcorn were. This would go on and on. "Ok now press 0. That looks like a circle or like a big O." Well, she couldn't identify shapes or letters, so that was a no go.

Let's say we were sitting down for dinner. "Isla, can you bring me four water bottles?" She would go to the fridge and bring back two. But if I changed the wording, she would get it right every time. "Isla, we are all so thirsty! I wish we all had some water." She would spring up immediately and happily bring four water bottles—one for each person.

Could she rote count? Sure, sometimes to 10 and sometimes to 20, depending on the day. But if you put a set of objects in front of her and asked her to count them, she would just keep counting without paying attention to the actual quantity.

I'm pretty sure you get the picture by now, but she was the same when it came to shapes. She could only identify shapes when you used creative associations. So a circle was like a basketball, a square was like the blocks, and an oval was like an egg. For some shapes, finding comparisons was just too tricky. In general, these were much harder for her than colors, but Isla did have excellent matching skills. Take, for instance, a page full of different shapes. I could point to a circle and say, "Point to all the shapes that look like this." She would do it and find every single one quickly. Matching was much harder for her with numbers and letters, but for colors, shapes, and objects, it was no problem.

She had very little recognition with letters, as well. That was probably the one that worried me the most, because it prevented her from reading and writing. So that meant it prevented her from learning how to use an iPhone to play or find music or the iPad to find her favorite YouTube Kids channel shows—things she loved to do. She would make a mess of the applications and settings because she had no idea what she was pressing.

If you asked her to write her name, you would get a paper with the capital letter I written about twenty times. If you asked her to spell her name out loud, she would do it correctly about half the time. The other half she would leave out a letter or two.

To this day, Isla's speech delay is the most immediate indicator of her diagnosis. If you ask her what her name is, she says, "I eeshla." She skips linking verbs when asking questions like, "Mom how your day work?" She speaks in descriptions because there are a lot of words that she has not or cannot store in memory. For example, one afternoon when she wanted to know where I'd hidden the Crystal Light single packs she asked, "Mom where the thingies?"

"What things, Isla?" I asked.

"Mom, those things put in water."

"Do you want ice?" I guessed.

"No. No. No," she clarified. "Mom, those things, sugar, shake water."

She is a master at charades, too, and as she described the item, she pinched her fingers together like she was opening a pretend packet. This was particularly heartbreaking when we couldn't figure out what she wanted, and you can imagine that it was nearly impossible for her to describe the songs or games she was learning at school for us to mimic at home. Fortunately, Isla's vocabulary had expanded tremendously through ABA therapy, and she did communicate pretty effectively by this time.

The moments of frustration were very few and far in between. She had also started using words correctly and in the correct context. One day she called me June on accident and immediately laughed out loud. "Oh, Mom, sorry. I so sorry. I confoosed." She continued to laugh and giggle. There was that light bulb flicker again.

Despite the communication challenges, her sense of humor has always been one of the most incredible things about Isla. She understands all sarcasm, all humor, all wit, all comedy, and all jokes, and she's almost always the first to laugh. It's actually pretty hilarious. I have mentioned before that she reads body language like no one else I know. She senses your attitude, your vibe, without you saying a word. When you get near her you can feel her scan your face. It's almost as if she knows she won't understand everything that comes out of your mouth, so she wants to get as many body language cues as possible before you speak so she can figure out how to respond. It's fascinating. Isla was and is fascinating.

As far as her interactions with kids her age there were three main issues we faced at the time: handholding, respecting personal space, and repetitive questioning. Handholding was something she had done since the age of two. It was her safe place, just holding someone's hand. It used to be that she would find the adult in the room as fast as possible—preferably the one who smiled at her first or commented on how beautiful she was—then, BAM! She wouldn't let go.

Most adults found that to be super cute, but I couldn't stand it because I knew it was how she started to manipulate someone. And it was especially an issue if the person she glommed onto was a fellow seven-year-old who didn't think it was so cool to hold hands. Isla would instantly process her chosen hand holder's face of disgust or annoyance and begin to hit or kick them to get their attention because she didn't know how else to do that. She had no sense of personal space and would sit on people or things with no thought at all.

She craved interaction but was not always tactful, so when she ran out of questions she would ask them all over again. Think back to chapter two where I mentioned that Isla said "Hi" a thousand times a day. As she developed more verbal skills, she replaced that with "Whad ah you doin?" over and over and over again. Now it had advanced to repetitive conversational questioning. Each day when we would get in the car I would give my kids a recap of the day ahead.

"OK, girlies, today is a fun day! First, we all have school, and I want you to remember the three things we do every day: do your best, obey your teachers, and be kind to others. Got it?"

"Yes mom," June would say, and then I'd continue.

"Then, when I pick you up from school, we have to get ready quickly to go to Daddy's football game. We don't want to be too late."

After about two minutes of silence Isla would ask, "Mom, today Daddy's game?"

"Yes, Isla," I'd say.

"Mom, football?" she'd repeat.

"Yes, Isla."

"Mom, you pick me up?"

"Yes, Isla."

"Mom, today Daddy have game?" and so on and so on.

She wanted to keep the conversation going, but she didn't know how, so she simply repeated. You can imagine that, when she would do that to children her age, they would get frustrated fast and determine that she was "weird" or "annoying." Then they would ignore her—or worse, make fun of her.

Needless to say with all of her unique strengths and weaknesses the ABA clinic had their work cut out for them.

Isla's first few months at the new ABA clinic location back in our hometown were going great. She was learning a ton, and she really enjoyed seeing new therapists and kiddos each day as the clinic grew. However, with each new therapist came a new opportunity to test the limits and boundaries of her behavior. Keep in mind that many of these therapists were in training, and if they responded even an ounce in their facial expression, body language, or speech Isla would catch on instantly and exaggerate her behavior. In about the second or third monthly parent training, I learned of a new behavior that was the most disturbing for me as a mother, a woman, and a healthcare professional.

We were reviewing the graphs of Isla's different behaviors, and the BCBA was showing me how they would spike when a new therapist came on board and then dissipate over time.

As she flipped through the charts I saw all of the behaviors I was already familiar with: Aggression, flopping, elopement, urinating off the toilet...some were getting better (elopement had clearly decreased), while some, like urinating off the toilet, clearly spiked with each new therapist. Flopping blew my mind because she only did it at school, but it was nothing new.

But then we flipped to a chart labeled "Disrobing," and I stopped in my tracks. "Whoa, whoa, hold on. What do you mean 'disrobing'?" Eileen explained to me that sometimes when urinating didn't work, Isla would take off her clothes because she knew the therapist would have to look away and stop the activity until she put them back on.

This one would definitely be added to the "uglies" list. My stomach went sour and I wanted to cry—and vomit—but I tried so hard to stay composed, because I needed to know the details.

"So do you mean all her clothes?" I asked.

"Yes," Eileen confirmed.

"No, hold on I mean do you mean she is completely naked?"

"Yes," she said again.

I was horrified. My mind started racing, and I pictured Isla standing in a room with therapists—men and women—completely naked. Wow. I should have mentioned earlier that the ABA clinic had continuously recording cameras in every therapy room and in every hallway so parents could request to see anything and everything we wanted.

I knew that from day one, so I never really worried about her being one on one with a therapist. I knew that was the setup she needed to learn and to avoid other distractions. But disrobing? I was paralyzed in my chair. My first thought was, *I don't care what the ABA rulebook says—if my kid is taking off her clothes, you damn well better put them back on quick! Call a female into the room and put her shirt back on before it escalates.*

But that was not the ABA model, and I knew that. I felt sick to my stomach and absolutely embarrassed. Ashamed. I didn't know that was happening. Was I supposed to allow that? Eileen caught on to my "I-am-about-to-throw-up" face quickly and paused.

With my eyes lowered, I quietly asked, "Are there shades on all the windows?"

Eileen said they had to get shades because of disrobing issues—not just with Isla but with other kids, too.

"So this is a typical behavior of autism?" I asked.

She said that while not all children do it, disrobing is not uncommon, and it typically happens as a response to frustration or sensory issues.

I walked out that day feeling totally defeated. I had no appetite that night, and I struggled as I tried to tell Greg what we'd discussed. He seemed to agree with Eileen that it was actually normal autistic behavior. It was far from normal Isla behavior, but what could I do? Apparently, my humbling process was not over, as I realized that day that no one was exempt from the ugly, scary side of autism. Nobody.

As was with each behavior, the disrobing escalated to an almost daily occurrence, then Eileen initiated a specific intervention and it improved and lessened over time.

But before that intervention, boy did it escalate. I was at work one day when I got a phone call from the ABA clinic. They rarely called me so I knew something had to be wrong. It was Michelle and she sounded nervous—not hysterical, but definitely nervous. She started with, "Everything is OK, but..."

Apparently, Isla was experiencing an extended episode and had remained disrobed for a lengthy amount of time. They were calling me because the therapist in the room had turned her back to allow Isla to get dressed, but when the therapist turned back around, Isla was not dressed, and the play dough that had been on the floor in front of her was no longer there. *Where was the play dough?*

I did that crazy speed walk to my car. You know, the one where you don't bend your knees and you want to make it seem you are not in a hurry, but you totally look like a fool in a hurry?

As I was driving to the clinic, I called Greg in hysterics. You have to understand that Isla did not act like this at home—ever. So when she did this during therapy my first reaction was anger. I was so mad at her. I wanted to spank her, yell at her, anything to make her understand that we would not tolerate that anymore. Greg, of course, was calm.

He told me to check her to make sure she had not eaten the play dough and reminded me not to let the therapists or Isla see how upset I was.

He said we would talk to Isla together at home. *Yeah buddy, easier said than done,* I thought as I hung up the phone.

When I walked into the school, Michelle met me at the door, clasping her hands and clearly feeling guilty for calling me. "I am so sorry," she said. "I just want you to check her to make sure—well, because we don't know what she did with the play dough, and we can watch the video back, but it will take time to load it and, well, I'm just so sorry."

All I could mutter was, "Where is she?" Michelle led me to a room, and I told her I wanted to go in alone. When I opened the door, my beautiful, tall seven-year-old girl, who was now fully clothed, stared back at me with big hazel eyes, nibbling on her finger nails. She was terrified. She looked so worried, scared, lost. It was a look I had gotten used to seeing, but this time it was intense. She didn't seem scared of me, but of the whole situation. All of a sudden all of my anger towards her—my rage towards autism, my embarrassment of her behavior—melted away as I knelt down and held her. We hugged each other tight and cried together. As I cried I quietly whispered, "God please help my little girl. Please don't let her suffer this anymore. Please help us, Jesus, to cope with this. Give Isla peace, please." Then I just kept saying in her ear, "It is OK. It is OK. Everything is OK."

It was one of the first times I felt that Isla understood that something was wrong with her and that she couldn't control it. She didn't fight it. She let herself cry and let me hold her and rock her.

After a few minutes, I pulled her away, looked right in her eyes, and said, "Isla I need you to tell me what you did with the play dough." She whispered back, "I not know." So we wiped our faces and walked to the bathroom together, where I undressed her and checked her head to toe. No play dough to be found.

I think it's also important to mention here that the ABA clinic team included a child psychologist who visited the clinic regularly, so I knew that Isla was getting psychological evaluations too. Then at one of the parent trainings, Eileen told me that one of her colleagues had a patient who had some pretty incredible results from something called "brain mapping" that helped shape his behavior plan. Brain mapping. The Googling started up again that night. I read articles, studies, research descriptions and summaries, blogs, and forums. You name it, I read it.

So the first question was whether the test was invasive or painful? No. Did I think it would help her? Maybe. Where was the closest we could get that done? About five hours away, where my little brother lived. Would insurance cover it? Yes. So we were going to do this? Yes.

Remember that Isla had already had an MRI that showed no damage and no growths. However, an MRI does not show neurological connections, synapses, oxygen and blood flow, or stimulation.

Brain mapping would tell us whether appropriate areas of Isla's brain were being stimulated depending on the source of information, and if she was using both sides of her brain to process information or just one.

It all gets very complicated, but because there were so many things Isla could do and so many things she could not do, we were still looking for the missing link.

So a couple weeks before Christmas I found myself in another prominent children's hospital waiting room while my little girl was having her brain examined. I was hopeful. It's such an odd predicament to face. I was hopeful to get an answer but scared for them to find anything wrong. I wanted her to be completely normal, but then again I knew I would be frustrated not to have an answer. There was relief in finding out what was wrong, and there was equal relief living in oblivion.

After several hours the physician who was performing the exam called me back. We discussed recent research utilizing brain mapping for autism and ADHD diagnosis, and in the end he told me that Isla's brain was functioning normally.

With the exception of some lag time in how quickly Isla responded to someone else's speech, everything was normal. All areas of her brain lit up when they were supposed to, and although there were some delays in time to respond, all was functioning normally.

He recommended we see a pediatric neurologist in the area who specialized in reading the results of the exam to see what he would recommend moving forward.

Brain dysfunction.

When we got back home I called the pediatric neurologist, only to learn that his practice was moving offices and I should call back in a month. A month later, I called back and booked the earliest available appointment, which was about four months away.

Meanwhile, I was getting to experience being an auntie for the first time. Our first nephew had been born mid-fall, shortly before Isla's brain mapping, and around the same time we found out we would be expecting a second nephew in the summer. We were thrilled! Greg and I had always said that we would not consider having a third child until our siblings started having babies and until we could mentally accept that it might be another girl. We had also promised not to have any more children after we turned thirty-five. But we were both thirty-three, and now were about to have two nephews. *Should we go for it?* Gosh, just thinking about it made me itchy.

Being a mom is no joke, special needs kiddos or not. I was alone a lot because of my husband's job, but my girls were becoming more independent and easier as they grew. *Could I do it all over again?* Knowing our history of taking forever to get pregnant, we decided to just get off birth control and see what happened. If by thirty-five there was still no baby, my birthday gift would include fallopian tubes tied up in a pretty bow.

We moved into our barn house on Valentine's Day, and it was by far the coolest home I have ever walked into. We all loved it, and we were proud to call the barn house home.

Back at the ABA clinic, Isla was doing great and really working hard to meet all her targets. She loved the program.

She would work hard to complete tasks, and placed tokens on her Velcro picture boards as she worked toward her reward of either iPad time, dance party time, or any other fun activities she had chosen. She loved it there, and they loved her. We did have several meltdowns a month during morning drop off, involving flopping, crying, and kicking at the door. I hated driving away when she was like that, but each day when I picked her up she was happy, skipping, and laughing.

The way I see it, Isla reacted the way we all want to some days. I mean, don't you occasionally feel like flopping on the floor, crying, and kicking when you have to go to work? But we don't, because we are adults, we are mature, and our brain allows us to rationalize that, if we work through it, the reward is to go home and get paid. Isla's brain had not learned to rationalize like that on a daily basis, so she would act out.

Around that time, we also hit a huge snag with insurance issues, and we ended up having to purchase separate insurance through the marketplace. Yes, Obamacare.

So wherever you are, President Obama, know that my daughter was able to continue her ABA therapy largely because of you. Once we met our deductible, the majority of the fees would be fully covered, but we were now looking at a huge deductible: thousands and thousands of dollars that we had not budgeted for that year. We needed the money and we needed it quick.

I was tired of loans and debt so I did something that was unconventional and a total shot in the dark.

Since college I had been on an e-mail group that advertised open casting calls for student projects, local commercials, and short- and feature-film extras. I received these e-mails constantly, but they rarely sparked my interest anymore. When I was in pharmacy school, I had been an extra for several different television series and feature films, and I'd even been in a commercial for the university. It had been a lot of fun, and now I happened to have two beautiful daughters who loved television, YouTube, and all the new social media. So why not? What would it hurt to take them for an audition when the right part came along? Around the time the big bill for Isla's school came in, I got a casting call e-mail looking for a Hispanic/Latina Mom in her 30's with two Hispanic/Latina daughters ages 3 to 8 for a commercial. It was almost too good to be true. The first step was submitting pictures, because you had to be invited to the audition. I submitted our pictures with a quick description of my girls, and a few days later we had an audition date. Our area of the country has no entertainment industry at all, so we would have to drive five hours for the audition. Looking back it sounds so crazy, but life is short and tomorrow is not promised, so we just went for it.

We packed up our vehicle and drove and sang and laughed and practiced saying our names and ages to a pretend camera. We traveled in pajamas and changed in the parking lot of a Wendy's. When we showed up, my girls were excited and giddy.

We stood in front of a camera, said our names and ages, and answered questions about what we liked to do for fun as a family. Guess what? Isla did awesome!

She was happy and smiling, and even though her answers were hard to understand, she was fascinated with the camera. The audition was all of five minutes and then we climbed back in the car for another five hours back home. Isn't that insane? Wait. It gets better.

Three days later I got an e-mail from the casting agency, and I was thrilled—until I opened it and read that we'd made the first cut and would have to go back for a second audition with the producers. I went to sleep that night thinking there was no way. It just seemed too crazy to go back all that way for just five minutes. They probably won't even pick us.

The very next day I got my third and last pink positive sign. I was pregnant with my third baby. My last baby. When I walked out of the bathroom the first thing I did was e-mail the production crew to tell them that that we would be there for the second audition. After another five hours, endless calories of snack food, and a little nausea, the second audition was even more fun than the first. The girls danced and ran for the cameras, and we got to talk to the production crew. The commercial would be for Legal Zoom, and it would feature us playing in a backyard. It sounded fun and easy, but again, we would have to go back home and wait. They had many others auditioning that day and would get back to us later. Ten minutes after we'd arrived, we started the five-hour trip back home.

It was the week of my husband's thirty-fourth birthday when we were told that we had landed the part. All three of us. We would be paid initially just for the taping day, and then we would be paid a higher amount if our scenes made the final cut. For the third time in two weeks, we took off for the ten-hour round trip.

That filming day was my dream come true. I loved it all. The crew was awesome, the clothing trailer and hair and makeup were awesome. They treated my girls and me so well and so patiently. My girls had a blast, and there was no pressure on them to say words or to really act. They just played. They wore ballet outfits and played in a backyard. I blew bubbles as they played and danced and held hands and twirled around.

They were beautiful. They were sisters, and they were perfect. I remember watching the playback on one of the crew's cameras, and I was especially drawn to Isla as her beautiful hair wrapped around her. She was full of joy and energy and beauty. Autism did not limit my Isla that day. My girls made me so proud.

When it was all over, we signed some paperwork and were paid our initial check. We were told that if we received a second check in the mail within the next two weeks, we would know that we made the final cut and we should start looking for the commercial on TV within one to three months.

Two weeks later we received the second check in the mail. The two checks combined covered our entire deductible for Isla's special school for the whole year.

A few weeks later, it was time for our appointment with the pediatric neurologist and brain mapping expert that would hopefully give us some insight into Isla's results. Unfortunately, the doctor was just as confused as we were. The brain mapping really did not show anything significant or helpful. He recommended genome mapping, which wouldn't help Isla a whole lot but may give us some answers. I wasn't so interested in something that wouldn't help us, but his second recommendation did intrigue me.

He asked why we had never given Isla an EEG. That seemed like an easy one. "Because she's never had a seizure."

"How do you know?" he asked.

"Because no one has ever seen her exhibit any kind of seizure-like behavior or activity."

Still, the doctor highly recommended that we do a forty-eight-hour EEG, which would involve Isla wearing a monitor for two days straight to see if her brain waves were appropriate for all times of the day, including when at rest and asleep.

I remember getting back in the car that day thinking that if I, of all people, had missed something like that, I would never forgive myself. What if, this whole time, each episode had been a seizure?

It was time for our third annual family vacation, and we were getting more and more ambitious with our destinations. This time we would be spending several days in Washington, DC, and New York City.

I was terrified.

I had daymares of Isla wandering the streets of New York alone and lost. I researched child leashes and read blogs by parents who were for or against them. I loved reading parent blogs. Most parent bloggers were so extreme and crazy that they made me feel so normal. In the end, I decided to buy a leash just in case, but we also bought some umbrella strollers because even though our girls were grown, it would be a lot of walking, and I was in no condition to be carrying kiddos. Well, guess what? Isla did great. With the exception of a short-lived meltdown at Ford Theatre, she did awesome.

She was fascinated with all of the different modes of transportation. She loved the plane and subway and trolleys. All of the hustle and bustle kept her entertained and stimulated just enough. I believe that Isla started maturing around that time. She still wasn't catching up to her age level, but still, she was maturing. The light bulb was flickering, and I started to see a glimmer of hope that once the little kiddo in my belly was grown, maybe we would be able to show our trio the world after all.

Chapter Nine: 8-9 years
Sand Dollar Child

The month of Isla's eighth birthday, we found out the gender of our baby. We wanted to be surprised, so I had blood work done and gave my brother all of the information to find out the result by phone. My brother and his girlfriend filled a large black balloon full of confetti and glitter and hung it from our front porch. Greg, our two girls, and I stood underneath it while he popped it open and confetti and glitter came floating down on us. I decided to make a YouTube video so that our family could all see it and share in the moment together without having to plan a big gender reveal party. I created a montage of pictures of my girls growing up and narrated the video, saving the balloon pop for the big finale. Here is the narration:

"Deciding to have another baby was not easy. We have been so blessed with two really beautiful girls who are happy and now very independent. Starting all over seemed crazy, but as you all know, for the last five to six years, most of the big decisions we have made for our home, our family, our jobs, and our lives have revolved around our Isla. As the years have gone by we realize more and more what Isla's future will be like. And as we get older and our kids get older, we just can't help but think of what's going to happen when we're not around anymore.

I know it sounds so crazy and so far away, but all of this made me think of my June. June is growing and learning so fast and will know and understand more about her sister very soon. So in the end, just like I wanted to have June to give Isla a partner, I needed to give June one, too.

My husband and I would just smile when people would say to us, "Well I'll be praying for your boy!" or "I am so glad you guys are trying for a boy!"

You see, when you know all of the reasons we wanted another baby, it makes sense for it to be another girl. I mean God always gives you what you need, right? Isla needs another sister for the future. June needs another sister to confide in and lean on. So in the early weeks I started praying for my girl. I prayed for a patient, kind, understanding girl, and then I started to feel guilty. I started thinking about some people in my life who are not my sister, but who love me like one and would take care of me like one if I needed it. I started thinking that I was not being fair because there are some boys that are very patient and kind and understanding, too, and maybe one day he'll marry somebody who loves and cares for my girls like her own sisters. With all that being said, we have the answer and are about to share it with you all right now. So here we go…"

The background music was set to the song, "Can't Wait to Meet You" by the Small Town Pistols.

My favorite lyric from that song talks about hoping that the baby would resemble somebody that we already loved. It was perfect, and I loved the whole idea of the video even more because I created the narration and chose the song all without knowing what the gender was.

That day when Greg popped the balloon, he, my two beautiful girls, my growing belly, and I were showered with bright blue confetti, blue streamers, and blue glitter.

Blue. A son. A brother.

By now June was four years old and involved in organized sports and activities like soccer and gymnastics. Isla was the best cheerleader, and she enjoyed the travel and hustle and bustle of practices and games, but she would occasionally ask me if she could get involved too. We had attempted enrolling her in gymnastics when she was younger, but that had resulted in many behavior problems and upset parents of kids Isla would hit or kick. Isla was physically strong but uncoordinated, and I knew we would have to wait for a team or sport that welcomed special needs and had a coach with a big heart and even more impressive patience.

It just so happened that one of the new therapists at the ABA clinic used to work at a local gymnastics center, and he volunteered to go with Isla one evening a week to supervise and help her adjust to the class. I knew that the ABA clinic offered off-site consultation to manage specific behaviors that occurred at home, at church, at the salon, or wherever.

But every week? He was willing to go every week? On a Friday night? This particular therapist was young and spunky, and I am sure he had plenty to do on a Friday night, but he chose Isla. He chose to spend an hour with Isla at gymnastics each Friday evening, and Isla was overjoyed. Oh, how she loved preparing for gym. She was so darn cute packing her gym bag on Thursday nights. "Mom, mom where my gym suit?" "Oh, Mom need water. Me and Coach Alan need water." "Mom these shoes good or no?" "Mom I so excited!" For Isla, that excitement never wore off. She loved her "coach" and would try to sneak snacks into her gym bag for him. Once she went to bed I would look through her bag and find all kinds of random food and drink choices. One time I found a granola bar that had been bitten and wrapped up again, so the next morning I asked her, "Isla did you get this from the trash?"

"No. No. No. Mom", Isla replied. "Mom that for Coach Alan, but he say it OK I try it first."

As far as the actual hour of gymnastics, Isla had good evenings and bad evenings at first. Sometimes she was tired and would just hold his hand, and other times she was full of energy and would prance around the gym like a gazelle with her mile-long legs. She was learning to do the splits and a bridge, and she loved jumping on any and all of the trampolines. Surprisingly, she also loved bar and beam, and on the way to gym every week she would ask me, "Mom, Mom, bar and beam or no? Mom, you not know? Mom, Coach Alan say yes today bar and beam. Mom, I so happy! I love bar and beam." She had become a real chatterbox.

After several months of shadowing her, Coach Alan started sneaking into the upstairs portion of the gym to see how Isla did without him. After a few more months, she was able to complete the entire hour on her own. By then she was comfortable with the other instructors and did not have to rely on her "coach" anymore. Gymnastics brought Isla joy and a feeling of independence and normalcy. And Coach Alan brought gymnastics to Isla. So for that, how could I thank him enough? He, too, allowed himself to be used, and in return he played a very special role in Isla's story. He can thank me later for saving him from half eaten granola bars, moldy yogurt, and hot water bottles with granola morsels floating in them.

Around that time, both Isla and June were due for the ever-dreaded dentist visit. Getting through these visits required so much encouragement, fake enthusiasm, and total hypocrisy on my part as I cheered and forced my kids to sit through something I myself absolutely hate.

No joke, I require almost full sedation for my own trips to the dentist. Yes, I ask for laughing gas just to get through a basic cleaning. Don't judge.

Anyway, the apple doesn't fall far from the tree. On this particular visit, we would experience something for the first time. I considered how to include this encounter in my story, and I decided the truest way to do it was to share the actual statement I submitted to the office manager the following day, with just a few interjections to further explain my crazy self.

My name is Lisa Peña, I am the mother of Isla Peña and June
Peña, both patients at your clinic. On --/--/-- both of my daughters
had an appointment for their regular dental exams and cleanings.
We were one of the first appointments scheduled that morning and
arrived on time. The first hygienist that helped us was kind and
courteous and explained that Isla would not need x-rays because she
had recently had a tooth pulled, and x-rays had been done at that
time. He was very kind and patient with June, as she was scared and
not very cooperative, but he was able to get one x-ray.

(In reality, June was screaming bloody murder, but "scared and not
very cooperative" sounded more politically correct for that document.)
We waited in the waiting room, and very quickly a dental hygienist
named XXXXXX called us and led us to an exam room. My
daughter Isla was first to lay on the exam table, and before the exam
began I was asked to come to the computers at the front end of the
exam pod to verify my daughters' medical history and information.
XXXXXX was sitting with Isla at the exam table, and I did not
catch the name of the other dental hygienist helping me at the
computer.

In front of both dental hygienists I verified that Isla is autistic and
has a diagnosis of Pervasive Developmental Disorder (PDD),
ADHD, and speech delay. I signed the electronic pad and sat down
as XXXXXX began cleaning Isla's teeth.

I was sitting where XXXXXX's back was to me and I noticed that she would very subtly slouch her shoulders or put her hands down from working as if frustrated that Isla was not cooperating. We have been to this clinic several times before, and although nothing was particularly wrong yet, I did notice XXXXXX's demeanor was not as cheery or patient as we have experienced with other dental hygienists. I decided to stand and try to comfort Isla, and XXXXXX began to make comments like: "She is not opening for me. She is just not opening her mouth enough." Again, this was not typical of my previous encounters, but I tried to encourage Isla to open her mouth more. XXXXXX then told Isla, "You have to open up so I can show your mom why she needs to start helping you brush your teeth."

(Ouch. It was this early in the encounter that my heart started to race. Let me just say that mommy shaming is real, and it hurts, and it is not helpful. It just makes a mommy really pissed. And when you piss off the wrong mom, things don't go well for you. Don't mommy shame. Strike one, lady. Strike one.)

I want to explain that a comment like this seems harmless unless you are a mother with a daughter with special needs. A daughter whose sensory abnormalities used to cause her to gag to the point of dry heaving every time I tried to brush her teeth. A daughter who experienced lockjaw when a tooth brush went into her mouth—sometimes with my finger inside and sometimes with just the brush.

A daughter who has had her teeth brushed by an adult her entire life and had to be put under full anesthesia at the age of six just to do basic fillings.

Naturally, I started to feel uncomfortable with XXXXXX and her insensitivity.

"OK, come on, Isla," I said. "Let her show me what she is seeing." I was able to help open Isla's mouth enough to see XXXXXX point out a molar that had plaque on it. XXXXXX then told me she could probably do the rest with just the toothbrush. She got out the toothbrush, and by this point Isla was already uncomfortable. Isla has always had this gift of reading people. She may not understand everything you are saying but she reads body language, eyes, expressions, tone, and demeanor, and if she senses you're frustrated, instead of trying to please you, she will shut down. She was not feeling comfortable, so she just lay there, refusing to open her mouth at all. XXXXXX then told Isla, "If you do not open for me we will have to call the dentist so he can come clean your teeth, and if you don't open your mouth for him we have straps we use sometimes, and we will strap you down if we need too."

(Whoa. Did you just threaten my kid right in front of me? With straps? Is there a camera in here? Am I on "What Would you Do?" because if I am being filmed, I am about to go to jail. Strike two.)

I blame myself for not stopping the exam at this point. This is where I should have spoken up and refused to allow anyone to threaten my daughter.

I was honestly just too shocked to react fast enough. So I agreed and told XXXXXX, "Yes, I think it is best we get the dentist over here."

XXXXXX then looked at Isla and said, "Yes, I am going to call him because you are acting like a 2 year old."

(Right now, wherever you are, Google "Mean Girls watering hole at the mall scene," and watch it. What happens in that scene happened to me instantly. I felt like an animal. I started to feel my chest rising and falling hard. It was a rage I had not felt before. A primal rage that made me want to rip the hygienist's heart out with my bare hands and throw it at her feet. If you are thinking I am crazy and unstable, then maybe you aren't a mom who has felt true rage before. Oh no, strike three.)

It is very hard to put into words all of the rage, confusion, disbelief, disgust, and sadness that I felt in that moment.

(It was not hard to put into words. It's just that the words were highly inappropriate.)

I did not know what else to do except remove myself and my daughters from the situation before I lost control. I told Isla to sit up. I took off her paper bib myself. I listed out loud to XXXXXX all of Isla's diagnoses as we packed up to leave. As I turned to walk away all XXXXXX could say was, "I didn't know." How could she not have known? This clinic specializes in pediatric dentistry, ESPECIALLY for children with special needs. Isla's folder is a different color, indicating that she needs to be given more patience and time.

Even if she didn't have special needs, what child should ever be made to feel like they are a hassle, threatened with straps, and bullied and called names by an adult in a healthcare setting that is notoriously intimidating even for most other adults?

I walked out of the building with my two daughters, and that's when my emotions overwhelmed me. As I was crying and putting my girls into my car, the office manager came out of the building to ask me what happened.

At this point I really can't remember all that I said to her, but I know I was too emotional and enraged to communicate clearly.

(I do remember some of what I said/screamed/hyperventilated. I don't regret it, necessarily, but I am not proud of all the words I used. "The hygienist was so rude and disrespectful to my daughter! She was annoyed and impatient and threatened to strap Isla down if she didn't cooperate. And then she told her she was going to call the dentist because she was acting like a two year old! Isla is autistic. She has pervasive developmental disorder and speech delay, so no shit she acts like a two year old! Thank you so much for the reminder!" Like I said, not a proud moment. My girls were both sitting in the car with the doors closed by that point, so I would like to think they didn't hear any of my hysteria, but they probably did.)

Since the age of two, Isla has seen and interacted with numerous doctors, nurses, hospital staff, medical technicians, dental hygienists, therapists, teachers, etc., and never have I felt that someone has disrespected her or bullied her like this.

We have had many encounters with this dental practice and interacted with several different front office staff, dental hygienists, and dentists, and we are always treated so kindly with so much respect and patience.

My daughter will never be like a "normal" child. She will never act or talk like anybody her age. This is a reality that my husband and I have not only accepted, but we have embraced. Yes, it is hard to know that your child will be bullied because of her special needs, will not go to college, will probably never be married or fully independent, will not have a normal school experience, and will not be in organized sports or extracurricular activities.

As parents we already have to try very hard to make her feel special but still excited for her younger sister who will be able to do all of these things. We are a family that has spent years praying, crying, begging, and searching for answers and help. We are a family that has been to hundreds of appointments for behavioral specialists, speech therapists, occupational therapists, neurologists, psychologists, MRIs, EEGs, brain mapping, genetics tests, allergy tests, and ADHD tests. We have completed trials of ADHD medications and dealt with all of the side effects that come along with them. We are a family that has moved away from our home, church, schools, jobs, friends and extended family to find special care and schooling for our daughter to help her reach her fullest potential.

We are a family that has been to more ARD meetings to count and now attend parent trainings at a specialized school that provides ABA therapy. How incredibly cruel is it to remind a family like this—with a beautiful, innocent seven-year-old girl like this—that she is like a two year old?

Regardless of what age Isla "acts like," she still deserves to be treated with kindness, tolerance, patience, and most importantly respect.

As a mother, as a medical professional, and as a patient I do not feel that XXXXXX should be allowed to manage, touch, communicate, or interact with children in any medical related capacity. I can only hope that there will be serious repercussions for her actions and hurtful, cruel words.

That is what happens when you piss of the wrong mom.

I got in the car that day and, through tears, told my daughters that we will not tolerate bullies ever.

Lesson one: do not let anyone bully you. I used it as a learning opportunity for my children that they should never allow anyone to bully, threaten, scare, or disrespect them no matter who they are, where they are, or how much older they are. Lesson two: do not bully others. More importantly, we as a family will never do that to others. We now know firsthand how terrible it feels, so we will respect and be kind to everyone, and we will not ever be bullies. Lesson three: if you don't like kids, don't work in pediatrics. It's not rocket science, people.

I felt it was important to mention the above story not to be unkind to anyone but to explain that I feel I did not handle the situation correctly. Reflecting back it was such an excellent opportunity to show my girls self-control, kindness, and tolerance for someone who was unkind and intolerant. I wish so much that I had had the composure and grace to share what I wrote in that statement with the dental hygienist right then and there. I could have turned that visit around, but instead I was a hysterical fool, and the worst part is that my daughters witnessed it all. I know that there will be many more experiences like this in my life, but I feel so much more prepared and empowered because of this first one.

When I dropped Isla off that morning at the ABA clinic, she was clearly shaken up. Keep in mind that both of my girls had braved the dentist's office and not even completed their cleanings. The dentist called me later that day and apologized, saying he felt so horrible about our experience. I was asked to please submit a statement for documentation, and the dentist assured me that the next visit would be better, so I rescheduled.

The dentist office handled the situation with such professionalism and kindness, and the staff loved Isla so much and was outstanding in all subsequent encounters.

For that particular rescheduled visit, Eileen and Michelle from the ABA clinic both showed up. They were on time, brought coffee, and talked and played with Isla in the waiting room.

They cheered her on as she sat in the chair for her cleaning and distracted her enough to get through the whole visit. Isla loved them, and just their presence put her at ease. I knew that Isla was starting to bond with this group of people in a way that blessed her and them.

Isla had always avoided screen time when she was younger, but this year, she really started to enjoy TV! Her favorite shows were anything on the Food Network, which she called her "cooking shows," and anything on HGTV, which she called her "house shows." She especially loved Fixer Upper, because we had modeled the décor of our barn house to mimic Joanna Gaines's farmhouse-inspired ideas, and she loved the cooking shows that featured one person cooking in their kitchen, like *Dinner at Tiffani's*, which was my personal favorite. I mean, who doesn't want Kelly Kapowski to cook dinner for them?

One afternoon in the early fall, while we were watching *Donut Champions* on the Food Network, a Legal Zoom commercial came on, and lo and behold, there on national television was my gorgeous June. She had a two-second spot where she had her arms lifted in the air and was twirling in the sunlight, trying to pop a bubble. She was smiling big with her beautiful gap in her front teeth, and that was it. Two seconds. In two seconds June paid for her sister to attend her special school for one year. It doesn't get more serendipitous than that. To this day I have been tempted to reach out to Legal Zoom to thank them for the commercial first titled, "Protect it" and later titled "Family" and then "Life of a Family."

They have no idea what those two seconds meant to us and to Isla. They probably also have no idea that twirling right there behind June was Isla, a beautiful girl with autism.

Shortly after the commercial aired, we scheduled Isla for the forty-eight-hour in-home EEG. I was completely amazed at the way my little girl handled the whole thing. She had to sit on a chair for almost an hour while the technician put on all of the leads, wrapped her hair, and set up her backpack with the battery pack. The technician was so kind, talking to her the whole time about every single thing he was doing. He was a true professional. He even brought her several backpack options so she could choose one that made her feel special. (She chose Hello Kitty.) He set up cameras in the living area and in Isla's bedroom. We were instructed to keep a log during the next forty-eight hours of what time she woke up, ate, went to school, napped, fell asleep, etc. We did one day at home and one day at school to get a good sample of her normal activity.

Each time she had an episode, meaning a behavior problem or meltdown, we were instructed to push a red button on the battery pack that would indicate that for the data collection. She could not take a bath, which she didn't mind, and overall Isla handled the whole forty-eight hours very well. She was so proud to carry the backpack around and even enjoyed wearing the pink bandana around her hair during those days.

We did not end up having to press the red button at home, but the therapists did press it three times while she was with them. It was about one week after the EEG that I got a call from the neurologist who had ordered the exam. I stepped out of my office at work and nervously huddled under a tree outside, listening to his every word.

"Mrs. Peña," he said, "I reviewed the findings from the EEG, and it did not show any seizure activity at all for the entire forty-eight-hour period, but it did show abnormal brain activity during each sleep event."

"What do you mean abnormal?" I was already feeling guilty. "And what sleep events? Do you mean naps?"

"Basically every time she slept, whether it was a short nap or night time sleep, her brain activity was extremely overactive."

"OK, so what does that mean?" I asked.

My mind was already backtracking to the sleep study we did when Isla was two. Didn't a sleep study monitor brain waves? Did they do an EEG during the sleep study to compare this to? Did the sleep study EEG show this overactivity and someone missed it? Or just didn't tell me? I was hating myself for not requesting an EEG sooner, but then again, was it my job to know to request that? Who was supposed to recommend that to me? The behavioral pediatrician? The regular pediatrician? The first pediatric neurologist?

"It means that right now there is not seizure activity," the neurologist explained. "But the overactivity could lead to seizures in the future, or it could improve by itself over time. Every patient is different."

"Listen doctor," I said. "I know I have been Googling way too much these days, but I keep coming across Landau-Kleffner Syndrome when I research Isla and the main delays she presents with."

"Yes, I thought of LKS at the first visit when you were describing your daughter, which is one of the reasons I requested the EEG. But really she doesn't fit LKS either, because her delays seem to have been present since birth, and her speech is actually improving, not regressing. She also seems to understand most conversation and instruction", he replied.

"So what do we do now?" I asked. "Should she be on an anticonvulsant?"

"It is an option. I can prescribe something, but I am not sure if you are willing to continue traveling for visits."

He was right. I told him I would feel more comfortable with a local doctor in case of side effects. He agreed, and he wished me luck before we hung up.

Yes doctor. Yes, good luck to me. And let's wish more luck to poor Isla.

This was another pivotal moment for me.

The old Lisa would have spent hours researching all of the pediatric neurologists in our area, reading about each one, calling people I knew to get recommendations, fighting to get in fast, and calling like a maniac to make sure they had my information and had verified insurance. But after eight years, I was tired. Why lie? I was tired of always fighting the system. So this time, I went to our regular pediatrician and just told him to refer us to someone. I didn't care where or to whom—I just needed a referral.

Like I had done so many times before, I spent the evening before our visit to the third pediatric neurologist making a timeline of Isla's history. Gosh, this was a long one. But in my mind, the physician would need to know everything to make the best decision. I had also worked through tons of red tape, countless e-mails, and a dozen phone calls to get a copy of the 48-hour EEG, which required access to a special physician portal. I was convinced I was being helpful by supplying timelines and detailed background information.

When we arrived we got the familiar stacks of paperwork to fill out, and I detailed everything I could and then I asked the front desk receptionist if she would please attach my timeline to the documents. She told me that anything I wanted the doctor to know would have to be written on the forms. I told her that it didn't have to go into her record—I just wanted him to get the whole picture. "Sorry, ma'am," the receptionist repeated. "You will have to write it all down."

I had four typed pages.

So I sat back down and encouraged myself. I reminded myself not to waste energy fighting the system when I could just play the game. I used the back of each form to write down my entire timeline.

When it was our turn, the nurse's first question to me was, "So what brings you here?"

I wanted to rip my hair out, but I reminded myself again just to play the game. I got out my four-page timeline and read the entire thing to her. She listened, made notes, and then called the doctor in.

So the doctor walked in briefly, looked at me and Isla from beneath his glasses, and started reading the nurses notes. Every few seconds he would make noises like, "hum," "uh huh," and "umm."

Once he was done reading, he looked at me from under his glasses again and said, "Sometimes we dig too much into why something is happening when we just have to fix the problems. Sometimes we do lots of tests, and they don't help us. Sometimes we have to just see what is happening right now and try to help right now. Right now Isla is not doing well in school, so we give her medicine to help her at school. But if you want me to prescribe medicine, she cannot go to other doctors. She will need to be seen here only."

Let me give you a summary of what he really saw in all those notes but wouldn't dare say: Crazy mom. Googles too much. Has money to get her daughter a lot of unnecessary, unhelpful tests. Impatient mom who switches doctors left and right to get what she wants, fast. All her kid needs is medication, and this mom is still looking for the source of the problem like it even matters.

I was officially a pain-in-the-ass mom.

Now, here's a summary of what I couldn't dare say: I love my daughter more than life itself, and yes, I am educated and smart, and if you paid attention to my timeline you would know that right in front of you is a medical mystery that you don't even care to figure out. I have only requested so much testing because Isla is not presenting in a clear way for any specific diagnosis, and yes, I do think that if I knew the source of the problem I could help her more. But I am only here because I cannot prescribe medication myself. So write down the name of the anticonvulsant of your choice on your stupid pad of paper, and I will blindly trust you and give it to my eight-year-old daughter so she doesn't develop seizures. You are why the RGV doctors get a bad reputation. Who in their right mind would tell a mom to stop trying to help her kid? Stop searching for answers. Just give in.

The only reason I even brought you a timeline was in the hope that you were part of the big plan. I keep hoping that someday some special doctor will read about Isla's case and be fascinated and be intrigued and want to do what they were called to do: help. Apparently you are not that doctor. Your loss.

But, of course, that was all in my head.

I was silent as he wrote a prescription for an anticonvulsant. Before we left he did mention that an ADHD medication may help with behavior during the day and even keep the brain calm at night. I mentally filed that away as something to consider once we got the anticonvulsant underway.

After one week on the new medication, Eileen pulled me aside with warm concern and told me that Isla was sad that day. There was nothing particularly wrong, but she cried at odd times, and she was just sad overall. I knew that depression was a side effect of the medication, but I didn't know it would present so early and in a patient so young. I told her to give it one more day because at home Isla had been great. But the next day was worse, and Eileen and the therapists were concerned. I called the pediatric neurologist's office and told them what was going on. After consulting with the doctor, they recommended I try half the dose.

Even on the half dose, the sadness did not dissipate, but this time I was the one who witnessed it. If you have never seen an eight year old be suddenly overcome with a wave of depression, I hope you never do. It happened on our routine trip to Starbucks, which Isla looked forward to every Friday. She loved the ambiance and aroma, and she always wanted to stay.

This particular week, everything was fine and dandy until the moment we stepped inside, when she just started weeping.

First, I thought she'd gotten hurt on something, but when I looked at her face, I could tell it was pure sadness. She had her arms and hands hanging at her sides with her palms facing forward and her head held high, and she was just sobbing.

"Isla, my love, what is it? What is wrong?" She just wept and then came close to me so that I could hold her.

I picked up my eight-year-old girl, carried her back to my vehicle, and sat in the backseat with her, literally holding her like a baby while she cried. As I cradled her, I watched her face, hardly recognizing my girl. This was not Isla's face. It was as if she was ten years older, and all the life had been sucked out. Her eyes were glossed over, and she looked somewhere off in space, just crying. She couldn't speak. All I could do was start singing. *"You are my afternoon, and day and night too, I'll stay up with the moon singing you a tune..."*

I was at a loss. Should I take her off the medication and just wait it out, pray she wouldn't develop seizures? What were the odds she would never progress that far? I wanted evidence and numbers and expertise. What was the likelihood that she would get a seizure one day? What was the likelihood that she would actually grow out of this abnormal brain activity? The doctor had mentioned ADHD medication. Were there studies that showed ADHD medication could help with overactive brain waves at night? During sleep? We had also started using essential oils and a white noise machine at night for her, so how often should we recheck the EEG to see what interventions were working? I had so many questions, and no one to ask but my sidekick, Google, who was sometimes mean to me, giving me misleading information and annoying advertisements about debt consolidation and women's Depends.

I called the pediatric neurologist again that day and told him I was stopping the medication and I wanted a follow-up.

When we returned to the office a week later, he glanced at his notes and then turned to Isla and asked three questions:

"Hi, what's your name? You like school? You like your teacher?"

Isla just stared at him, smiling, so he wrote a prescription for an ADHD medication and then proceeded to tell me that from what he was seeing Isla was not autistic—she was probably just MR.

Oh, OK, you knowledgeable doctor, you. Let me get this straight. In two quick visits that lasted five minutes combined, with three questions and no formal testing, evaluation, or observation of any kind, you decided my kid was MR?

No guys. I didn't say that out loud. Instead, I smiled a sarcastic, totally fake smile. You know the one. It's the smile where you squint your eyes a little, press your lips together, and force the corners of your mouth upward.

The definition of *mental* is "relating to the mind" or "relating to disorders of the mind." The definition of *retarded* is "less advanced in mental, physical, or social development than is usual for one's age," or "foolish or stupid." So you know who is really MR? Every single person who spreads hate and has no tolerance, acceptance, or love for anyone who is a different color. You know who is MR? Every single person who is selfish, greedy, power hungry and doesn't care if they have to hurt others to get what they want.

Wait, what's that you say? The phrase "mentally retarded" has been replaced by "intellectually disabled?" Oh, OK, no problem.

The definition of *intellect* is "the faculty of reasoning and understanding objectively," and synonyms include *reason, understanding, brainpower, sense, judgment,* and *wisdom.* The definition of *disabled* is "having a physical or mental condition that limits a person's movements, senses, or activities," and synonyms include *impaired, defective,* and *abnormal.*

People who practice and spread racism, bigotry, sexism, misogyny and hate have a mental condition that limits their senses and an impairment and defect that prohibits them from reasoning and understanding, so they are *intellectually disabled.* Those people have a foolish and stupid disorder of the mind, so they are *mentally retarded.* Isla may be severely academically challenged, but she is not mentally retarded. My daughter may have a significant speech delay, but she is not intellectually disabled.

By that point I was so tired I did not care what he said. I knew he didn't know my Isla, and I just needed him for the prescription, so I got what I wanted. You already know that Isla was much more verbal by this point. Her vocabulary was expanding, and more and more the therapists, my husband, and I noticed that the ADHD really was the biggest problem. She was constantly distracted, unfocused, and all over the place, and I just wanted her to rest both her body and her brain. We decided to do a trial of ADHD medication again because now she could verbalize her feelings and thoughts a little more, and we had started considering something we had been dreading for years: transitioning back to public school.

It was that time of year when all of the changes to insurance plans around the country were starting to come out.

The insurance we had purchased from the marketplace would no longer cover ABA therapy, but the federal insurance plan changed and included ABA, so my insurance would now be our primary insurance. However, that meant a co-pay per day of service, which was pricey for a whole month, and honestly I was wondering whether Isla had plateaued at the ABA clinic. She had made tremendous gains in regards to behavior, asking for breaks when she was tired as opposed to acting out and making everyone guess when she needed a break.

Her trademark behaviors had all but disappeared, including my favorites: urinating off the toilet and disrobing. When they did happen, it was usually just one time with a brand new therapist.

We had to constantly reevaluate what was best for Isla. That's one of the hardest parts of being a parent of a child with special needs. Many times you don't know what is "best," and there is no one to help you. It is lonely and scary and a tremendous responsibility, and the worst part is that for some, the child can't be a part of the decision. Some can't verbalize their feelings, worries, and fears to the extent that other children can. All I knew was that when we committed to ABA therapy, I promised myself to stick with it for two years. That was the evidence-based recommendation, so that was what we went with. It had now been two years.

As much as I loved the ABA clinic and their incredible team, I knew the potential that Isla had, and I knew that I needed to continue challenging her and giving her as many real-world experiences as I could. One of those real-world experiences was public school.

So again, I jumped the gun. Now seven months pregnant, I decided to make the rounds and visit the more prominent elementary schools. I reached out to each principal by e-mail and scheduled appointments to visit with them and the special education teachers. I knew that once the baby came I would not be able to get around as much, so whether we transitioned Isla after Christmas or for the next school year, I wanted to be prepared ahead of time. I visited new campuses and older campuses. I saw some special education classrooms that were unorganized and chaotic and others that were strict and quiet. I met with teachers who had master's degrees and numerous years of experience and teachers who didn't recognize the acronym PDD.

I saw bare classes and cluttered classes. I saw classrooms with few to no resources for the kids and other classrooms that were fully digital, complete with iPads and Smart boards. I saw classrooms with all boys, classrooms with too many students to count, and classrooms with less than a handful of students.

Let's say you move to a new town and want your children to attend the "best" school. What do you look for? You find the zip code with the "blue ribbons" or the "exemplary" campuses, right? If their scores are the best in town, they must have the best teachers, best administration, most resources, and brightest kids.

Well, what about parents whose children need special education? What about the families that know their child will be in a self-contained Life Skills class? How do we know how to choose a school? Testing scores? Puhleese. They mean nothing to us. How do I know which special education teacher has both the most compassion and the highest expectations?

How do I know which school has the special education teachers with the most training in the type of learning style my child responds to best? How do I know which special education programs are kind and respectful and won't be run by rude or impatient staff who will just make Isla put her head down all the time? And I haven't even mentioned paraprofessionals yet! Anyone who is anyone in the public school system knows that a paraprofessional can be critical in a child's well-being, success, and progress—especially in special education. So what about them? Is there a rating system for accountability? Kindness? Education? Training?

Does everyone see the biggest problem here?

We send the children who are the least verbal, who cannot come home and tell us about what their teacher said or how they were treated, and who need the most help—academically, socially, and physically—to the one department of the public school that has no accountability scale, test, rating score, or process. At first I thought that wasn't fair. But really, it's more than that. It's not right.

So I did the only thing that I could do. I visited every single school, saw the classrooms myself, talked to the teachers myself, and chose the program I thought had the most organized and knowledgeable teacher, most reasonable class size, most impressive classroom décor (which I assumed translated into attention to detail and emphasis on environment), and most exceptional principal.

So we were ready to transition Isla, but the ABA clinic was not so sure. Eileen had a heart to heart with me one day and sincerely told me that Isla was not ready.

Eileen had twenty-plus years of experience and had transitioned many children into public school, so just like I had to trust every other health care professional in this story, I had to trust her, too. We all decided to work for the next few months to better prepare for a public school classroom and transition Isla in the fall for the new school year. Meanwhile, we had started the new ADHD medication, and it was not perfect but it was a much more positive experience than the last attempt. Right away we noticed a calmness about Isla. As the medication peaked each day, she did have moments of being a bit whiny, but she never complained of stomach pain, and while she would skip lunch, she ate well at breakfast and dinner and had some snacks in the afternoons. The medication didn't magically turn on the light bulb, but it helped her to focus, lessened distractions, and allowed her to be in the moment rather than looking for what was next. I thought it also helped her act more age appropriately in her responses, excitement level, and demeanor.

The ABA clinic went above and beyond to get my kiddo ready for public school. They simulated a real classroom inside the clinic and incorporated circle time and preschool basics. They started lengthening learning sessions and incorporated the other children in the clinic for more social time and team building exercises. Isla loved all of this, but only in short spurts and for limited sessions per day. She was learning and adjusting, and it was all because of that incredible team of people at the ABA clinic.

Before I get off the "I love the ABA clinic" train, let me share one other thing. I was at one of Isla's gymnastics sessions one evening when I saw a familiar-looking young woman walk in.

It was Lorraine, a therapist from the ABA clinic, but I assumed she must be there watching a relative or a friend's kid. Nope. She was there to see my Isla. Just like Coach Alan had, on a Friday night when she could have been doing so many other things, she came just to watch Isla. And boy did Isla light up when she saw Lorraine. Oh, she loved the attention, and she just giggled and jumped and smiled and waved so very proudly. And the visits didn't stop there. Over the course of the next couple months, three different therapists made the trip on Friday evenings to watch Isla in her one-hour gymnastics class. Let me tell you what this is. It is not work, and it is not therapy. It is love.

Eileen had a child in dance at the same gym, so we would see her, too, almost every session. Isla loved Eileen and would always ask about her and search for her.

Isla wanted to make her therapists proud, and that simple little gym class would prove to be so vital in making Isla independent. It taught her self-control because she had to contain her excitement so she could "perform" for them. It was proof that some of life's most valuable lessons are not learned in the classroom. If anybody has taught me that, Isla has.

It was around this time that I was able to put my newfound skills in dealing with situations like the dental drama into action. The valuable lessons I had learned that day all came in very handy one evening in the bathroom of the gymnastics gym. Isla and I walked into the bathroom to change her for her class, and we saw a young girl around Isla's age getting her hair brushed by her mother. I recognized them both and nodded hello just before the young girl blurted out, "Hey Mom that's the girl that bit me when I was little!"

I had just placed Isla's gym bag on the counter to start changing her when the little girl said this, and I immediately picked the bag back up and started scanning the bottom of each stall to see if one was open. The mother said nothing, so the little girl repeated herself. "Mom, remember? That's the girl that bit me when we were in Ms. Salazar's class. Mom, remember?" By this point I'd found an open stall and thrown the bag in. Isla stayed standing in the middle of the bathroom, staring at the little girl. She was reading her face, her attitude, and her body language, looking back and forth from the mom's face to the little girl's face and back to my face.

She was stuck and didn't know how to respond, but she absolutely knew there was tension building. She could feel it, and she knew it was all because of something she had done. The mother said nothing. She pretended like nothing was happening. I put my arm around Isla and led her into the stall. I was scrambling to do the right thing. I considered poking my head out and saying, "Her name is Isla, and I am very sorry if she bit you many years ago. A lot of children bite when they are small." I also considered poking my head out and saying many other things that I am too ashamed to admit here.

I took a deep breath as the little girl repeated herself for the third time. "Mom don't you remember? When I was in Ms. Salazar's class I got bit, and that was the girl that bit me. Mom, remember?" The mother did not utter a single word the entire time. It was a moment when I had to accept that things like this would happen probably for the rest of our lives with Isla. There would always be children who don't know any better and parents who decide children with special needs don't concern them and it is best to remain silent.

I also accepted that although I cannot control others' behavior I can always control my response, and I can always control the kind of person that my children see and hear and learn from.

I knelt down and started to take off Isla's shirt and shorts to change her into her gym outfit. She was burning a hole through me with her eyes as she watched my expression change from surprise to anger to rage to pensiveness to calm.

"Hey, Isla," I said, "did you know that you have the most beautiful hair?"

Isla looked at me totally confused. "What?"

"Yes!" I said. "Isla, when you were in my tummy I prayed that you would have super beautiful, big, curly hair, and you do! I love your hair, and so many people wish they had hair like yours." Isla started to giggle, so I continued. "Hey, Isla, don't you like this new gym outfit? Gosh, you picked a good one, girl! I love the color. Doesn't it feel so good on your skin?"

Isla rubbed her tummy to feel the spandex. "Yes, Mom! It feel nice!" We finished dressing, and I hugged her tight and told her I was proud of her and that I loved her. She told me she loved me too, and we walked out of the stall. I was not expecting the mom and daughter to still be standing there, but they were. They just stared as we walked out, and as we left Isla smiled and waved at them.

"Have a good evening," I said quietly. By this point I was super-de-duper pregnant, so thank God I didn't let my hormones get the best of me that time.

Throughout my pregnancy we had many discussions about the baby. June was head over heels in love with my belly—so much that I was worried she would miss it when the baby came. She would rub my belly and talk baby talk to the mystery boy inside.

While I helped the girls brush their teeth each morning and night, they would both rub the belly and giggle. It was fun and special and exactly what I wanted for them during that time.

Isla was not as attached, but she was still excited. Every once in a while she would get a glimpse of my side profile and place her hand over her mouth and giggle. "Mom, oh my God!" I would laugh and ask her what she meant. "Mom, that big baby!" Oh, yes. He was big, and he was coming.

The new baby was having much more of an impact on June than on Isla. June was my baby, and it was a turning point for her—a maturing time. I was sad sometimes, and she was too. She would ask me questions like, "Mom, are you still going to read me books when the baby comes?" "Mom are you still going to sing to us at night when the baby comes?" I knew that the reality was it would be tough. Having a newborn can be hard on everyone in the family, so I was careful to reassure June and show her as much love and attention as I could in those last days when it was just us four.

Greg Major was born the week before the Super Bowl. I am going to say two things about his delivery: First, he was very big, and we elected for a cesarean section with a glorious upgrade to tubal ligation. Second, if I ever hear anyone say that a cesarean section is the easy way out, I will punch them in the face. That's all.

Major was born beat up, splotchy, yellow with jaundice, rashy, swollen, and huge. He had hair that looked like he'd been growing it for years and dimples on both cheeks and his chin. I have a picture of Isla and June and Greg all hunched over, looking at this chubby little guy in his plastic box on wheels. In that moment, we were complete.

My recovery was brutal, but my baby boy was perfect. I was so lucky to have such a good baby for my third. He never cried. He was always content. He slept well, ate like a champ, and was all smiles at just five weeks old. He was strong and would use his legs to stand on me at almost a month. And with my mother in law as my witness, he rolled over at four weeks.

Isla and June were in love from day one. They hardly ever gave me problems when it came to Major. They loved on him so much, and as he grew their bond got better and stronger every day. Isla loved that little baby boy. She played with him, sang to him, talked to him, wanted to push him in his stroller constantly, and loved to feed him. She was his little momma. We did have moments when we had to stop her or remind her that he was not a doll, but overall, she was amazing. At just a few months old, Major was already shaping up to be another excellent at-home therapist for Isla. A very handsome therapist with great hair, I might add.

Isla did struggle during these months a little bit because I was not around as much. My mother helped me drop off and pick up the girls from school for a few weeks while I was not able to drive. But without me there, Isla would act out and flop and be defiant at each drop off and pick up time, so at a mere two weeks post C-section, I stood at the door of my SUV wondering how I was going to lift myself up.

With no makeup, severe sleep deprivation due to breastfeeding on demand, questionable deodorant, legs the hairiest I have ever let them get, and still-swollen ankles and feet, I hoisted myself up into that SUV and drove my kiddos to school and back. I know those therapists saw my toughest days and never judged.

After a few weeks back in our routine, we started to see Isla make big improvements weekly and even daily. Through discrete trials, Isla was learning to tie her shoes! She was also requesting breaks on a consistent and appropriate basis. By this point we had converted the loft in our barn house to the girls' bedroom and added a Dutch door. Pretend play was now in full swing, and it was so fun and funny to listen to. The girls played nursery, grocery store, and house, and it was just awesome to hear Isla play appropriately and hold small conversations with June. Isla was maturing, and it could not have come at a better time. One of the great things she also began doing on a consistent basis was telling me when she was tired. At the end of each day, she knew when she had had enough. She *wanted* her bath time. She *wanted* her bedtime. Any mom can appreciate that. By far the biggest things the ABA clinic gave her were her voice, her vocabulary, and the power to verbalize how she was feeling. That is priceless to a momma who has a child with special needs. Priceless.

It was the end of the school year and time for June's dance recital. She would be performing a ballet number and a tap dance number, and the whole family showed up to support her. We got there super early to save seats, and Isla was totally in charge.

She would stare at the door, and every time she saw a familiar face that belonged to our group, she would wave her arms high in the air and call out to them. She would stand in the center row and direct them like she was directing traffic.

She loved this. She loved family. Even though sometimes having *all* the family together at once proved to be overwhelming, she didn't want it any other way.

As the auditorium lights dimmed, she wiggled in her seat and leaned over to me. "Mom I so excited June! Mom, you tell me when June come, OK, Mom?" So in the dark I tried to keep her on track with all the performances so she knew when to expect June. June was beautiful and on point, as always. Isla cheered, clapped, and yelled, "Go June!" Then suddenly she was anxious, and she started asking to leave. This was typical for Isla. The crowd, the lights, sitting for lengthy amounts of time…it all becomes too much. Greg and I worked together to distract her so we could make it to the finale without a total meltdown. The finale song was Isla's favorite: "Can't Stop the Feeling." It played loudly, and the whole crowd started clapping to the beat. Each performing class came on stage one at a time to bow, curtsy, and wave at the crowd.

I watched the edge of the big red velvet curtains intently, not wanting to miss June because I didn't know when her class would be up. But after a few moments, I realized that Isla was gone.

I looked down the aisle, behind me, and around me at each family member. I was on the verge of panic, but Greg, who is much taller than me, spotted her quickly. He pointed down the center row, and there was Isla, oblivious to the crowd. She was clapping her hands big and high in the air to the music. She was bobbing her head up and down and inching her way to the stage. I grabbed Greg's arm and shriek-whispered, "Oh my God go get her!"

Greg thought this was great. He waved at Isla and smiled and encouraged her to keep dancing. "Lisa, she is fine. Let her have fun."

I am all about having fun, but not like that.

Not everyone there knew Isla, and she looked so normal, and I didn't want her to look dumb or slow, and there are strict rules and etiquette for recitals, and I didn't want us to look like bad parents for not stopping her and— I suddenly started crying. I still really don't know if I was mad, embarrassed, ashamed, or worried. Part of me knew that if the audience knew even half of Isla's story they would all have gotten up and danced with her. But they didn't, and when some see Isla act like Isla, well, they judge. They judge her and her parents. Isla did not make it to the stage that night, but she got close. When the music ended, she knew to join us to go look for June and congratulate her. I wiped my eyes quickly before the lights came on and pretended nothing had happened.

This was also the month of Isla's big end-of-the-year gymnastics performance.

It was an evening when the parents and families could come into the gym and see their children show off the skills they had learned. Everyone would cheer and clap, and all the gymnasts would get medals, and it was just fun all around. Isla was beyond thrilled for this, of course—mainly because she wanted to show off in front of her therapists. That's right, on a Friday evening five of the most influential therapists in Isla's day-to-day life showed up to cheer her on. She did amazing, and as I watched her that day and then panned the room to see the group of therapists, I realized something. I didn't choose for Isla to have autism. I didn't pray for God to send me a child with special needs. As horrible as it may sound, the truth is that no one wants that. No parents ask for that for their children. As I watched the faces of each therapist, I could tell that every smile, every clap, and every giggle was genuine. They chose my Isla. Even with all her oddities and challenges, they chose her.

They chose to dedicate their lives to working with Isla and children like her. I honestly can't think of many other careers as honorable or selfless. I mean, I have always thought I had a big heart, and I was taught to be kind and show compassion to others, but this was a whole different level. I was so emotional that day as Isla hugged them and they each gave her flowers and gifts and she stood there among them, so proud, so happy, and so joyful with her #TeamIslaLove.

Before we knew it, it was summer and officially beach time. We had a family routine: on Fridays as soon as I got off work, we would load up and head to the beach for the evening.

We would get there about 5:30 or 6:00 p.m., which was the perfect time to have kiddos out in the sun without worrying about big-time sunburns. Isla loved the beach. It was sensory-friendly for her, and I think it encompassed all that made her calm. The texture of the sand on her feet, the sound of the water and seagulls, the activities, and the people watching soothed her and kept her just stimulated enough.

After a few hours we would head upstairs to the big beach bar and restaurant deck to clean up and sit down for dinner. There was a live band each night, so we listened to music and ate and enjoyed the evening, which always included fireworks. And every Friday night, Isla was a dancing machine, just like at June's recital. She had no fear, no hesitation, and no worries. She would go right up to the stage where the live band was and dance her heart out to every song. She couldn't care less if she was alone or in the middle of a crowd of families, tourists, couples, and drunks. She didn't care. She would bob her head up and down and clap really big and hop from foot to foot. She would spread her arms and twirl and laugh at others who were dancing silly.

She would often grab the attention of fellow dancers who would hold her hand as she mimicked their dancing.

One routine Friday evening in beautiful South Padre Island, as I watched my island girl sway to the music, I had "aha moment" number three. For many years I had worried about Isla not being free to live the life I wanted for her. But I was starting to see that of all of us, Isla was the most free. She was always herself, take it or leave it.

She lived as she pleased, danced as she pleased, loved as she pleased, and was 100 percent free. Interesting, huh? If only we could learn to enjoy life as adults the way Isla enjoys her life. If only we could live freely as adults, just like Isla, with no fear of judgment from anyone. That summer was the first time in eight years that I knew we would be OK. I was going to be OK. Isla was going to be OK. It was that summer that I decided to write this book, because I realized how far we had come as individuals, as parents, and as a family. I didn't want to forget all that was Isla's story, and, more importantly, I wanted June and Major to know how it all started and how important they were to our family's story.

Early that summer, a local news station approached me to see if I would be interested in sharing Isla's story. The news station was doing a series on autism—it's effect on families, the lack of resources available, and the challenges and small victories that came with it. They specifically wanted me to share our story of moving away to attend the ABA clinic and working to bring it back to our hometown. I was hesitant. I worried about how they would portray our family, and especially Isla. I knew that the media usually skewed stories to their advantage, but in the end I decided to do it for one reason.

There is a scripture that reads, "Speak up for those who have no voice" (Proverbs 31:8). I had to think about Isla.

If she could speak for herself, would she want to tell others like her about the ABA clinic? Yes.

If she could speak for herself, would she want to share her story and help others gain independence and learn coping skills through ABA therapy just like she had? Yes. So I did it. I was Isla's voice. I wanted this to serve as a thank you from her to all of the therapists and Eileen, but there was so much that I said about the ABA clinic that did not air. I know that the clinic received several inquiries in the days after the news story aired, and I can only hope that we helped at least one family. We recorded the story on DVR, and Isla asked to watch it over and over. She called it her "commercial," because we would often see June on her commercial. Each time I replayed the news story, both girls would jump and cheer, and Isla would run to hug the TV screen when Eileen came on.

Throughout that year, as June grew and matured, we tried to start conversations with her about Isla. June was smart, but she had just turned five, so at that age everything was still very literal. These conversations started when Isla was invited to a special needs rodeo where she could dress up like a cowgirl and go into a rodeo arena to practice lassoing a toy cow, pet the rabbits, and ride on a hayride. I knew I would have to prepare June for the kids that she would see with Isla and explain why she could not participate. My attempt turned into my first total mommy fail of a conversation as I totally underestimated my June.

"Hey, June, have you ever noticed anything different about Isla? Like, do you think she is different from you?"

"Oh yes," June said innocently. "Mom, Isla has curly hair, and I wish I had curly hair."

I was one question in and already tearing up.

"Well, yes, her hair is curly and yours is straight, but that's good. It is good to be different, and your hair is beautiful, too. But do you think that Isla acts different? Like when you play with friends or your cousins?"

"Yeah, she is not shy like me. I wish I wasn't so shy," June said.

This was fascinating to me. I grew up with two brothers, so I was not familiar with the sister dynamic. All I knew was that my older daughter had special needs, which meant sometimes there was disturbing stuff happening in the background, but her little sister had no clue. Isla was June's norm. That was all June knew a big sister to be. Like any little sister, she wanted to be just like her big sister. You would think I would have gotten the hint and moved on from the conversation, but then I went and made it worse by trying a different angle.

"June, I want to tell you something about Isla. Isla is different. You know how she goes to the special school with her therapists? Well, she is special and needs special people to help her learn."

June was clearly offended. "Wait. So I am not special?"

Insert foot in mouth. Wow, I'd really messed that one up.

I could lie and tell you that I took all the time I needed to explain and really drive home the point, but this kid was out of my league, so I hugged her, told her she was amazing and special, and got her an ice cream cone quick.

The special rodeo confused June. Initially, she was just sad because she wanted to participate too, but as she watched all of the children that were going in with Isla, something didn't add up for her.

She started pouting, so I sat next to her.

"Hey, June, are you OK? Do you remember the other day, when I was talking to you about Isla and how she is different?"

"Yes," said June, with a look on her face that said she was trying hard to make sense of everything she was seeing.

"Well, these kids that are in the rodeo are like Isla. They learn differently, and some of them have different kinds of therapists and teachers to help them learn different things in different ways."

"But, Mom, Isla is not in a wheelchair, and her legs work."

I never could have imagined how hard it would be to explain autism to June. It was complicated, and I was obviously not prepared. I would continue trying over the next few months to introduce these ideas to June. When the news story aired, she heard the word "autism" for the first time and asked me if autism meant Isla couldn't learn. That was a very hard thing to explain. Keep in mind that Isla looked completely unaffected by any disorder. She had no stimming tendencies and no physical features that would indicate anything abnormal.

Then again came my saving grace, the ABA clinic, to the rescue. In late summer, about one month before we were set to transition Isla to public school, the ABA clinic held "Sibling Week." For the entire week, June went to the clinic with Isla and spent the day with her. Somehow they did it. June came home talking about zebras and the autism stripe from the book they read, and it just seemed to make sense all of a sudden. I truly believe that seeing it first hand was what she needed.

We were a few weeks away from the new school year, and I was starting to panic. The ABA clinic had a program where they would send a therapist to the public school with your child for six months to help them transition.

But Isla's school district did not allow this due to legalities, so I set out to convince the new special education teacher to either allow the therapists to come meet with her or—even better—to visit the ABA clinic to see Isla in action and complete a "warm hand-off," so to speak. The weekend before I was planning to meet with the new teacher, I learned that I had chosen poorly. Through a family friend who had substituted in many special education classrooms in our area, we heard some things about the special education program at the school I had selected. My intention is not to hurt anyone or be unkind, so I won't go into the details. But after the conversation was over, I knew in my heart I had judged poorly. More importantly, I knew I could not send Isla there.

There are so many analogies that I could use here, but the one I think fits best is one my Dad will appreciate: it's the scene in Indiana Jones when he has to identify the Holy Grail. The villain chooses the cup that is sparkling, shiny, made of solid gold, and encrusted with emeralds—the cup of a king. He chooses poorly. Indiana Jones chooses the cup that is modest, worn, and made of battered clay—the cup of a carpenter. He chooses wisely.

When I set out to find a school for Isla, I'd been determined to find the prettiest classrooms in the best-known neighborhoods. I was wrong. When I really thought about what was most important, I realized I wanted the program that practiced the most patience, attention, respect, and love.

The new school that I chose had a Life Skills class with only five students, including Isla, and the teacher was more than willing to visit the ABA clinic for that warm handoff I needed for her. I had a very lengthy conversation with the teacher because I needed her to understand that she was getting a very unique student.

I wanted her to know all of the most disturbing behaviors so she would be aware and prepared. She assured me that she had dealt with many challenging behaviors before, and this would be no different.

Now, Isla would be going to a school where we had family teaching and attending, which was a blessing bigger than I have words to describe. Such a blessing that I couldn't help but wonder about June. June was still enrolled in that day school that we loved, and she was registered to start there in a few days.

I began to wonder whether it was time for the girls to go to the same school, but my super smarty, June, beat me to it.

"Hey, Mom, what's going to happen to Isla when she goes to big school?"

At first, I wasn't sure where she was going with this. "What do you mean? She'll have new teachers, and she'll do well."

"No," June said, "I mean Isla won't have one teacher just for her right? There will be one teacher for all the class. What if Isla needs one just for her?"

"Oh June, you don't have to worry," I said, getting a little emotional about her concern for her big sister. "Isla has a small class, and the teacher can still help Isla while she's helping the other kids."

"Hey, Mom! I have a great idea!" June bounced up and down as she made her pitch. "Maybe one day when I'm bigger, I can go to school with Isla, so if she needs help I can help her because I am her sister!"

Withdrawing June from her day school was a different experience that time around. I felt at peace. Even though, as a mom, I never know if what I am doing is right or best, I knew in this case that I was following my heart—and June's. The same headmaster who had been so influential before came through again.

I knew from experience that she would be supportive and encouraging, and that was what she was. She did not make me feel guilty or wrong.

The week before Isla's ninth birthday, something happened to Isla and me that had never happened before.

We were on our way to drop off Major at daycare one morning when Isla noticed a vehicle in front of us.

"Hey, Mom," she asked, "that your friend?"

"Uh, no, Isla, but you are right. It looks just like my friend's car."

"Mom, what her name?"

"Sueli."

"She have babies, right, Mom? Remember, Mom? I go to birthday party her babies?"

"Yes she has two daughters. You're right." I'd been a little sleepy when Isla asked the first question, but by now I was fully alert, fascinated by her recall.

"Mom, what their name?"

"Elise and Mia."

"Oh, Mom, that pretty name. Mom, they so cute! I remember I see them at party! You remember, Mom?"

I couldn't help but giggle at Isla's excitement. "Yes, Isla, I do remember! They are super cute, and they do have pretty names!"

"Mom, who take them?"

"What? Who takes them where?"

"No, no, no. No. Mom, who take care them?"

"Well, Elise goes to a day school, and Mia stays home with her family. She doesn't go to day care like Major."

"Oh. That nice, Mom."

I leaned back in the driver's seat, realizing that I had just had the first full conversation ever with my first-born daughter. It was a real, beautiful, normal, appropriate first conversation with no repetitive questioning and with Isla herself initiating every thought. I was stunned. I just laid my hand out on the middle console, and Isla placed her hand in mine and smiled. I remember wondering how many people were having conversations with their kids on the way to school that morning, who had no idea what a blessing it was.

It was time to say good-bye to the ABA clinic, and I'd known since I'd enrolled her two and a half years before that this would not be easy. How could I possibly thank them? They were invested in Isla. They had invested time and tears and studying and planning and cutting and pasting and talent and energy in Isla for almost three years. They were silly and fun, and that was how Isla preferred to live life. They let her paint their nails and style their hair (neither well) as rewards for tasks completed. They went to gymnastics to cheer for her, showed up to dental appointments to comfort her, and went out of their way to give her rewards that were fun and special to her. They'd each cleaned urine-stained carpeting and bagged urine-soaked clothes. They'd dealt with disrobing and fits and meltdowns and yelling and kicking and crying. They made her song playlists and hopscotch patterns and taught her to tie her shoes and helped her enough that she could now have a full conversation with her mom.

They respected her, never mistreated her, and were happy to see her every morning regardless of her demeanor or the way she had treated them the day before. Isla impacted their lives. Isla had inspired some of them to change their career paths to help others like her for the rest of their lives.

Isla cared about them and loved them. She would ask them about their days and evenings and compliment their new shoes or new haircuts. Isla always remembered the special events in their lives and would congratulate them and be genuinely happy for them.

And I haven't even begun to talk about the leadership at that clinic. I have been a part of many companies, teams, programs, committees, and organizations, and I know that success or failure can always be traced back to the person in charge. Eileen trained twenty to twenty-five therapists in the course of two and a half years! It's incredible to consider that, for every amazing therapist, there was one leader who was tireless in her work, endless in her love for all of the kiddos, and patient enough to train that many different personalities to reach a common goal.

How do you thank someone for changing your daughter's life?

I started by sharing Isla's story. During each of Isla's last nine days at the clinic, I shared one chapter of her story with the therapists who had been most influential. It was the only thing I could think of to help them truly appreciate how far we had come because of them. I also wanted Isla's story to be a reminder that every new child enrolled in the clinic has a story.

Not everyone will tell their children's stories like I do, but everyone has a story. I hope all the professionals who played roles in Isla's story will remember that so much happens to every family before they get to your doorstep.

Isla's last day was one big party. Greg and I, June and Major joined in for the fun. There were balloons, cookie cake, songs, dance parties, and tears. There were gifts for Isla and kind words shared all around.

Isla walked down the hall for the last time with a graduation hat on, dancing to the song, "Can't Stop the Feeling!"

Then she went outside and threw her hat in the air, and everyone cheered and clapped and cried.

I knew I wanted to give my friends at the clinic something to remind them of Isla every day. More importantly, I wanted them to have a reminder to continue sharing their love and devotion with each child that walks in those doors, just like they did for Isla.

After a lot of consideration, I finally decided on the sand dollar.

When I moved away from home to attend pharmacy school, I bought myself a gold sand dollar pendant at James Avery. I chose it as a reminder of my home, my dreams, and all that I was working toward, and I have worn it around my neck every day since then. My home was near the beach, and my dream was to come back home, have a beautiful beach family, and maybe even own a condo on the beach one day. I knew it was a beautiful reminder of all of that, but at the time, I did not know how much meaning there really was in a sand dollar.

If you look on the front of the sand dollar, right in the center you will see a star. It represents the Star of Bethlehem that led the wise men to the manger. Around the star is an Easter lily, which is symbolic of the resurrection. Then there are five holes: four on the sides and one in the center. These represent the four nails in Jesus's hands and feet and the spear in his side. Now flip it around, and you will see a poinsettia, which represents Christmas and Jesus's birth. If you break a sand dollar, five little chips that look like white doves will fall off, representing the Christmas doves of peace and joy.

And, of course, there was the connection between Isla's beach name and the fact that sand dollars are only found at the beach.

You know what else they say about sand dollars?

No two sand dollars are exactly the same. Just like our Isla, sand dollars are one in a million.

So I found some really cool decals of sand dollars and ordered them in mint green, which was the consensus when I asked the therapists what color most reminded them of Isla. The decals were made to be used anywhere—on laptops, phones, cars, windows, and anywhere they would want them. But in honor of Isla, I asked them to place one next to each light switch in each room of the clinic as a reminder that each child in those rooms is one in a million, and that each therapist who walked into each room was playing a big role in turning on their light bulbs.

I hugged each therapist that day and told them all through tears that I loved them for loving my Isla all those years.

Then we all got into our vehicle and, with more symbolism than I could have planned myself, we headed straight to Isla and June's new elementary school for "Meet the Teacher."

As we drove up, Isla and June were giddy. They were in awe of the big library and the big cafeteria and the halls and the endless rooms. Isla's teacher was happy to see us, and since Isla had met her before, she was comfortable and all smiles.

What would this new part of Isla's life bring? Would this new teacher be the final piece to the puzzle? Or was this all just another beginning? Would Isla surprise us and jump right in? Or would she become defiant?

The teacher had forms on her desk for Special Olympics. How would Isla handle that? Could she handle that?

Would this be the year the light bulb turned on?

Chapter 10: 9-10 years

Let's Get Gritty

"You are Magical!" was the theme of Isla's ninth birthday party, which took place on a Sunday, just a few hours before my girls' first day of public school. Her aunt threw Isla a unicorn and rainbow party at her house with close family. I learned that these more intimate parties worked so much better for Isla, as they were less stimulating and overwhelming than the large-group events. We sang and cheered, and she loved it all.

When we got home that night we looked through all of Isla's gifts, and one stood out to her. It was a card she had received in the mail from the ABA clinic headquarters which had a ten-dollar prepaid debit card inside. When the girls were in bed after songs and prayers and books, I asked Isla what she wanted to buy with the ten dollars. She smiled coyly.

"Mom I know. I buy pampers Major."

"No, Isla!" I said, laughing. "It's your birthday! You have to buy something fun like a toy or something you want for you."

June was giggling in her bed thinking of all the things she would buy and pampers were for sure not on her list. But when Isla realized I really didn't want her to use her gift card on diapers, she became stern.

"Mom. Mom. Mom, I buy pampers or baby food? Which one you need? I not know."

"OK, OK, Isla, it's your birthday, so you can buy whatever you want," I said. Isla went to bed happy that night, knowing she would spend her ten birthday dollars on her brother.

I felt good as we drove to school the next morning. I felt at peace, like all of this would be OK. But as soon as we parked, I was queasy.

As I opened Isla's door, I sighed a big sigh. I kissed her forehead and whispered, "Oh my God, in the name of Jesus."

"Mom!" Isla laughed out loud. We all laughed as June got out of the car and started adjusting her backpack.

For the first time since I'd left two-year-old Isla at daycare seven years ago, I cried after dropping off my girls. The image of June, so small and innocent, walking into this big building with so many people and kids and rooms was just overwhelming. As she walked away with her ponytail swinging, I prayed that I'd made the right choice for her.

It's funny how, no matter how hard things got and no matter how helpless things seemed or how impossible a situation became, I was always so hopeful. I am not sure if it was my faith in God, my personality, or the way I was raised, but I left that day thinking that maybe by some miracle our trials were over. Maybe Isla was ready, and she would do awesome, and it would be like nothing had ever happened.

When I picked up my girls after school, they were both all smiles and chatterboxes, and I was so relieved.

But then I opened up the notebooks the teachers used to record the students' behavior each day. June's class would use smiley faces or sad faces, and a parent would be responsible for signing the face each afternoon. June had a smiley face. Signed. Then I opened Isla's. I was excited. I wanted to read awesome news. I expected it.

"Overall, Isla transitioned well." The report started off as I'd hoped, but took a quick turn. "She did struggle throughout the day when it was time to work. She also kicked two different students and pulled hair as well as pinched a few times. Please have a talk with her about her behavior. "

I started to feel that queasiness again. It was the first day of school, and my daughter had made several kids' first day awful. She was hurting others, and that was something I was not prepared for. I read the teacher's notes out loud to Isla and asked her what happened. I asked her why she was hurting her friends. She scowled. "I not know. Mom I do good. I not bad."

I couldn't figure out if she didn't remember or if she was outright lying. I went to bed that night feeling so horrible for those kiddos and their parents. I knew that, for now, the priority had to be teaching Isla to function in the classroom without laying a hand on anyone. That was goal number one in my mind, for now. The next day was a little better, and the teacher noted that Isla got work done but did not eat all day and had difficulty during lunch and recess when there were a lot of kids, too much noise, and no structure. OK. *But she didn't hurt anyone*, I thought. I knew I had to take each day one a time. We all did.

With the start of the school year came the time to choose which extracurricular activities to put my kids in. Gymnastics was a given because my girls loved it. June was getting strong and flexible, and I liked this type of exercise for her. As for Isla, besides the thirty minutes per week she got at school, it was really the only occupational and physical therapy she was able to participate in, and she was already so well adjusted to the class and instructor. We had also decided to enroll her in the Special Olympics. That was something Isla and I were both anxious and excited for. The first sport would be bowling, so I figured it was a great way to ease her in and get to know the coaches and kids who would be participating.

Another thing my husband and I had talked about with friends and co-workers was karate.

I did not grow up around martial arts, but I had heard some great things about the program's knack for building self-confidence and self-control and teaching kids how to (peacefully) manage bullies. I wanted all of these things so badly for June. I was bullied pretty consistently when I was in junior high, and to this day I wish I had learned better ways to handle these situations. I think back now on how easy it would have been to just raise my voice, look someone in the eye, and say, "Stop." That's it. We were raised with the "turn the other cheek" mentality, which is important and good until it means letting someone walk all over you, belittle you, embarrass you, and harass you day after day. I believe that God wants us to be kind but strong.

It was a great balancing act that I wanted June to learn because I had not until I was much older.

But should I put Isla in karate, too? I have always been mindful that I don't want to limit Isla. I want her to have the same opportunities as her sister and brother even if it leaves me broke in the end. I am sure you have heard that children with autism usually have one "thing." Maybe one is a great singer and another is a mathematical wonder or a piano prodigy or has a photographic memory. Well, how would I know what Isla's "thing" was or if she even had a "thing" if I didn't try everything? My gut told me not to enroll her. My mind told me differently. I mentioned to the instructors that Isla had special needs and asked if she could just be on a month-to-month contract because I didn't know how she would do. But the dojo was firm. All students enrolled were placed on a six-month contract, and there would be a pretty big fee to cancel early. Rules are rules, so the girls had a short one-on-one introduction with an instructor, and they both did great, so we signed them up for thirty-minute classes twice per week.

Week two of public school was a bit of a toss-up. The teacher wrote things like, "Isla had a much better day today. Completed all her work and even earned her free time." Then, further down the page, I would read things like, "She did begin to pinch/hit when a teacher would sit with her to work. At one point we did have to have the other students leave the room due to her behavior being a distraction."

Sometime during that week my husband and I were called in for the first ARD meeting of the year. We were told it would be a quick meeting to sign consent forms for Isla to be fully tested by each specialist. When my husband and I entered the conference room everyone was seated and attentive with their notes ready. After introductions, everyone took turns speaking. Everyone knew their roles and what they were in charge of. Everything was correct on the paperwork. It was super organized and efficient. My husband and I signed all of the required paperwork and headed back to work, immensely relieved. I cannot fully express how much of a difference it makes to a parent attending an ARD when the simple things are done correctly. Being punctual shows that you respect parents' time. Being prepared shows you care about your job and what you have been called to do. Being organized shows that you are professional and take pride in your work. Being attentive shows parents you care about their child and want to help the best you can. This particular ARD was just a formality, but it impacted me nonetheless.

Meanwhile karate was going...well, it was going. At the very first session I knew it was not going to work for Isla.

The first class started with the instructors standing on each side of the room and throwing a large rubber bouncy ball at the kids' legs and feet to try to get them "out." They played music while the kids dodged and jumped, but my Isla just didn't get it.

When an instructor had the ball, the object was to get away from the ball, but Isla would just laugh and smile and stand there next to the instructor, running the opposite way from the other kids. Of course the instructors were kind and wouldn't get her "out" right away, but after the first few minutes I am sure all the parents watching realized Isla was different. Karate at this facility was fast paced and loud, with music playing during drills. Even June had trouble catching on at first, so imagine Isla.

By about the third or fourth time we went I was starting to feel embarrassed for her, and you already know how much I hate admitting that. She would never stay in line, she was extremely uncoordinated, and she didn't take anything seriously. When it was time to concentrate silently, Isla would shout, "Kai ya!" She would laugh and giggle when she was supposed to be serious. She did it on purpose. She was impulsive, and it was funny to her. No one got after her or acted upset with her, but it was obvious that she was just there to mess around.

During one lesson, the instructors lined the kids up in front of a punching bag with instructions to jab, cross, and knee strike and then go to the back of the line. The music started, and the kids took turns, each waiting anxiously in line. Meanwhile, Isla was chewing the life out of her white belt. To the point that it was dripping with saliva. She was excited and smiling but not paying a bit of attention to the drill. She would bob her head and dance because the song was so good, and when it was her turn she would go up to the bag, smile at the instructor, and flail her arms for a few seconds.

She would then head to the back of the line, put the white belt back in her mouth, shoot me a big thumbs up, and start dancing again.

I know you might be laughing about all that, and I did too, at first, but it really was a tough place to be as a parent of a special needs child. Was it OK to allow her to look "slow," "off," "silly," or "undisciplined?" Should we make her participate in everything, even if it seemed unkind to portray her a certain way? She had no idea how she looked to people, but I did. Was I being mean? But on the other hand, shouldn't I protect her from people who would judge or think she didn't belong? These are very tough questions, and I don't know if I will ever know the right answer—or if there even is a right answer. A huge part of me wanted to start dancing with her, laugh and enjoy her silliness. The other part of me said, respect Isla, be wise, and don't waste money on something she cannot correctly participate in. At least one instructor would have to stand right next to her to direct her for everything, and when they had to work in pairs, I would get so scared that Isla would hurt someone right there in front of all the parents. She had no impulse control, and that was what karate was all about. She also seemed to want or need to do the opposite of everything that was requested. I could see it all over her face. When the instructor would tell the students not to hit the bags their partners were holding, I just knew that Isla would punch as hard as she freaking could.

Oh and the gloves. Sometimes in the middle of a session they had to go to their backpacks and put on punching gloves. Keep in mind that Isla had almost no control over her fingers separately.

Putting on gloves was impossible. It would take a patient instructor trying to get a stupid glove on one hand and me, holding Major on my hip, working on the other glove while everyone waited. It was ridiculous. Even after all that, I still didn't want to be a quitter. But then came nunchuck day.

Yes, I said nunchuck. When the instructor told all the kids to go get their nunchucks, I almost passed out. Isla came running—no, sprinting—to me with wild eyes and grabbed those suckers out of the bag with force. I couldn't watch. I went to stand next to the door, thinking that as soon as she hit someone I could sneak out and pretend I hadn't seen. The nunchucks were covered in hard foam, but they still had the potential to hurt. When they started the drills, Isla just couldn't hold her place in line. They had spaced the kids out enough not to hit each other, but Isla would drift closer and closer to the little girl in front of her with each instruction. I swear my blood pressure was through the roof by the time it was all over, and I had palpitations for at least a half hour afterwards. The very next day, we paid that big fat fee, and we got her out of karate.

It was also within that second week of school that I had to deal with something I had not dealt with since high school. Homework. The moment I sat down with June to do her first homework assignment, I realized how incredibly nerdy I actually was. Don't judge me, people, but I was excited. June was sharp, and I was amazed at how fast she was learning.

She'd gotten good at remembering the date each day, and she was actually reading some words. Wow! And the next day, to see the homework come back with that exquisite red check mark…Let me tell you, when a big red check mark makes you all warm and a little giggly, that's when you know you're a nerd. For me it was a combination of nerdiness and the fact that, in nine years of being a mom, I hadn't seen a single big red check mark. But nothing—not even that check mark—compared to hearing June read her first book. It went like this:

Sam.

Sam and Cat.

Mat and Cat.

Sam, Mat and Cat.

Cat sat on Sam.

Mat sat on Sam.

Sad Sam. Sad Mat.

Sam sat. Mat sat.

O.K., Sam. O.K., Mat.

The End.

Music to my ears. I never imagined loving a Sam, a Mat, and a cat so much.

Isla's homework time, however, was brutal for us both. During this time the teacher was trying to figure out Isla's academic baseline to see how much homework she could manage. So she started with just one assignment each night. Monday was usually a tracing exercise with the words of the week.

Tuesday was a matching worksheet where Isla had to draw a line from a word to the corresponding picture.

Wednesday was some kind of cut-and-paste work related to the same words, and Thursday--oh Thursday. Lord have mercy. Thursday was when Isla had to trace her first name thirty-five times. It was only one page, and it seemed so doable, but the first week we did this work together was truly heartbreaking. It is one thing to know that Isla has delays in academics, fine motor skills, and attention span, but to see it firsthand made me so sad for her every time.

Here was a typical homework scene:

"Oh, Mom! Mom. Mom. Mom I have do my homework, OK, Mom?" She'd start out so excited. "Mom, I get it. I get my work. Mom, you have pencil, Mom? Oh, Mom, I have pencil. Mom, you have sharpener, Mom?" Isla loved sharpening pencils, so even when they were sharp enough to poke an eye out she sharpened them more.

"Alrighty, Isla, let's start," I'd say, matching her enthusiasm. "These are the words of the week. Let's start by tracing the top word, and we will work down to the last word. OK, the first word is sister. Oh, Isla, you have a sister!"

"Yes! June! June. June. June you my sister!" Isla would giggle at this, and June would be in the background smirking. Then, Isla would get down to business. "OK. OK. OK. Uh, Mom, I start here? OK. Um. OK."

Isla would put her pencil to the first letter and not move it.

She would start to tap her pencil on the table and look at me and smile and then put her pencil down again to trace and start tapping again. "Mom where Major? Major OK?"

"Yes Isla." I'd try to get her back on track quickly. "Start with the first S. It is squiggly, remember? Like a snake."

"Like a snake? Oh, Mom, what that noise? Mom, that a train? Mom, I not know what that is. Mom, you know?"

The train was seriously miles away, but Isla was right. It was passing through.

"Yes, Isla, that is a train. OK, you have to finish this work so we can have outside playtime. June is putting on her shoes, and I want you to go play too, so let's start."

Isla would start to trace with no regard to the dots. She would draw a letter S but not directly on the dotted letter and usually much larger than the dotted letter.

She would tap her pencil after each letter, usually refusing to even look down at the paper while she was tracing.

"Mom, look!" she'd say after finishing one word. "Look. Look I done? Mom, that good?"

"Woohoo!" I'd cheer. "Yes. OK, there are nine more words, Isla, so let's keep going."

I could go on like this forever. If I wrote down each word and distraction and comment and diversion from Isla, the transcript of just one homework session would be longer than this book.

The bottom line was that she remembered she had homework every day, and every day she wanted to do it even though it was brutal. In fact she *asked* the teacher for homework daily. She was trying, and I was OK with that.

In the third week of school, something started happening that I was not OK with. Isla started hurting herself. The first day of that week, her folder had nothing but good reports from the classroom, but it did mention difficulty when she went for speech therapy. I figured that was probably because she was not yet familiar with the speech therapist on campus.

Then there was this report: "She did have a difficult time in the afternoon. She refused to work, and instead she began to stomp her feet, bite on her arm, whine, and ask for her parents to be called to pick her up."

By that point we were getting after Isla daily. Each night my husband and I would talk to her, asking her to explain herself and threatening her with no gymnastics or no iPad time when she had a bad report. The problem was that by the time we picked up Isla from school she was happy as could be. It was so hard to be consistently pissed off at this little girl who was so joyous all the time.

I started noticing that Isla was more than happy—she seemed relieved. She didn't care if we were mad or upset or whatever, because she was home and at peace. She had a sense of utter relief about her, which I thought was a little weird.

Then, about the fourth or fifth week of school, the honeymoon period ended abruptly, and everything spiraled out of control. She was refusing to do work, throwing things, kicking, screaming, pinching her cheeks, and yelling at the teachers that it was OK because her mommy would pick her up. These daily reports were wearing on me, and I was really starting to feel the weight of it all.

Drop offs were also starting to be so difficult for Isla. She would get ready each morning with such joy and happiness, but as soon as we would turn onto the school's road her demeanor would change in an instant. I realized I was seeing something in Isla that I hadn't seen before. It seemed like anxiety. *What the heck?*

These new signs of anxiety and the increase in Isla's overall aggression had me worried enough to make an appointment with the pediatrician. At the time I thought the stimulant she was taking for ADHD was most likely the culprit.

A week before the pediatrician appointment was Isla's first Special Olympics bowling practice. As I sat at a table scanning the room, I was overwhelmed, just like I had been when I was in the waiting room with Isla the day we first got her diagnosis. Some students had severe delays, and some had physical impairments. Some of the students, like Isla, didn't have any immediately identifiable special need. They were all unique and all excited to participate in their own way.

By this point I had already started writing this book, and I was obsessed with people's stories. Every child there had a story—a mom, a dad, a family, and a past—and I wanted to know them all.

This first bowling experience brought up some feelings that are definitely a touchy subject. I think many of you will be able to relate, but others may judge me, and that's OK, too. If you aren't used to being around children with special needs—and except for Isla, of course, I really wasn't— it can make you feel uncomfortable. Some of these children are very friendly, wanting to start conversations or hug everyone they see. Some have no sense of personal space. Some are big, and some are small, and they range widely in age, and sometimes it's hard to tell who can be trusted.

As I sat there at Isla's first bowling practice, several of the other children approached me, and I will admit that at first I felt a little uneasy. But I surprised myself. I was a pro at interacting with Isla and distracting her when necessary, and I soon realized that I could use the same skills with the other children while still acknowledging them, respecting them, and showing them kindness.

I could almost instantaneously shift my focus by thinking about how I want Isla to be treated when she approaches someone. So as a young boy barreled up to me and tried to take Major out of his stroller, I was calm. I reached for Major's little arm and lifted it up. "Hi! This is Major," I said. "Do you want to give him a high five instead?" The young boy laughed and gave Major a high five. Then I asked him what his name was, and he mumbled something I didn't understand and moved on to the next table. But when he saw us at other practices, he would always say, "Major give me high five!" Major, of course, would be all smiles with his little hand raised in the air.

Situations like that get touchy because I can see how it could scare or upset someone to see a big, strong, child with a severe mental delay come charging in to try to pick up an infant. But ever since that fateful diagnosis day, I always keep in mind that every brain can be trained. Many times these children don't act the way they do because they want to but because they can't help it. And you know what? They deserve just as much love, respect, discipline, and praise as any other child. And you know what else? If you are a person who becomes uncomfortable in these situations, you deserve some grace. This will not come naturally unless you practice, and that's OK too.

Isla was a star at bowling. She sat in her assigned seat and waited her turn. Her new coach would help her with the ramp when it was her turn, and she would smile and clap and beam with pride. She would cheer and encourage her classmates when it was their turn. She was amazing.

However, as incredible as she was in bowling, Isla's classroom behavior was getting worse.

The Friday before we were scheduled to see the pediatrician for a possible medication change, I was out to lunch with a good friend of mine when I got a call from Isla's teacher. We usually communicated through text, behavior reports, and during drop offs as needed, but she didn't usually call me. Apparently, Isla's aggression was at its peak, and after a one-on-one compliance session with the teacher, she went after another student so violently that she needed to be restrained. *Restrained.* Physically restrained.

The friend I was at lunch with knew Isla's story, and she was patient and quiet as I listened to the teacher's recap of the horror Isla was causing in the classroom and to that poor student that day. I was quiet. I didn't want to discuss it then and there, so I just asked the teacher if the student was OK. She said the student was fine and was being checked by the nurse, who would contact the parents.

I simply said, "Thank you for letting me know," and I hung up. I put my phone in my purse and looked up at my friend, who just gave me a knowing smile before she did the best thing a friend could have done. She waited a few seconds to see if I would say something, and when she understood that I was not going to talk about the phone call, she picked up our conversation right where we'd left off. She knew that if I wanted to share I would, and I wasn't ready.

I definitely don't know everything about special education, but I do know from what I have gathered from friends, family, and my husband that a kid has to do a lot to get restrained. I mean, a kid has to present a real, serious danger to the staff, other students, or themselves in order for anyone to legally lay a hand on them.

I got in my car after lunch, and I looked up at the roof. "WHAT MORE DO YOU WANT FROM ME!!!" I screamed it. I growled it. I yelled it. I yelled it to God. I yelled it to the universe. I yelled it to Isla. Believe it or not, I was still not at my lowest point, but I could feel that point approaching.

I called the teacher that afternoon to explain why I'd been so quiet during the call, and she told me that after the restraint incident she thought it was best to work on compliance training one-on-one with Isla for a couple of days, separate from the other students. Instead of doing any academic work, Isla would work on everyday directives and compliance with behavior and rules.

The teacher assured me that she'd had to do that for many students in the past, and for most kids it would take a couple of days before they realized what was expected.

When I picked up my girls that day, the first thing I did was go through Isla's backpack to find the message for the day, which was accompanied by "the letter." When your child is restrained at school, at least in the state of Texas, you receive a letter. It is mainly for legal purposes, and it reads like this:

As outlined in "Procedures for Use of Restraint and Time-Out," restraint of a student with a disability may be used only in a clearly defined, emergency situation. Schools must inform parents when it becomes necessary to use restraint in an effort to protect the student or others or prevent serious property damage. This information is provided for your review and to seek your input into this situation.

Seek my input. The whole letter was just one big "ugly".

Then I opened June's backpack, expecting to just sign the smiley face like I did every day. But there was another letter attached.

I signed the smiley face quickly and opened the letter to find a request for my permission to have June tested for the Gifted and Talented program. I couldn't decide whether to cry or laugh. In my left hand I held a "your-kid-is-so-bad-she-had-to-be-physically-restrained" letter, and in my right hand I held a "your-kid-is-so-smart-we-want-to-put-her-in-Gifted-and-Talented" letter. This mommy roller coaster ride of mine was only beginning, but quickly intensifying.

Day 1 of Compliance training: Isla lost her shoe privilege. Yes, you read that correctly. She could no longer wear shoes in the classroom because she was taking them off and throwing them at people.

Day 2 of Compliance training: I sent Isla to school with socks and crocs. She had another difficult morning being defiant and throwing fits, but in the late afternoon she started to work alone quietly and earned some stickers to enjoy snack time with the class.

Day 3 of Compliance training: Isla had a great morning. She earned more stickers and enjoyed some time with classmates. But after lunch was a different story. She was defiant and refused to do any work.

Day 4 of Compliance training: Boss day. This was the day that Isla decided to tell the teacher, "You are not the boss. I am the boss." Well, how do you like that? I could hardly recognize the girl the teacher was talking about in these reports. Never—and I do mean never—has Isla ever told me she was the boss.

I picked her up early that day because it was time for the pediatrician visit. In that exam room, my beautiful Isla was at ease, happy, and eager to see the doctor.

As I explained all that was going on, I remember wondering what Isla was thinking. She was clearly hearing me, but she seemed just as removed from the person I was talking about as I did when I read reports about her. The pediatrician prescribed the same non-stimulant medication that I had recently read up on and we headed straight to the pharmacy to have it filled.

Day 5 of Compliance Training: This was the first day Isla took the stimulant and the new non-stimulant together. Again, I drove her to school with hope and anticipation that this would be the winning combination. It was a good day. The teacher mentioned that Isla was very quiet, completing each directive and waiting patiently for the next one. However, she did not eat, and she scratched her chest and nostril all day until they were red.

When she got home I checked her nostril and chest, but I didn't notice anything unusual, so I didn't worry.

The next Monday would be the second day Isla was on the new combination. After a weekend to recharge and a nice church service on Sunday, again, I was hopeful. When I dropped her off Monday morning, she was content and happy, giggling because we had been singing "This Girl Is on Fire" in the car at the top of our lungs. I should explain that Isla fixates on songs. When she hears a song that she likes—regardless of genre, artist, or theme—it becomes the song of the week or month or longer.

We have gone through, "All About that Bass," "Sugar," "Can't Stop the Feeling," "Staying Alive," "Let Me Love You," "Diamonds and Daughters," and a gospel song called "Into my Heart". So after Isla, June, and I belted out "This Girl is on Fire" about five times straight, we parked at the school and Isla got out of the car laughing.

I had hoped that laughter would set the tone for a great day, but the report that afternoon said she'd had an "off day." She did well until it was time to work, and then she refused to do anything. The note also informed me that Isla had picked at her belly button until it bled. She also had an accident that day involving a bowel movement in her pants. I could feel my stomach turn as I opened June's notebook to sign the inevitable smiley face. *What was going on?! Skin picking?!* God, how much more could we take?

We got home, and I asked Isla to step in the bathroom. I slowly lifted her shirt to see her belly button. It was raw, bleeding, and sensitive to the touch. The tears started rolling down my face as I cleaned up the area and applied some antibiotic ointment.

Isla touched one of my tears as it lay on my cheek and said, "Mom I not know happen. I sorry." "No Isla," I whisper-cried, "I am sorry. Mommy should know how to help you and I don't."

I spent the evening researching the medications again, and I decided that I was not going to give her the stimulant anymore. The non-stimulant medication was approved to be used alone for ADHD, and the skin picking fit the side effect profile of the stimulant.

I wrote down some ideas I had to review with the pediatrician regarding timing of the medications to reduce side effects, and then I fell asleep reading journal articles and clinical trials.

The next day, we got another report of noncompliance, refusal to do work, and saying no to everything. But there'd been no skin picking. In her mind, at least, Isla had learned how to cope with all the pressure and demands.

By this point she knew, it would all be over at 3:00 p.m., so until then she just had to refuse. When they tried using rewards like ice cream as an incentive for good behavior, Isla would say, "It's OK, my abuelo gives me ice cream." If they told her she could not participate in PE that day because she was kicking or hitting she would say, "It's OK, my mom take me to gymnastics." She had a response for everything.

The next morning when I dropped off Isla, a paraprofessional walked her inside and Isla's teacher came out to my vehicle to talk to me. She told me they were working hard with Isla, but they had to call a second paraprofessional into the class for almost two weeks now so the teacher could just be one on one with Isla. The principal had started to get involved because she needed to see why Isla needed so much attention and why, even with a class of just five, the special education teacher was asking for more help. "I think it's time you really think about what you want for Isla," the teacher said. I was taken aback. *What did she mean by that?* Then she told me how Isla was basically refusing everything at school because she knew she would get to have fun at home without any academic demands.

The lump in the back of my throat grew bigger and bigger. I assumed we were on the same page the whole time, but could she possibly think I was not doing my part as a parent? Was I supposed to take everything away at home, too? Not take Isla to gymnastics? Not let her go outside or play with our animals or her cousins? Not let Isla help her abuelo on our little ranch? Not let her go to her dad's football games and pep rallies? I mean, I have other kids, remember? Did they have to stay home too so Isla would see that she couldn't get what she wanted at home, either? Oh my God.

I explained to the teacher that some of these things were just our everyday life and I had other kids to think about. Not only that, but since I got off work at 4:30 p.m. each day and school was over at 3:00 p.m., Isla and June's grandpa or great aunt and cousins would usually pick them up. That was also rewarding for Isla, so what was I supposed to do? Was I supposed to ask to get off work early every single day to pick her up as a punishment? The teacher suggested I find someone to babysit Isla at home while we went on with our evening routines and football games. She told me it would only take once. I felt my face scrunch up hard into the ugly cry, and I just told her that I would talk it over with my husband. She said she was sorry—for making me cry, I assume—and I drove to work.

I called Greg and started firing off questions to him. "Are we not doing enough? What are we supposed to do? Do we really have to find someone to stay with Isla while we go about our lives without her?

All for what? So she will behave in class? So she will do work in class? Do we have to find someone who will be super strict and stern with her? Are we seriously talking about using our home as punishment?" I was just in utter disbelief. Here I was thinking that I was going above and beyond in every way, but could it be that the teacher thought I was part of the problem? Or at least not helping with the solution? I knew I was partially at fault for this lack of communication, because I never verbalized to the teacher how much the daily reports were wearing Isla and me down. This conversation made the pot boil over, but the teacher had no idea how much we were struggling emotionally because I hadn't shared that with her.

Greg was notably upset, mainly with Isla. He told me to check on Isla at lunch, and if it was a bad report he was going to start going to the school himself every single day she misbehaved to put her in her place.

Sure enough, lunch brought more bad reports, so Greg drove to the school and asked to speak to Isla alone. I don't know exactly what he did or discussed with her that day, but when he left Isla did three activities on her own in less than fifteen minutes. On my end, I decided to be honest with my supervisor. I told him we were facing something with my daughter that would require daily intervention, and I apologized. I felt so unprofessional and stupid, but what choice did I have?

It was a Wednesday, which meant outdoor play with cousins, feeding the animals, and riding our golf cart around to visit family members who lived around us.

Isla would not be allowed to do any of that. When we got home I sent her to her room. She was sad and cried and pouted as June got to do all of the things Isla loved. I stayed inside to watch Isla and made her eat in her room and stay in her room all evening long. She fell asleep unbathed with her plate next to her. It really made me sick to think that Isla had a crappy day at school with people pushing her to do stuff she didn't want to do and her dad getting mad at her because she wasn't doing school work that we didn't know if she was even capable of doing, then coming home to find that her mother (who by that point was always mad or crying) was refusing to let her enjoy her family or the outdoors. The entire day she was disciplined for things I didn't know for sure she could control.

On the way to school the next day, the whole vehicle was somber. No singing. No music. I could feel resentment building toward everything and everyone. Right before I parked to let the girls out, Isla turned to me and said, "Mom, I hope today good day." I didn't know what to make of that. Did it mean she knew she really couldn't control herself? Was she messing with me?

Both of my girls walked into the building, and I drove to work totally confused, expecting another horrible day for my Isla. It was a Thursday, and the next day was a big pep rally and football game for my husband's team.

That was Isla's incentive all week. She needed to obey her teachers and change her attitude in order to go to these fun events. And sure enough, Thursday's report looked better.

"Isla did have a difficult morning. After talking with her, the behavior changed. She did very well. We did talk about behavior at home and at school and how certain behavior makes people feel. We are working for girls' time tomorrow. We will paint our nails, watch videos, dance, and invite June and her cousins to join us in the afternoon if Isla has a good day."

So all it took was one day of not letting Isla see her family and friends and cousins or go outside or eat with us, and it was all fixed? I was relieved. I hugged Isla and told her I was so proud of her and that I was so happy, and Isla was incredibly proud. She was beaming as she showed me the work she had done in class, and I texted her teacher to thank her and tell her I was hopeful for another good day tomorrow. I will never forget the teacher's response: "Yes, I am very happy she had a good day, and I'm even happier for June." *What? June?*

She explained that, since the very first day of school, June had been going to Isla's classroom at the end of each day to check on her sister and ask the teacher how she'd done that day. June would knock on the door and quietly ask if Isla had a good day. The teacher was always honest, and when she said "no", June would turn away sad and disappointed. My heart broke as I read these texts.

I had no idea this was happening. So the day before that good day—the day Greg went to the school and the day Isla had to stay home all night—when June went to the classroom to see how Isla did the teacher said June cried.

She said that June walked in and sat next to Isla and told her that it made her very sad when she made bad choices. The teacher said it was obvious that June was really hurting, so she followed June out of the classroom and June told her that she didn't understand. June told the teacher that we prayed every night for Isla, and she didn't know why our prayers weren't working. The teacher said she reassured June and explained that we are all special and we all learn in our own way and at our own pace and that we needed to keep praying for Isla and everyone around her because it was going to require everyone working together to help Isla make good choices.

So on Thursday, when June came and knocked on the door, the teacher told June Isla had done very well, and June was so overjoyed that her eyes and mouth opened wide and she jumped up in the air with her arms up and yelled, "YAY!" and ran to hug Isla. Then my five-year-old girl sat with her nine-year-old big sister, asked her to show her all the work she had done, and praised her for it. I had no idea this had been weighing on June throughout the day.

June was doing amazing in school. She had blossomed since the first week, and she came home every day with so many stories of friends and schoolwork and the things she was learning.

But while the trouble with her sister was not affecting her academically, it was affecting her emotionally. I started to think about what she must have been seeing all those nights when I looked sad or when she caught me crying as I washed dishes or when I sang their bedtime songs.

I took time to love on June a little extra that night. I was emotional as I told her how proud I was of her, and I had to explain that my tears that night were happy. I told her that she was so special to me and that Isla was so lucky to have her as a sister.

I told her she was tough and strong and that I was so proud that, as Major got older, he would also have a sister and friend and protector like her.

The next morning was Friday: game day. We blasted the music and sang out loud. "THIS GIRL IS ON FIRE!" We danced in the car and talked about all the fun we would have that day. June was excited to spend time in Isla's class that afternoon but, again, all of this would depend on Isla's behavior. I went to work feeling hopeful. Oh old hopeful. I had even dressed up a little that day thinking that I would spend time with my husband at his work while we watched the pep rally. Then, in the early afternoon, I got a text:

"The day has taken a pretty big turn. Isla's refusing to follow any directives. She says that she wants to have a bad day and does not want to have a girls' afternoon and does not want to go to the pep rally or football game."

"She's even saying she does not like June or Mom or Dad and wants everyone to be sad. She is saying 'call my Dad to come get mad at me because I don't want to make good choices.'"

I took a screen shot of the text and sent it to my husband. We were both so disappointed because that meant no pep rally and no game. I would have to stay home with Isla to stick to my word. That was the deal. Greg decided to pick up June that day because we didn't think it was right for her to be punished for Isla's actions. June went to the pep rally with her dad, and with some help from my good friend, who was also a coach's wife, she got to attend the game, too.

Meanwhile I requested to leave early from work again, embarrassed and so incredibly bummed. Isla and I did not say a word to each other when I picked her up. I drove her straight to the pediatrician's office and asked to be seen as a walk in. It was probably the first time our pediatrician had seen me like that.

I was emotional, scared, confused, and for once I had absolutely no idea what to do or what I was even asking for. I tried to explain to him what was going on, and only God knows what I rambled about, but I remember asking him about mental health issues and medications and a psychiatry consult, and I remember saying I was worried because maybe Isla was bipolar or schizophrenic or—God, I just didn't know anything anymore! After some discussion we decided to try a different stimulant in combination with the non-stimulant she had been on for several weeks, and he agreed that Isla may benefit from seeing a child psychiatrist.

We left, and as we drove to pick up Major from daycare, I was just so angry. I felt like I was the one who was going to need a psychiatrist, and quick.

I was dreading the evening ahead—sending Isla to her room, making her eating alone, hearing her crying to come down, and waiting as she fell asleep unbathed and alone. I was dreading my own evening watching Dateline specials instead of my husband's football game. Everything just felt wrong. I was so pissed that, when I pulled up to Major's daycare, I got out of the car, slammed the door, and walked away without even waiting for Isla. She got off on her own and jogged in behind me. I told her to sit on a bench in the lobby, and I walked the hall to Major's little classroom looking like Ronda Rousey walking into the octagon.

And here is where you come in, my Major boy.

Even at just eight months old, my little boy, my son, came to my rescue. I opened the door to the class, and when I caught his eye I could literally feel my face soften. As soon as our eyes met—and I know this sounds so cheesy—I just felt pure joy. He smiled so big and bright and wide that his cheeks hid his eyes entirely.

He clapped a big, wide, forceful clap, bounced up and down in the bouncer, and when the daycare worker set him down, he sprint crawled across the room in sheer excitement. He stood up on the border of the play area and lifted both hands up to me, still sporting that ear-to-ear grin. I jokingly said, "Hey I know you! Are you my little son-son, Major?"

He shook with happiness and almost squealed for me to pick him up. I reached down for him, and he clung to my arms and then my chest. I held him close and felt his chubby legs around my waist and his chunky arms and hands around my neck. He was smiling and laughing as if everything in the world was wonderful and right.

Major saved me during those weeks and months. He saved me. I don't know where the darkness of that day would have taken us if it were not for my sweet son. He was my reminder that there was still joy and happiness in the world and that I was loved and cared for and depended upon and that I was a good mom. He was my reminder that I could not allow myself to be overcome with depression or grief or helplessness, because I had other children besides Isla. He was my break. He was my timeout from all the mind games my life with Isla was throwing me. I hope that one day he realizes what an impact he was in my life, especially in those months. It was not by coincidence that he was brought into our lives during that specific time.

On that day, as I walked the hall back to my vehicle with Major in my arms and Isla trailing behind us, I started to cry. My heart was full but breaking at the same time. We drove home in silence, and as soon as we parked outside our home Isla started to whine, groan, and complain. She started to talk non-stop regardless of whether I answered or ignored her.

"Mom, I go to game. Mom, I not bad. Mom, why you mad? Mom, where June? Mom, I so sorry. Mom, where Dad? Mom, I change my mind. I go to game too."

It went on and on and on, and I couldn't utter a word. I didn't want to. I was exhausted and sad.

As I sat there in my living room that night playing with Major and trying to ignore Isla's relentless talking and pleading and moodiness, the bitterness and resentment started to settle in.

How dare Isla act like that? How dare the teacher make me feel like I had to stay home when Isla didn't behave, which would probably be every day? How dare God ignore me when all I did all day and night was pray for answers? How dare He leave me hanging?

Isla fell asleep very early that night right after she ate dinner. I bathed Major and rocked him to sleep in silence because I got too choked up every time I tried to sing to him.

It was pretty early, about 8:00 p.m., when I sat down on my sofa and stared at the floor, wondering about the football game and thinking of June. I was starting to regret the punishment we had agreed to. It didn't feel right. How could punishing Isla by taking away things that define our family be the right answer? Again this may really make the most sense for a coach or a coach's family, but there is something sacred about Friday night football in our family.

Friday night *is* about family. Friday night is about watching and celebrating and supporting our daddy. Friday night is when we get to take part in his life and when we get to take part in a different family: our football family. My football family in the stands is awesome.

I sit with the other coaches' wives and their families in our small reserved section, and in that circle I don't have to say a word to be completely understood. We stand up for the national anthem, and we always look for our daddy because that is the time of pregame when he looks for us. My girls feel so special as he waves to them in the crowd, and they jump and cheer and wave back.

Under the Friday night lights, Isla is not a girl with autism. She is not delayed or disabled. On Friday nights Isla is part of a bigger family. On Friday nights Isla can be herself as she claps and sings and dances and cheers.

Nobody judges Isla on Friday nights, because trust me, grown adults act all kinds of foolish themselves during these football games, me included.

I sank back in my sofa and decided that I would not miss another game, and neither would Isla. Family time and football time would be off limits for "punishments" from now on. Period. Since I now had the rest of the night to myself, I decided to devote some time to my faithful friend Google. I started looking up bipolar disorder in children, mood disorders, schizophrenia, etc. I'd been splitting my focus between Google and Dateline for about an hour when I happened to click on a link that sent me on a path to finding answers I had been searching for for nine years.

I clicked the link because it had the words "autism" and "Jekyll and Hyde" in the same sentence, which really described Isla at that moment.

The link took me to a blog devoted mainly to those who were experiencing or who had children with "atypical" autism. One particular comment mentioned some research being done in London, and I clicked it, mainly because the word "research" always intrigued me. These words popped up big and bright on my phone screen: "The National Autistic Society: What is pathological demand avoidance?" That article described Isla in such a clear way that I could not have done it better myself.

Pathological Demand Avoidance (PDA) is a profile of behaviors some people on the autism spectrum exhibit. The article mentioned that the distinctive features were resisting and avoiding the ordinary demands of life, using social strategies as part of avoidance, appearing sociable but lacking understanding, and exhibiting excessive mood swings and impulsivity, and that all this behavior was rooted in an anxiety-based need to be in control.

It went on to say that people with PDA can seem controlling and dominating when they feel anxious or out of control but totally charming when they feel secure and in control. I put my phone down and thought, *did I just diagnose my kid!?* I picked up my phone again and read a segment called "PDA in the early years." PDA was founded and is researched at the Elizabeth Newson Centre in London. Elizabeth Newson proposed the PDA profile in 1980, and her colleagues have continued the practice.

According to the Centre, many people with PDA exhibit what is called "passive early history," meaning that as infants they dropped or didn't reach for toys, just watched instead, and they were delayed reaching milestones. My mind instantly flashed a slideshow of my life's past images and scenes. The piñata scene, with Isla just staring at the candy. Isla watching the liquid spill out of the cups she would constantly drop. I started having *deja vu* of all the delayed milestones I wrote down for every doctor—sitting up, crying, speaking, rolling over, smiling. I kept reading, now fully enthralled. Next section was "The characteristics of PDA." The first sentence said that the main characteristic of PDA is exhibiting a high level of anxiety under demands.

Uh, demands like sitting at a desk to do school work that you don't understand, knowing you will get it wrong and then feel embarrassed and dumb?

First characteristic: Resists and avoids the ordinary demands of life.

When someone with PDA is trying to avoid a demand they distract the person making the demand, and they may physically incapacitate themselves.

Like peeing on yourself or disrobing so the person has to stop the unwanted activity and clean you or dress you?

They also may use physical outbursts or attacks.

Like kicking, hitting, and pulling hair enough to be restrained?

Then I read that the straightforward refusal or outburst of explosive behavior, including aggression, was a form of panic and was displayed when the patient's anxiety was so high they "exploded" or had a "meltdown."

Did that mean we were disciplining Isla for having panic attacks? Oh my God.
Hot guilt. Oh, the guilt was intense. So intense that I had to take a
break. I got a bottle of water and went up to Isla's room to check on
her. I peeked in, but she was so beautifully asleep that I just closed the
door and ventured back into Google.

Second characteristic: Appear sociable but lack depth in
understanding.

People with PDA are usually not diagnosed with autism initially,
because they appear to be very social and people-oriented. They learn
social niceties but have difficulty seeing boundaries and taking
responsibility for their actions. This section mentioned things like
confusing behavior and hugging one second and pinching the next. It
mentioned PDA children lacking a sense of pride or embarrassment
and behaving in uninhibited ways. Lastly, it said children with PDA
may not exhibit a sense of authority or recognize "a pecking order,"
always clinging to adults because they feel they are adults, themselves,
and treat and talk to others as such.

My mental slideshow started again. I thought back to when Isla was
three or four and everyone would compliment me on teaching her such
excellent manners.

Isla would constantly say things like, "Oh thank you much," "E'cuse
me," and "Oh, I so sorry." Everyone was impressed that she knew how
to be so kind at such a young age. Next scene: holding the hands of
each and every adult in her path. Oh, yes. Isla was always clinging to
the nearest adult.

It was her safe zone, and yes, she always seemed to assume she was an adult, too, which is why she was confused when she was told she couldn't do adult things. Like buying pampers with her birthday money.

Third characteristic: Excessive mood swings and impulsivity.

This part mainly focused on difficulty regulating emotions, which was common in people with autism. Basically mood swings can be in response to real or perceived pressure, and again they're driven by the need to control.

We rarely saw this at home, but at school, oh yes. That would explain why I never did recognize the little girl they were talking about in those daily reports.

Fourth characteristic: Comfortable in role-play and pretend, sometimes to an extreme extent.

Early studies of children with PDA reported that a third of the subjects confused reality with pretend and that this could be severe and cause huge conflict during play time with other friends or family. Isla was not one of these children, but she did really enjoy pretend play, and she always wanted to play the part of the adult—the store owner or daycare worker or whoever was in charge.

Fifth characteristic: Language delay, often with good degree of catch-up.

Another prominent characteristic that presents in the majority of children with PDA is some delay in speech and language development, which is usually dependent on their intellectual ability, and often there is a sudden degree of catch-up.

These children have a more socially acceptable use of eye contact and conversational timing than others on the autism spectrum. I could feel myself sinking lower and lower in the sofa as I read that some of these children become fluent in using expressive language but can have problems with comprehension.

They can have difficulty processing what they hear, and they need additional time to do that. This can lead to misunderstanding and disruption to the communication process, which can contribute to their anxiety-driven behavior.

I could not keep up with my own mental slideshow. Slide after slide and scene after scene of Isla being told she was not autistic because she had looked a person in the eye. Slide after slide and scene after scene of the brain mapping that was completely normal except that it showed delays in how fast she processed others' speech. I seriously could not read the article fast enough.

Sixth characteristic: Obsessive behavior, often focused on people.

It mentioned that some people with PDA may have a strong fascination with pretend or real characters and people.

Isla did show some obsessive behaviors in relation to songs, objects, activities, or fictitious characters. For example, for a while she was completely obsessed with Santa Claus because she found an app where you could "call" Santa, and hear him ask you if you've been naughty or nice. Isla would call and recall and talk and laugh and have conversations with this app over and over and over, and then she'd pass the phone around so we could all join in.

Seventh characteristic: Sensory differences.

Just like all other children on the autism spectrum, children with PDA can have difficulty processing everyday sensory information and can also have balance or body awareness difficulties. Cue slideshow of Isla's continued clumsiness.

Isla was so lanky that we assumed it was just awkwardness, but there were so many images in my head of her falling off a chair when she seemed to be perfectly seated or missing steps up or down stairs or falling backwards because she couldn't gauge whether the sofa was directly behind her or not. Oh, and her clothes. Scene after scene of trying to get her to feel that her entire dress was in her tights and her booty was proudly revealing itself. And the times when she would have clothes and shoes on backward and not realize it. Isla could have hair all over her face, a wedgie that was out of this world, or drool all over her chin and not feel a thing.

Based on what I read, Isla was considered a proprioceptive under-responder in some respects—she was very heavy footed and she was most comfortable with heavy blankets completely surrounding her while she slept—and an over-responder in others—she showed difficulty knowing where her body was in relation to space or to others. Think back to "aha moment" number one when Isla sat right on top of a child on the circle time rug. Tactilely, she was a hypo-responder—since she was very small, she'd had a very high threshold for pain. Isla also loved messy play. Remember the cookie crumbles and juice at the classroom Halloween party? But these days, she engaged in messy play more frequently at home, especially when she was bored and knew she was not being watched closely. In those moments, she would often empty entire bottles of soap or shampoo, or sometimes even glue, into her hands, on her bed, or anywhere else that she decided was a good place for a mess.

Eighth and final characteristic: Severe behavioral difficulties.

The studies showed that a large majority of children with PDA had great difficulty controlling and regulating emotions, specifically anger. That usually resulted in prolonged meltdowns, and it was important to see those as extreme anxiety or panic attacks and treat them appropriately. The article suggested using reassurance, calming strategies, and de-escalation techniques. I dropped my phone. *What had I done? What was I doing?* My daughter was having panic attacks, and instead of helping her I was taking away the very things that made her feel safe.

No football games, no dinner with family, no ice cream with her abuelo, no outdoor play time…nothing, nothing, nothing! My daughter was having panic attacks at school because she was so anxious, and instead of helping her the teachers were separating her from the other students and forbidding her from going to recess or PE or having fun Fridays. My face felt flushed and I wasn't sure if I was going to throw up or scream or pass out.

I was weak in the knees as I walked upstairs to Isla's room. I crept in and knelt next to her bed. She stayed asleep, and I just put my head down on her bed and cried. "Isla, you have to forgive me. Oh my God, Isla, I am so sorry, my love. I am so sorry."

It was not time to fight Isla. It was time to fight *for* Isla.

Before I turned off my phone for the night I read the rest of that last paragraph, which mentioned that many times PDA signs and symptoms are more severe in one particularly stressful location. Children like Isla, for whom the demands of school were particularly anxiety inducing, typically became "school refusers." The next sections went on to give parents and teachers strategies for dealing with PDA, including links to three books on the subject. I bought them all that night, and I bought extra copies for the teacher and therapists.

I was so overwhelmed that night that I waited until the next day to talk it over with my husband. It was all so spot on that I could not refrain from filling in Isla's teacher, too. I sent her a text with the link to the article I had read, and after a while I got her response. "OMG this is Isla to a T."

We texted back and forth for a while about how to approach the week, because a lot was happening in the next few days. First, Isla would start her new medication, so now she would be on the new stimulant and the non-stimulant together. Second, the big ARD meeting was set for that week. Isla's testing was complete, and Greg and I would finally learn what labels would follow Isla for the rest of her public school educational experience. And on top of that, now we had new information that could potentially change the way we approached everything about Isla. The teacher told me she wanted to take it slow and not change the class or the environment too much too quickly. She also recommended that we be careful how we mention PDA in the ARD because it was not a diagnosis accepted by the Texas Education Agency (TEA) or by DSM-V.

Remember that earlier I mentioned my frustration with the latest and greatest trickling its way to us? Well, in the case of PDA, that "us" wasn't just the Rio Grande Valley but the entire United States. PDA was only recently being recognized in Europe. I wanted to know why. If PDA was so incredibly unique and distinguishable, why was it not accepted by DSM-V? Why wasn't there more being done in regard to researching, diagnosing and treating PDA in the United States? I Googled to see if there were trainings that were available for Isla's teachers. Only in London. Awesome.

Then I came across an article from the PDA Society website, with a sentence on page seven that floored me: "When parents discover PDA it is like a 'light bulb moment,' a label that describes their child to a 'T'.

It immediately makes sense and adds understanding; it feels like a tailor-made diagnosis." A "light-bulb" moment. This was the phrase I'd been using all along as I told Isla's story to doctors, teachers, therapists, and in early drafts of this book. I had always said we were waiting for the light bulb.

But it was not Isla's light bulb I had been waiting for. It was mine. And now it was my job to turn on everyone else's light bulbs.

I went to bed a little sick that night, thinking of all the terrifying things I'd been Googling only moments before I stumbled upon PDA: mental disorders, bipolar disorder, and schizophrenia. I was reviewing antipsychotics in children and cringing as I refreshed my memory of the possible side effects. What if we'd started experimenting with those? How would that have affected my beautiful girl? Don't you get it? This is why a *correct* diagnosis is so important. This is why anyone who tells you that a diagnosis doesn't matter is wrong. I started to think about other children out there. If PDA is not widely known or accepted, are there other children out there on antipsychotics as a result of a misdiagnosis? Are there kids out there who everyone just assumes are "bad" or "troubled," who are not being supported the way they need to be, and who are living with anxiety and stress and side effects of medications they don't need while everyone around them assumes their behavior is just noncompliance?

The following Monday was a holiday, and I spent it reading the first of the books I had ordered about PDA.

I was fascinated with every single page.

There were separate sections for teachers and parents, and as I read I realized that, through trial and error with Isla, I had stumbled upon many of the strategies they recommended. For example, children with PDA have to feel like they are in control and can't always process or respond to the pressure of "demands." So the book recommended rewording demands whenever possible so that they did not sound like demands. I'd been doing this with Isla for years. Instead of saying, "Isla clean your room please," I had already learned to reword it.

"Gosh, Isla," I'd say instead, "I have no idea where these pillows go. I wish I knew where to put them."

Isla would immediately spring up, grab the pillows from me, and say, "Oh, Mom, I know. I know. I know. Here, Mom. See? Here, Mom, right here on bed."

Then I would keep going. "Oh man, Isla, I am so glad you knew where to put them! Mommy forgot. Silly mom. OK, now what about all of these crumbs on the floor? I don't know if I should get a broom or—"

Isla was always quick to respond. "Oh, Mom. Mom. Mom, look. Mom, look. I vacuum. I do it, Mom? Mom, I do it."

This, my friends, was how I was already living my life with Isla. We all were. We didn't realize it but we were using effective strategies for PDA. Changing the demand to a question or posing the demand as a request for help immediately put Isla in control, making her feel proud and accomplished because she was able to fulfill someone's need.

I thought back to that water bottle scene I mentioned earlier in the book, where rewording a request even helped her count correctly. Instead of asking her for four water bottles, I told her we were all thirsty and wished we had some water.

I realized that this was how the teachers were going to have to approach Isla from now on. The therapists, too. I thought back to all of those failed speech and occupational therapy sessions, which amounted to hour upon hour of demands.

I went to bed that night wondering how I could change the DSM-V, thinking of how I could come up with the money to take us all to London for an official diagnosis for Isla and training for all her teachers, and realizing that I had stumbled into something much bigger than me and way out of my reach. I went to bed that night realizing that I may not be able to change the world, but I definitely was on the right path to changing Isla's world.

The first day we tried the new stimulant in combination with the non-stimulant, we got this report in her notebook:

"Isla had a fantastic day. She participated in group activities and completed individual work with no help. She did listen to a book being read by the paraprofessional, then she answered questions and took an accelerated reader test. She did get a 100%. We're very proud of her."

As I read that entry I could feel my shoulders loosen and my neck relax.

I cannot explain how incredibly stressed and tense I would get waiting to read the reports that came home in Isla's backpack each day. So reading that brought on such a sense of relief. I texted the teacher and asked if Isla seemed happy that day. Did she eat well? Did her stomach hurt? The teacher said Isla did smile a couple times. She did not eat much, but she did not complain at all of stomach pain.

It was time for the big ARD meeting. And once again, I was so impressed with the way the school administration and Isla's team handled the meeting.

There were a total of eleven people in the room: an administrator, a regular education 3rd grade teacher, the school psychologist, the school diagnostician, the school occupational therapist and her intern, the school speech therapist, two special education teachers including Isla's, and my husband and me. For over three hours we listened to each person review their testing of Isla. The psychologist told us that this time Isla did absolutely test autistic according to ADOS-2. He explained that sometimes as children get older, the diagnostic criteria are easier to detect and some tendencies become more apparent. As usual, some things were hard to hear, but for the most part nothing surprised us.

One particularly interesting part of the meeting involved the occupational therapist's testing results. She spread out some examples of work she was doing with Isla to improve her fine motor skills, focusing on tracing and writing.

The page she put in front of us was too good to be true. It was the same page that I had seen weekly as Isla's homework—ISLA PEÑA written 15 times in dotted lines for Isla to trace. But this sheet was perfectly traced. "So you are doing these activities hand over hand?" I asked. The occupational therapist clarified that these were done without her help. Isla's teacher and I were equally perplexed. She got out a sample of tracing from her class, and we compared the two. Then we spotted it: on the occupational therapist's pages, the areas Isla was to trace were highlighted yellow. The teacher's sheets were just black and white. *Hum, that's weird.* This was another mental file I would have to unpack later.

After we'd heard all the reports, the teacher and I introduced our newfound discovery of PDA and explained why we were convinced this was Isla's diagnosis. Everyone was intrigued. Everyone took notes and wrote down the titles of the books that I'd ordered.

They all listened intently as I explained Isla's history and why she matched up so well to that diagnosis, and they also listened as I shared some of the ways we manage Isla at home, such as rewording common demands to help with compliance.

After everything was said and done, it was time for the diagnostician to tell us what labels they would be documenting on Isla's official education record. Her labels would be Autism Spectrum Disorder – Pervasive Developmental Disorder Not Otherwise Specified, Attention Deficit Hyperactive Disorder, Speech Delay, and my favorite: Intellectual Disability.

The diagnostician was very sweet, and it was obvious that she rushed through that last label. She said it sweetly and quietly and quickly. I smiled, and said, "You know that is an "ugly" right?" The group all looked at me kind of nervously.

"Excuse me?" said the diagnostician.

"You know that, for a parent that is a very ugly word, especially when it is not correct. I mean, your testing is all correct, and you did a fantastic job, but the word is wrong. It's a terrible label."

The administrator smiled. "Yes, I agree. It used to be much uglier."

"Yes I know", I said.

"What do you think the label should be?" asked the administrator.

"I think that all special education programs should use diagnoses, not labels. A label tells me what my daughter is. A diagnosis tells me what my daughter has. But since you asked, there should be a label of "academically delayed" because for Isla, that is the only delay that presents at school."

Everyone agreed. These people looking back at me were some of the best I had encountered. Their reports were spot on. They took time and attention with Isla, and they wanted to be correct. Yes, my reputation for "knowing my stuff" had preceded me, but I don't think that was the only driving force. These educators all wanted to do right by Isla. Every single one was slowly and steadily becoming invested. The administrator praised their hard work. My husband and I made sure to thank them all for such professionalism and respect for Isla through all of their testing—however difficult she'd made it for them.

For the rest of that short week, we got nothing but good daily reports, and on Friday my second PDA book arrived in the mail. As I began to read, I recognized that the author's child was dealing with a much more severe form of PDA than what we were seeing in Isla. However, there were too many similarities between her stories and mine to be mere coincidence, and that book was what I needed to seal the deal. Isla had PDA. Here are a few characteristics that Isla had in common with the child in the book:

Both seemed to enjoy not following orders, specifically when it came to academics. If we asked Isla what color the apple was, she would grin and say, "blue" without even glancing at the object in question. The child in the book was unpredictable at school, with some days being awesome and some days being horrific. For both of them the most interesting part about that unpredictability was that no matter how hard we tried, we could never identify a specific trigger. The mother, like me, had tried issuing time outs and taking away things and rewarding positive behaviors, and nothing worked for very long.

Just like the child in the book, Isla has always done well in situations with a lot of things to do and very few boundaries, like playing in a park or play area.

However, a confined setting like a restaurant was more difficult in the early years. This has improved drastically, but she used to constantly interrupt our adult conversations and make frequent trips to the bathroom to remain in control.

Then came the obsessive requests for things that she just couldn't let go of—like going outside. She was relentless. There's no other word for it.

The mother who wrote the book and I shared a heavy responsibility to help our children become people who would be socially accepted. But also we agreed that their young minds just seemed to be wired differently, and when anyone asked them to play by "regular" rules, all they could see were demands to do certain things or behave certain ways that made them feel completely out of control. That's when they would start to act "naughty." This other mother shared stories of her child urinating on clothing and picking at her skin to keep the anxiety at bay, and she perfectly described that "frightened animal" look I dread to see in Isla's face after a meltdown. I didn't know this lady, but I felt so connected to her. I could empathize with almost every single paragraph of her book.

Then I stumbled on something new. When the child in the book was between four and six years old, she started complaining that certain colors bothered her eyes. The eye doctor diagnosed the child with Irlen Syndrome and prescribed a pair of glasses with colored lenses that helped to calm whatever overstimulation the child was seeing when she tried to read or when she was in fluorescent or harsh lighting. I immediately thought back to the ARD meeting just the day before. The occupational therapist. The perfect tracing. The yellow paper. *Oh my God!* Irlen Syndrome?

I practically flung the book across the room and frantically searched for my cell phone in the sheets of my bed. The first thing that popped up when I Googled Irlen Syndrome was this description: "Irlen Syndrome is a perceptual processing disorder. It is not an optical problem. It is a problem with the brain's ability to process visual information." Holy smokes! I could not believe what I was seeing. I read reviews and articles and studies and success stories and failure stories. I read that Irlen Syndrome could affect academic performance, behavior, attention, ability to sit still, and concentration. I read that, for people with the syndrome, black and white print may be indistinguishable or appear wavy or distorted. Was that why my Isla hated—and I mean hated—worksheets and flashcards? Was that why, as a baby and toddler, she fastidiously avoided staring at the TV screen? I read that light sensitivity was common with this disorder and that glare or fluorescent or bright lights could cause physical symptoms such as fatigue and irritation. Was this why Isla had such weird daytime sleep issues? I read that attention and concentration problems were especially prominent in academic settings, and that, as a result, many children with Irlen Syndrome are given ADHD medication unnecessarily. (Ouch. That one hurt.) I read that the disorder caused writing problems—including the inability to copy or trace accurately. This often resulted in the student tracing the letters in the right shape, but with unequal letter size or spacing. Cue those homework scenes! Lastly I read that the disorder could affect depth perception and cause clumsiness and difficulty catching balls or judging distances.

The very next morning I searched for the closest Irlen Syndrome diagnostician. I found out she was five hours away from our town, and I booked the first available appointment.

I called Isla's teacher and asked if this kind of testing was done within the school district. We later found out that the public school system does not provide official Irlen Syndrome testing, but they do lay colored vinyl sheets over books and worksheets for special needs children when needed. It was the second week of the new medication combination, and we were still seeing good reports daily. Isla would usually have some tired or uncooperative moments, but as soon as she was provided choices and given options, she would choose to be compliant.

The day before Halloween, Isla was involved in her first Special Olympics bowling competition. Isla had the option of being dropped off directly at the bowling alley or being dropped off at a local middle school where she would get to ride a bus there with the other participants. Isla bravely and happily got on the bus and waved goodbye to me for her five-minute bus ride. I arrived at the bowling alley, where my parents, my husband's father, two of the therapists from the ABA clinic, and Isla's teacher were all waiting to greet me. Isla had a cheering section! When she arrived, my poor girl was completely overwhelmed. There were so many schools and children packed into one bowling alley, and as Isla's morning medications kicked in, I could tell she was struggling to cope with it all.

She was happy to see everyone, but she had that blank, frightened look on her face much of the morning. When someone snapped a photo with her standing next to an administrator and one of her classmates, I cringed, because Isla was not Isla in that photo. She was scared and overwhelmed, and I knew it would end up on the school district Facebook page. It did.

The competition started off with an "opening ceremony", during which each team marched with its school banner for introductions.

Once everyone was standing in line with their banners, Isla started to ease out of her trance and become herself. Then one of the athletes lit the Flame of Hope, which symbolized respect and inclusion and shined a light on the talents and abilities of people with special needs (and which was faux for obvious reasons). He then recited the Special Olympics motto: "Let me win. But if I cannot win, let me be brave in the attempt." Having gone through what I had gone through, and knowing that that room was filled with close to a hundred parents who had been down their own difficult paths, I couldn't think of a more appropriate motto than that. The place was filled with incredibly brave parents, teachers, and children. I had chills just taking it all in as we sang the national anthem.

Once the ceremony was over, the children and their cheering squads returned to their assigned lanes, and the competition was on. Isla was in a group of five other female athletes, all her age, and she did fantastic. She was patient and attentive throughout the entire competition, and in the end, she won first place.

She was all smiles as she accepted her medal, and she beamed as she took pictures with her family and friends.

That day would mark the last "good" day for Isla for many months to follow.

Isla's daily reports took a very sharp turn for the worse: "Extremely rough day…" "Keeps saying NO!" "…gets very upset…" Then we entered the "I hate everyone" phase. Hate was not a word we used at home—we just didn't have a need for it. But suddenly, Isla was saying she hated her classmates, which meant she had to be immediately removed from their area.

Isla also started to say she hated "all of us," meaning my husband, June, Major, and me.

One day, the teacher sent me an audio clip of Isla proclaiming that she hated all of us as she named us one by one. It broke my heart.

The voice I heard was not my Isla. The voice I heard was angry, lost, defiant, and trapped. I went back to the pediatrician the day I heard that audio clip. Together we surmised that Isla's body and mind had adjusted to the low dose of stimulants, and we decided to follow guidelines and increase her dosage, rather than starting over entirely. Her first two weeks on the medication had been so amazing that I was hopeful we'd have some luck once we got the dosage right. Instead, things got worse.

The day we increased the medication, Isla started having crying spells. The first one lasted literally all night long. She'd fallen asleep as usual that evening, but shortly afterward, she woke up and came to my bed crying.

I couldn't get her to say anything, and I was so half asleep that I just let her lay down with me. I wrapped her up in my blanket, spooned her, and let her cry quietly. I was in and out of sleep, and every few minutes I would wake up to her sniffling, wipe her eyes and nose, and just hold her. I called the pediatrician the next morning, and we decided to reduce the medication to the original dose. But still, every day got worse and worse. Isla was refusing everything and defying every single demand. She was taunting others so much that she had to be removed from class all together. Isla's disruption was causing flare-ups in her classmates' behavior too. Then after, ten months with no incidents, Isla used her old friend, "escape by urination," again.

It is very difficult to put into words the despair and loneliness that I felt during this time. I think it had been bubbling under the surface for years, but now a new sense of hopelessness was at the forefront, and it consumed me daily.

Each note from school reignited the feeling that I had to do something or I wasn't doing enough. I started to worry about June and Major and what must they be seeing and hearing.

Would this be the memory of their mom? Sad, depressed, and angry?

I had also committed myself to two different volunteer organizations a couple years before, and during this time I was heavily involved in planning major events for both of them. I was overwhelmed, and my heart was just not in it. I dreaded every meeting and every task, which was not like me at all. I was in survival mode.

During one particular volunteer meeting, I waved hello to a friend who had just walked in. As she approached me her smile turned into a concerned frown. "Oh my God, what's wrong?" she said. I thought I'd been putting on a pretty good "happy" show, but everything had become so all-consuming that I just couldn't fake it anymore. For years I'd been able to hide the fact that I was constantly sad and worried about Isla. In fact, it wasn't until I was writing this book that I realized just how often I pretended nothing was happening. But now it was written all over my face and my body. I couldn't pretend anymore. I didn't want to pretend anymore. I stopped sending Isla's notebook back each day. I didn't want to read or hear anything. I couldn't bear it anymore, because I had already tried it all.

The only option left was not an option at all, thanks to the stupid, irresponsible decisions I had made eight years before she was born.

When I was in high school I never considered the amount of money it would take to accomplish my goal of becoming a pharmacist.

When I was in undergrad, I never thought twice about taking out loans, and once I got into pharmacy school, I took out even more. It was a no-brainer.

That was what everyone did. The problem was that I didn't just borrow what I needed. I borrowed what I *wanted,* and I never worried about the eventual repayment, because pharmacists get paid well, right?

What's worse, I knew we wanted a family, but I never considered what that family would cost, and I never ever could have fathomed the financial strain that raising a child with special needs would bring. I began to hate myself.

Isla needed to stay home, but I could not afford to quit my job. Isla needed to be home schooled, but my student loans were monstrous. Isla needed to learn in an environment where she was not stressed or anxious, but I would not be able to make that happen. It was one thing not to know what was best for Isla. It was another thing not to have a choice.

I am no Dave Ramsey, but if I could send a message to every single person out there racking up student loans—and especially those in the medical fields where the education costs are even more exorbitant—my message would be simple: You never know what life has in store for you. You never know what cards you will be dealt. You never know what kind of care you or your family will need. So if you are going to have a partner and you do want a family, the smartest way to live is as if you depend on one person's salary. That way, you will never be trapped. That is the only thing in my whole life that I sincerely and tearfully regret and would do over a thousand times.

The burden and guilt of my student loans is crushing, and while at one point it only limited how many nice things I could have, now it was directly affecting what I was able to do to help my little girl.

It was about this time that I started thinking about what would happen if I died.

Let me be very clear: I was not suicidal at all. I did not want to die or to hurt myself, and I especially did not want anything to happen to my children. But I did think sometimes that, if I did die, it would be OK. I mean, Greg would get a truckload of money, pay off my student loans, and hire a full-time caregiver for Isla.

June and Major wouldn't remember me much, so hopefully they wouldn't have memories of me being so miserable, and I would get to rest and be at peace.

I know what you are thinking. This is crazy talk. Well, you are right. It was. But I think it is important to share this because I've come to understand that a lot of people deal with that feeling daily, whether they're parents of children with special needs, parents of neurotypical children, or not even parents at all. At one time or another, many of us have issues that seem so overwhelming that our minds play games with us. I believe it was the guilt I carried for feeling so helpless and out of control that got me to that point. It was ugly and dark. But what was even uglier was what was happening to Isla.

She was changing. She was not eating and not sleeping well. For a whole week she cried every day before and after school, begging me to please let her go to sleep.

She didn't want to be out and about or go outside or do anything she usually loved, and others were noticing, too. I got a text one night from her gymnastics instructor saying her heart was broken over how sad Isla was and that she was praying for us and all the decisions we had to make daily for her.

That same night, Isla fell asleep early, but she woke up after just an hour.

I was getting ready for my shower when she came into my bedroom. She was crying, but it wasn't her usual, quiet cry. This time she seemed panicked, and she was hyperventilating a little bit. She seemed desperate as she sat down next to me.

"Mom, peese. Mom. Mom, peese I not go that school no more. Mom, peese."

"Oh Isla," I said, "Every single kiddo has to go to school, my love, but listen, you have to tell mommy why you don't want to go to that school, and I can help you."

Isla pouted, frustrated.

"Listen, Isla, think very hard. Try to think of the words you want to say. Why don't you like school?"

Isla just continued to cry.

I tried a different way. "Isla, do you think that someone is being mean to you at school?"

Isla said no.

I asked the same question individually about each teacher she worked with. Were any of them mean to her? She said no every time.

"Are the students or your friends being mean to you?"

Isla said no.

"Isla is *anyone* being mean to you *anywhere*?"

Isla said no.

At that point, if we're being honest, I was not such a great mom. My fuse was short, and I was dealing with my own issues, so I got frustrated.

"You know what, Isla? I am trying to help you. Every day I want to help you, but you are going to have to tell me what's going on and why you don't like school so I can help you. Let me know when you know." She stomped away mad and crying and frustrated, and then I had my typical shower sob session, hating the world and myself for being such a jerk to her. When I got out, she was in my room.

Isla very calmly said, "Mom I need talk to you."

I sat down, positioned her right in front of me, and looked right in her eyes. "Ok, Isla, I am here. Tell me."

"I no like my friends look at me," she said.

"What? You don't like when your friends look at you?"

Isla put her head down and repeated herself. "I no want my friends to look at me."

My mind started backpedaling to the PDA books I had been reading about how these children can have very low self-esteem, and they often try to mask their lack of confidence with distraction or charm. Could it be that Isla was embarrassed daily? Humiliated, even?

I mean, she was frequently separated from the other students, stuck in the corner with her classmates looking at her, fully aware that she wasn't behaving and could not participate. For the first time, I thought about it through Isla's point of view. She's self-conscious of her poor academic performance and the restrictions PDA imposes, so she starts acting out in order to avoid embarrassment. But as a result, she is separated from the students and forced to sit in a corner while they're staring at her intermittently the rest of the day.

Wouldn't you be embarrassed?

All evening, Isla continued to beg me not to make her go back to school, and we had "cry night" number two, spooning, sniffling, wiping tears, and in and out of sleep. For the second time in her life, Isla was feeling depression, and I didn't know if it was her medication or her school or the PDA or just Isla or what. It was one thing for me to be depressed, but I couldn't bear to see Isla that way for one more day. I needed to know if the medications were causing the depression, so the next day I did not give her the stimulant. I did give her the non-stimulant, because it affects blood pressure, so I wanted to wean her off that one slowly.

During my lunch break I drove to the ABA clinic for a heart-to-heart with my buddy, Eileen. We laughed and talked and got teary-eyed together as we agreed that, no matter what kind of kiddo you have, being a parent is hard. A parent's responsibility to maintain a child's sanity and happiness can be a big load to bear, and it sometimes comes at the expense of the parent's own sanity and happiness.

This is especially true when it isn't clear what's best for the child. We reviewed Isla's insurance profile for the year and talked about her coming back to the ABA clinic. It was an option. When I left, I was still confused about what to do, but I was relieved that at least we had another option.

I told Greg that night that I was going to withdraw Isla from public school. As always, he served as a good system of checks and balances, and he told me that he was really OK with whatever we decided, but we should at least give the school an opportunity to tell us what our options were. The very next morning I spoke to both the assistant principal and principal about the notebook.

I told them that for twelve weeks now we'd had nothing but sad, disappointing, disturbing reports of Isla's behavior, and I just could not handle anymore. Even worse, I told them that the Isla they knew was not my Isla. When she showed up to school so stressed and anxious each day, how could she be herself? I made sure they knew that I did not think this was anyone's fault. I knew that the teachers were doing all they could. I was not upset, and I was not blaming anyone. I just needed to take action, because Isla and I were not doing well mentally, emotionally, spiritually, or even physically.

The principal, together with the two special education teachers, proposed a schedule change that would give Isla breaks every thirty- to forty-five minutes. They also proposed a co-teacher approach in which the two special education teachers would switch throughout the day to give Isla a change of pace, personality, and location.

It was a great idea, and even though I wasn't sure if it would work, I was very appreciative.

They were really trying their best and giving their all for Isla. At the end of the conversation, the principal talked about the school's goal for all its students: to make sure they had the skills and tools they needed to be functional in the world. He said that it may take weeks or months or years for Isla to catch on, but it would require tough love either now or later.

I left the school that day feeling happy that they were willing to try something new, but I was also a little perplexed by the last part of the conversation.

Did we really have to keep pushing for Isla to conform to the public school model? What if that was not possible for her? What if she couldn't conform? My intention was always to break her *in,* not to break her.

I was really starting to question the whole "tough love" idea, mainly because of all I was reading and researching about PDA. Then I smiled to myself, wondering if perhaps Isla was the one practicing "tough love" on all of us.

Isla would not be able to start the new schedule until we had another ARD meeting, which they could not schedule until the following Wednesday. But for Isla, every day was critical. She was so miserable—and so was I—that I seriously considered keeping both of us at home those days.

My heart was screaming at me to take Isla out of school. Take her back to the ABA clinic. Make Isla Isla again. I just wanted to see her smile and laugh and sing and dance again. I just wanted her to be at peace and content. But my head said to stick it out. Let the school give it all they got. Even if Isla had to suffer for a couple more days, we had to stick it out. I discussed the proposed schedule changes with Greg and Eileen, and we agreed that it was a good model and worth a shot. More importantly, with someone like Isla, we would know very quickly if it was a good fit for her.

Isla had been off the stimulant for a day or two when we left on our trip for her Irlen testing. It was just Isla and me on this trip, which I hoped would be happy, silly, and carefree, with no talk about school or behaving or notebooks. Typically, Isla absolutely *loved* road trips. She loved the ride, the videos, the snacks, the music and the anticipation of staying in a hotel or a relative's home. Not this trip. She slept the whole way, and when she was awake, she complained that she wanted to go home. I spent most of the trip worried that I had set Isla on a path to permanent depression.

The Irlen testing would be a two-day event. The first day would be to determine whether Isla in fact had Irlen Syndrome and, if so, what colors her eyes and brain preferred.

The second day would be to determine the right shade—meaning how light or dark—for her colored lenses. Here was the problem: Isla couldn't read. If someone was able to read, the Irlen test was incredibly simple, but for Isla we would have to approach it very differently.

The Irlen diagnostician and I had spent some time on the phone before the appointment reviewing all the things that Isla could do so that the test would be accurate.

The first day was great. The Irlen diagnostician tested Isla by taping sheets of white paper under fluorescent lighting and natural lighting. These white sheets of paper had different shapes or designs or pictures in black print. She used Irlen colored overlays and asked Isla to look at each sheet and tell her which one was easy to see or which one looked better. She did this many, many times to be sure Isla's color preferences were consistent. We narrowed it down to blue, purple, and yellow. The next step was to hold lenses in these three colors up to Isla's eyes as she looked at the pictures.

We first did blue and purple, which continued to invoke similar positive responses from Isla. Then we added yellow into the mix, and I was surprised at the way her eyes darted when she first looked down through those yellow lenses. She had her head down, but her eyes were not looking at the paper. I put my finger on the paper and pointed to the object. "Isla, look right here. Can you look here?" Her eyes just didn't want to focus. This didn't happen with the blue or purple lenses. The diagnostician and I looked at each other and smiled. OK, then, blue and purple it is!

The second day did not go so well. Isla was moody, tired, resistant, and stubborn. The whole goal of finding the right shade was to ensure that, when the person looked through the lens, they didn't see the color of the lens.

But Isla can't identify colors consistently, so when we would hold up the lenses to her eyes and ask her what color the tree looked, it was always a no go. "What about the leaves, Isla? Which color makes the leaves looks clear and sharp?" Clear? Sharp? No way. We agreed to try a happy medium tint. We were given an estimated time of three weeks for the glasses to come in the mail, and we took off. As I buckled us up to get back on the road, I tried to push down the gut feeling that we had just wasted seven hundred bucks. Again, Isla slept during the entire five-hour car ride home, convincing me that it was time to start tapering off the non-stimulant.

We had three days to get through before we could be cleared to start the new schedule, and every day started with a pep rally, which, frankly, was as much for me as it was for my girl. I constantly reassured Isla, telling her I loved her and that I knew she could do it and that soon she would get to leave the classroom more often. I encouraged her through her tears and complaining and whining and sadness.

I was relentless in trying to get her to eat, begging and pleading and letting her pick anything and everything she wanted when she was hungry for even a quick minute.

Finally, we made it to Wednesday, the day of our third ARD meeting in two months.

This particular ARD was put together very quickly, so there were different people in attendance, but it was important and effective, and the first time Greg and I felt it was necessary to make sure everyone knew where we stood in regards to discipline and medication.

The second special education teacher who had been getting involved with Isla led this meeting. She reviewed the Functional Behavioral Assessment (FBA) that they had completed in an attempt to find out why Isla acted the way she did. An FBA has two primary components: First, to identify and track the common behavior that needs improvement or correction. Second, to try different strategies to improve the behavior and track the success of each. Sound familiar? This was exactly how the ABA model worked. The co-teacher explained that they were starting to notice that Isla required very high energy and very high motivation from the teacher in order to perform. She said they had to be like cheerleaders all day, with upbeat attitudes and happy-go-lucky body language, and Isla needed constant chatter and songs to stay engaged. Greg and I smiled, and he said, "It sounds like you are starting to figure Isla out." Then the co-teacher said something that gave me a totally new perspective on the past month. She said that regardless of what Isla was doing in class or the challenges Isla brought on daily, she really had started to enjoy working with Isla, and she felt blessed each day she worked with my girl. "Isla expects us to act like we should act and live our lives every day," she said. She was right.

We should live with joy, happiness, and an upbeat attitude, as though there are no worries in the world. We should live with a song on our tongue and a dance in our step every day.

At the meeting, we also established a new way to communicate about Isla's behaviors.

The principal had shared with the teachers that the daily behavior notes were wearing on all of us, so they proposed a plan to make a worksheet with sections for each part of Isla's day. If she did well in a section, she'd get a smiley face; if not, the teacher would check one of three boxes—"Listen to Teacher," "Do My Work," or "Sit Quietly"—indicating the main issue. I would get these worksheets every Wednesday and Friday to review, instead of every day.

When it was time for Greg and me to chime in at the end of the meeting, I said two things. First, that we were never giving her medication again. Isla would be totally medication-free until the day that she could come to me and say, "Hey, Mom, I have been researching and reading, and I think I want to try this particular medication to see if it helps me in class so I can focus a little bit more." Second, we had decided that we were no longer going to take away home time, family time, or family outings as "punishment" for what Isla is doing at school. If we need to take away the iPad or other material things, that would be fine, but if Isla's abuelo wanted to take her for ice cream, she would get to go for ice cream. If we were going to a football game, Isla would go to the football game. We reiterated that Isla is different, Isla is special, and Isla is our family, and this would not change no matter how hard or bad the day was.

My husband then reminded everyone at the table that, although we agreed with the behavior plan and understood that all they were doing was the best for Isla right now, we could not forget that the underlying problem was not a behavior problem.

Isla had a learning disability that we had not identified yet, and that was the root of the problem.

Also, one of the biggest challenges with PDA is that what works one week may not work the next week, so the co-teachers would have to really try to make things new and exciting for Isla every day to continue seeing results.

The night of the third ARD meeting was the first time in almost a year that we did not give Isla any medication at all. That night I also started telling Isla the same thing I tell her every night, to this day. "Good night, Isla. I love you no matter what." Now when I say, "Hey, Isla, I love you," she replies, "No matta what."

I mentioned very early on that I sing each night to my kids. It's always the same songs, one being the Miss Love song, and the second is one that I made up on one particularly endless night when Isla was an infant.

"I is for I love you, no matter what you do.
S is for the smile Jesus gave to you,
L is for the laughter you've brought into my life.
A is for always—I'm always on your side
Isla, Isla, Isla, Isla girl."

That's right. No matter what. I am always on her side. Since the beginning, and forever.

Just twenty-four hours after we stopped all medication, I had my Isla back. She had a full week off for Thanksgiving break, and she was back to her old self.

She was my smiling, laughing, singing, dancing, silly Isla, full of joy and eating like a champ. The crying stopped, and the sadness disappeared. Isla was back.

The new schedule worked well for a while. The teachers were cheerful and upbeat every single day, and I started seeing more smiley faces than I'd ever dreamed of on papers that didn't have June's name in the top right corner. Isla was still a kid, and some days would say she didn't want to go to school. I would just laugh and tickle her and say, "I don't want to go to work either, crazy girl!" She would laugh, we would just blast "This Girl is on Fire," and all would be forgotten. There were some days when the teacher would literally have to lift her out of the vehicle, but her resistance lasted all of five minutes before she would settle into her new routine.

A couple of weeks after Thanksgiving, Isla's new glasses with blue-purple lenses arrived. I don't know if I will ever know for sure if Isla has Irlen Syndrome, but I do know that the glasses ended up being too much of a distraction. She would put them in her mouth or on her head like sunglasses, and sometimes, when things got really heated, she would throw them in the trash. We agreed to only present the glasses to Isla when she had to complete worksheets, participate in flashcard activities, or use the computer. The teachers stayed positive, knowing that for someone like Isla it may take many weeks or months to adjust. Through some of the darkest times of my life I learned that, as parents, we will always feel our children's pain or sadness. That is inevitable.

However, as much as we feel compelled to help our children find happiness and joy, we have to show them by example how to find happiness and joy even in sorrow and pain. I was not that example for Isla for a long while, and it required a huge shift in my attitude to become that example.

Now when Isla has a rough day I hug her extra tight. I make sure she sees me smile and hears me tell her that I love her no matter what.

I make sure that she knows that with every sunrise come a new chance and a new day, and that tomorrow will be great.

Over the Christmas and New Year break we got approved to send Isla to the ABA clinic for a few days while school was out. We decided to focus strictly on behavior therapy with no academics to keep the school and the clinic separate. I was starting to feel like maybe Isla needed both, and now the ABA therapy could serve as a supplement to school, with a focus on anger management, impulse control, and her worsening indecisiveness. Those days during the break, Isla did amazing at the clinic. The therapists were blown away by how much she had learned and how linguistically expressive she was becoming. The experiment went so well that we decided to keep it up, so Isla started getting ABA therapy for about an hour and half each day after school while I finished my work day.

We also experienced Special Olympics for the second time, and this time it was just so memorable. Here is the essay I wrote about that super cool day for the Today Show Parenting Team:

"We have a shelf in my daughters' bedroom that is filled with treasure. It has knickknacks from our last vacation, the random water globe the girls begged for at God knows what store, an odd ceramic something or other that was way too expensive (because one of the girls hand painted it at one of those paint-while-you-wait mall places), plus hair clips and rubber bands galore. But it also has trophies and medals. June is five years old and has three trophies and four medals. Isla is nine years old and has just one medal.

You see, regardless of how equally and fairly we try to treat our children, when one has special needs, it won't ever be equal or fair. Equal and fair opportunities don't always exist for them. So God bless that one medal. God bless Special Olympics.

When Special Olympics was formed in 1968 by Eunice Kennedy Shriver, I don't know if her initial intent was to change the world or just to change her sister's world. What I do know is that, fifty years later, for about four weeks, twice a week, five to six men have gotten together in a middle school gym with a bag full of basketballs and practiced dribbling, shooting, and passing with about thirty special needs children in our school district. Some of the coaches have jobs in the district related to special needs, and some are dads that volunteer, but they all spend a couple of hours a week whooping and hollering for every single kiddo that enters that gym.

There are high fives, smiles, victory dances, cheers, and nonstop clapping and words of encouragement. The kids *love* this time. No. The kids *crave* this time.

It gives them a rare opportunity to participate in something that all their neurotypical peers can participate in effortlessly. It gives them an opportunity to be on the "other side," with their siblings sitting in the bleachers cheering for *them* this time.

I am going to attempt to describe something to you that really must be seen, heard, and felt to understand: Special Olympics Competition Day.

As I poke my head into the very busy gym where the competition is being held, Isla spots me in an instant. She stands and waves both arms high in the air, and she smiles. But oh, how my girl smiles. She has a small cheering section of family members who have come with my husband and me, and I wave and quickly make a beeline to her. I just saw her thirty minutes ago when I dropped her off with the coaches to ride the bus, but we still hug and kiss like it's been days. Her love for her daddy and me never wavers. It is always strong and always excited and new. As we sit with her team we hug and greet the other mommies and daddies and discuss our mornings.

Some dealt with meltdowns. Some dealt with anxiety.

Some let their kiddos ride the bus for the first time, and others had to drive at the last second because their kiddos were just not feeling it that day. But it's all good. For us these unpredictable mornings are...predictable.

The gym starts to fill up with athletes from eight years old to over thirty. Some athletes' diagnoses are apparent, but others' aren't so clear. Today it really doesn't matter. They are all unique and all equally important. For us spectators, things don't feel too emotional until all of the athletes line up with their schools or teams and proudly hold up their banners. There is a high-spirited announcer that welcomes everyone, and my eyes start to well up just hearing and seeing the Special Olympics athletes react to this welcome. How do you describe pure joy with just words?

The crowd in the bleachers stands, and one by one the schools and teams are announced, and they walk to the front all together holding their banners. One preteen girl is so overcome with happiness that she covers her mouth with both hands as she giggles and throws her head back with laughter. She waves at the crowd, practically skipping. Then a young man who is probably late teens pretends to dribble a ball through his legs and jumps to shoot an invisible basket. He looks at the crowd and lifts his arms up and down, signaling us to stand up and cheer, people! The teachers and coaches smile and wave, and some are even jumping up and down alongside their students.

Then here comes the cutest little boy *ever,* and he is just leaping up and down as high as he can with both arms lifted in the air. "Yeah, baby!" he yells out loud.

Then there is a group of three young adult ladies that walk side by side, each holding up one hand with the "I love you" sign. I almost choke on tears as spectators who don't even know these sweet gals sign "I love you" right back.

"Eye of the Tiger" blares in my head when I see a middle-aged athlete with his arms raised and his hands in two fists above his head like Rocky Balboa.

The innocence is *beautiful*.

The *love* in the room ignites all kinds of emotions for many of the parents in the stands.

As for my little girl, she is so ecstatic she can hardly stand it. She is supposed to be helping hold the school's banner, but she is so excited she can barely hold her hands up, so a teacher gladly lends her a hand. They choose an athlete to say the Pledge of Allegiance, and when he forgets a word no one bashes him on Twitter or complains to each other. Instead, everyone cheers. "You can do it!" "Try again!" and "You got this!" He responds so well to the encouragement that he gets through the whole pledge with a big smile on his face. When he is done, he walks back to his teammates, who gather around him and give him high fives and hugs. He is loved. He is important.

Then they choose another volunteer to say the Special Olympics motto. "Let me win, but if I cannot win, let me be *brave* in the attempt." Oh yes. Yes! *Yes!* They use a faux torch with a cellophane "Flame of Hope," and four or five athletes spread out and run to each corner of the gym, passing the torch one to another.

All the spectators are on their feet, cheering and clapping for each handoff. Once the ceremony is complete, it's time for all the kids to break off into groups and start the basketball skills competition. Just as I think I'll finally be able to stop crying like a fool, I notice that all hundred or so of those volunteers in yellow shirts are *high school students*.

You high school kids get a bad rap these days, you know? Teachers, parents, and administrators around the country write and talk about how you have become disrespectful, rude, selfish, and entitled. Well, I am not a teacher or an administrator, but that is not what I saw that day. That day I saw almost a hundred high school students getting involved in a way that warmed my heart. These kids had no incentive for volunteering, except maybe missing a class or two, and they weren't standing around bumming it. They were hustling, checking lists, leading the Special Olympics athletes, and best of all, they were cheering.

That may not sound like much at first, but imagine the coolest kids around—star athletes, cheerleaders, leaders of clubs, honor roll students, all kinds of kids from all kinds of homes and all kinds of abilities—cheering for our athletes. They would clap nonstop for a kid that was doing a skill they themselves could master with one hand and their eyes closed. They didn't know my girl. They didn't know her diagnoses or our story. But it didn't matter. That day they were lifting up their peers who may never have the opportunities they had, and for one day they were giving back. And yes, they may have been there for volunteer hours or college resumes or just to hang out with their girlfriends, but I guarantee you that regardless of the original intent, those volunteers couldn't help but build character that day.

Some of these kids were so genuinely involved I couldn't watch them too closely because I knew I would start to ugly cry which would totally freak them out.

So all you high school kids, imagine what this feels like for our athletes. The same kids they watch under the Friday night lights, the same kids they watch lead the student council, the same kids they look up to in the hallways are cheering for *them*. These Special Olympics athletes long to be like you, and I don't mean necessarily that they want to play sports.

It's deeper than that. Some of them long to be "socially acceptable" like you. But your cheering shows them they are more than acceptable to you no matter what their diagnosis is, and *that is powerful*. Never forget that being a high school athlete is not a right. It is a privilege.

When it's all over, we head outside to the awards ceremony. There is another group of student volunteers and a super pumped up volunteer announcer who calls out each Special Olympics athlete's full name and the school or team they represent. With her family, friends, and coaches looking on, Isla receives her second medal ever. And you can bet it will go on the shelf right next to her first, which was for Special Olympics bowling.

So I say *kudos* to all of the parents of these exceptional high school kids. I say *bravo* to the school board, administrators, and staff who said yes to Special Olympics at their campuses. I say *you rock* to every high school guy and girl that cheered for my little girl that day. I say *you are making a difference* to every coach, volunteer, and teacher who had anything to do with this event. If you and your kids have never attended one of these events, I challenge you to put it on your to do list for this year.

Once the newness of the modified schedule change wore off, Isla was right back at it again, defying requests, kicking, yelling, having meltdowns, ripping her clothes, and all her usual "tactics." This went on for several weeks, and I tried very hard to maintain composure and my positive façade for Isla's sake. But it all peaked when I got called in for a meeting with the two co-teachers. They sat me down and informed me that the parents of the other students in her class had started calling the school about Isla. Their children were coming home reporting that Isla was kicking them and biting them and pulling their hair. One child had even told their parent they were scared of her. Some parents had called more than once. There was that good ol' queasy feeling again. Out of everything that happened during this whole crazy year, I don't think anything hurt me as much as hearing that other children were afraid of my daughter. My beautiful, loving, funny girl. It was just sickening.

That same day when I picked her up from school, her teacher showed me a picture that would start us on a new journey with our girl and this school district. It was a picture of a bite mark that Isla had inflicted on the forearm of a paraprofessional. I was disgusted. It was gruesome, showing every single one of Isla's teeth. Just a millimeter more pressure would have broken skin all the way around.

Had this happened earlier in the year, my mind would have jumped straight to anger and discipline. But by this point, my outlook on Isla's behavior issues had started to change, and I just became sad.

I remember thinking, how trapped and misunderstood she must have felt, how lost she must she have been, and how frustrated she had become to act out so violently.

That day, Greg and I decided enough was enough. We would formally request a one-on-one shadow for Isla. I had heard of this before, and I know how it usually goes. Parent request a shadow, school district denies shadow because there is supposedly no money, parent gets mad and gets a lawyer, and then parent and school district spend crap loads of money that neither of them have to argue whether the child needs a shadow or not. The parents usually win, though they're broke by the end, and they can't guarantee the shadow that is selected by the school district will be a good fit for the child's personality—or even whether they'll be trained properly. Meanwhile the relationship between the parent and the district has become strained and weird. But what choice did we have? My child was physically harming others. Shouldn't the school have jumped to assign her a shadow before I could even ask? I didn't understand why this process was so difficult for others when it seemed so clear and necessary to me.

I also knew that the district could not use the "we don't have money" excuse. You see, this particular district was very well known in our part of the state, and it took pride in having the greatest innovations in education. It spent millions on a specialty high school, STEMS junior high, and new elementary schools with focuses on fine arts.

It was building new buildings and expanding facilities left and right, so surely, *surely* they would be innovative for their Special Education students, too. Surely there would be money for a sensory room if I asked for one, and a shadow, and training for the paraprofessionals, too, seeing as I was quickly learning that Special Education paraprofessionals—who spend the most time with the students—do not receive the same training as Special Education teachers. I knew I was good. I wasn't asking for anything more than what was sensible and reasonable. This would get approved, because this district had it together, and I would get the satisfaction not only of having made a huge, important change for Isla but also of ending this book on a note of joy and triumph.

All that hope and certainty only served to make the disappointment that much worse.

First, I wrote up a formal request for the principal of Isla's school. I had a section detailing why I was asking for a shadow, a section listing all of the functions I thought the shadow could assist with, and a list of the personality traits that I felt best suited Isla for a one-on-one aid. The principal was aware of the parent calls and told me he would pass my request to the district special education administration department right away.

The school district decided it was appropriate to start with an evaluation of Isla, which would involve observation from a behavioral specialist, an instructional coach, and one of the directors of the special education department.

About four weeks later I was called in for the results of their findings.

One of the special education directors told me from the get go that the one-on-one aid was not approved. I didn't panic right away, because surely they could not ignore the fact that Isla was hurting others, so I assumed they would unveil some innovative evidence-based behavior plan instead. Then the behavioral specialist took over, and I learned she had been able to observe the side of Isla that we see at home. The beautiful, calm, funny, helpful Isla. The behavioral specialist explained that the fact that Isla was so observant to their presence and the fact that she modified her behavior to please them when they were there showed great cognition and potential. I wholeheartedly agreed. The behavioral specialist said that they did not observe *any* behavior issues and suggested that the teachers and paraprofessionals could benefit from more training.

Next up was the instructional coach, who showed me a box of hands-on activities he had made for Isla. The instructional coach explained that it was obvious that Isla got frustrated easily with worksheets and difficult material and that it was best to use as much hands-on learning as possible with her. No surprise there. So the district specialists would give the box and its contents to Isla's teachers, and they would also provide further training.

"So you are telling me that all of this…Isla's outbursts and violence and meltdowns are all due to a lack of training?" I asked, and each of them immediately said yes.

"So are you OK with all of this?" one of the special education administrators asked.

"You mean am I OK with you saying no to my request? Well, of course not, but you are the experts, and if we have to work on training and making more things hands-on for Isla—and if that corrects the behavior—then go for it." I was all for giving it our best shot. But was concerned that nobody had mentioned anything specific in regards to training. What would the paraprofessionals and teachers be trained to do when Isla was having a meltdown or biting or kicking?

When I asked them these questions, the only answer I received was, "We can look into that."

Um, OK. I ended the meeting by saying, "Look, I don't pretend to know what it is like to have to teach Isla in a classroom, so I am OK with all you're proposing to do—if I can hear her teachers agree that it is possible and reasonable to do all of this in the classroom with the resources they have."

The next step was to take all of these findings to another ARD meeting so that it could be implemented.

However, neither the behavioral interventionist nor the instructional coach showed up to the ARD meeting. I had wanted them all together in a room to agree and show me this was best for Isla, and I did not get that. I heard later that tensions were high, as the teachers felt they were being asked to do everything a one-on-one aid would do for Isla, but without a one-on-one aid.

During the ARD meeting I stressed my concern about the initial problem of Isla hurting others, as well as the potential, kneejerk reactions of anyone she hurt.

Anyone's reaction to a bite like the one in the picture I'd seen would be to swat the offender away, and understandably so. It really began to scare me, not only for others' safety, but for Isla's, too. I also learned that the worst of her behavior usually occurred when the teacher had stepped out for a meeting or ARD or training, leaving the paraprofessionals alone with the children. So I asked if the paraprofessionals were trained to manage behavior problems. I was told they were currently receiving training. Then I asked if they were restraint trained, and I was told no. I was assured that for the next few weeks until school was out, the behavioral interventionist and the instructional coach would visit Isla frequently to work with her and to train the teachers and the paraprofessionals.

In the week following the meeting, Isla's reports showed about 50% smiley faces and 50% sad faces. I asked the teacher how the hands-on learning assignments were going and how Isla was responding to them. Unfortunately, she reported back that there was only one hands-on activity Isla could do in the entire box. The rest were way too difficult for her.

What?

So I got back in my car, thinking surely the instructional coach had observed Isla to figure out her academic or educational or motor skills level *before* making that box of hands-on assignments. Right?

Surely when he was done creating all these neat projects, he'd tested them out on Isla to make sure they were appropriate for her learning level.

I did not want to believe—no, I *could not* believe—that a top-level professional who'd beaten out many highly qualified applicants for a job would implement learning materials and train paraprofessionals on how to use these materials without actually trying them out on the student first. I assumed there must be some mistake.

Then came the fateful day…

About a week later—two weeks after the ARD meeting—I received a phone call about 2:00 p.m. from the instructional coach and the behavioral interventionist. They were calling me to give me an update on Isla's progress. They used the words "amazing" and "well-behaved," and "cooperative." They said Isla had had "no violent outbursts at all" and that their visits with her were going great. I knew that not all of Isla's behavior reports were "amazing," but she probably was very "cooperative" when they were around. Then they asked me if I had any questions or concerns, and I nicely mentioned that the teacher had told me some of the hands-on materials were too hard for Isla. Again I should have been more honest, but I was careful. The instructional coach told me that they would tweak the hands-on materials. I hung up the phone, still skeptical, but reassured, nonetheless.

That reassurance was short lived.

I went to pick up Isla from school and saw the teacher walking her to the front office with a look of exhaustion on her face and a totally sad-faced behavior chart in her hand. Isla had had one of her worst days since school had started. She was noncompliant; she was defiant; she kicked, screamed, bit, and punched; she was out of control. I looked at this behavior chart in disbelief.

"I don't understand this. I just got a call an hour ago from the behavioral interventionist and the instructional coach, and they both told me Isla was doing amazing."

"What? They were here today." The teacher looked as confused as I felt.

"Wait. What? They were here? Today? Did they see Isla misbehaving?" I asked.

"Mrs. Peña, they didn't even come into the classroom."

I was upset now, but I held it together while I tried to wrap my mind around the facts. "Whoa. Hold on. This can't be right. Why would they call me and tell me everything is wonderful when they didn't even see her?"

"They stood in the hallway the whole time they were here, and they pulled the paraprofessionals out to talk to them. While the paras were outside, Isla started hitting and kicking, so I held her hand and poked my head out the door to ask for help. The paras came back in the classroom, and the district team left."

The teacher went on to say that she sent both of them and their supervisor an e-mail shortly after the incident requesting clarification of their roles, as that moment would have been a perfect time to witness Isla's behaviors and use their expertise in behavior management to help.

"Did they know that it was Isla that was giving you a hard time?" I was stupefied. "I mean I guess it doesn't matter right? They should help no matter what student was involved. But did they know Isla was with you?"

"I was holding her hand. They had to have seen her."

So the behavioral interventionist and the instructional coach had gone to the school, but did not go into the classroom, much less help when they were needed. And then when the teacher had sent an e-mail to them and their boss, they'd decided to call me with wonderful updates to make sure I didn't find out? Or to get to me first?

I felt like I'd been duped.

I called the instructional coach back right away and asked if they had indeed gone to the school that day. The answer was yes. I asked if they'd seen Isla that day. The answer was yes. I asked if they'd actually gone into the classroom with Isla. The answer was no. I asked why. The answer was because Isla had been sitting on the circle-time rug, well behaved, and they didn't want to disturb her. I asked if the teacher had indeed come out to ask for help. The answer was yes. I asked if they'd known it was Isla the teacher needed help with.

The answer was that the teacher never said which child was acting up—just that she needed help.

"I apologize for my tone," I said, "but I am very frustrated. How can I get two drastically different reports, all within one hour, about the same little girl? What is going on?"

Mommas, why do we apologize all the time? Why do we always want people to like us, even when we are justifiably mad? Let me answer that for you. We are avoiding the unavoidable: Crazy Mom Stigma.

Remember the school I'd decided not to send Isla to at the last minute? I'd recently learned from an insider at that school that one of their representatives had called the school in which Isla was transferring to to warn them about me when we transferred. "Watch out," the message was. "You have a real bitch coming your way."

To whoever called me a bitch, let me tell you something. Are you reading this? Man, I hope so.

Forget about the fact that this is probably the most unprofessional thing you could do; forget the fact that I love Jesus and He loves me, and I am a human being who deserves respect; forget the fact that the last time I was called a bitch was by a pimply eighth-grade bully; and forget the fact that you probably know *nothing* about being a parent of a special needs child in a public school system; and forget that I wasn't even involved with that school long enough to do anything "bitchy".

Now that you have read 319 pages of my story can you see why this is so hurtful to a momma like me?

What you noticed was probably sheer, practiced confidence. Did that make you uncomfortable?

Now let's make some more people uncomfortable. Ready? All I ask is that you're honest with yourself. Have you ever heard someone talk about a mom like this? Have you ever talked about a mom like this?

"Ugh, here she comes again. She thinks she knows everything."

"You better make that mom happy, because we don't want a lawsuit."

"Puhleese. She thinks just because she is educated that she can get whatever she wants."

"Crap the ARD is tomorrow. You'd better make sure those reports are correct, because that mom will bite your head off in front of everyone. "

"Oh man watch out that mom is a total bitch."

Any of that sound familiar?

Instead of calling us "bitches" or "difficult" or "demanding," please throw your arms to heaven and thank God that our child, your student, your patient has a person in their life who loves them so much they are willing to carry these stigmas freely and gladly.

Be thankful that you have an educated, invested parent who's desperate to work with you—in the career that *you* chose—to get the best and most out of their child.

Yes, I know not all of us are as nice or courteous or patient—and I know I've had my moments—but most of us do try very hard to be kind.

But being truly kind means we have to be honest, which is not always easy. Do you think we like to be the moms everyone talks about? Do you think we enjoy confrontation and awkward conversations with grown adults? Come on. We didn't ask for this role. We were given this role, and we have learned to embrace this role. But more importantly you need to understand that when you give us this stigma, those around you feed off of it and may judge us unfairly, which could ultimately affect our children's education or the care they receive or the way you view them. If you are working in a school district, please, for the love of God, do not "warn" other schools about what you consider "bitch" moms. It is degrading and wrong, not to mention immoral and unethical, and it hurts our children. Please. *Help a sister out.*

And now, back to the mommas. Listen to me. Enough is enough. *Stop apologizing.* Stop being fake nice and fake sweet to people because you are scared they won't like you. Instead, work hard to be kind by always being honest. The kindest thing we can do—for our children and everybody who works with them—is to put it all on the table. Put it all out there—your heart, your feelings, your fears, your requests, your decisions, your opinions—without hesitation and as respectfully as you can. The more you make yourself relatable to the teachers and staff, the more they will respect you and your children.

And let this be your wake-up call: It is time we stop broken medical systems, broken special education systems, and broken societal systems from convincing us that our children are broken.

That night we decided that Isla would need to be transferred to another district. I was sick about this because this district was awesome in so many ways. It was perfect for June, and the Special Olympics program was stellar, but the teachers and paras were not getting the support or training they needed in the classroom.

We decided to transfer both of our daughters to the district where Greg was employed. My husband had had a great experience with the administration there, and we'd heard great things over the course of the year, even from surrounding districts' personnel.

I went to meet with the director of special education services for this district, and as soon as introductions were over, I cut to the chase. "OK, so everyone says your special education program is so great. Why? Why are you guys so innovative and other districts are not?"

His answer was spot on. "Most districts hire administrative positions without regard to their backgrounds. But the last four directors here, including myself, have extensive special education backgrounds within classrooms, as diagnosticians, etc. So we know what is lacking, what is needed, and what to change, and we are more receptive to teacher requests for resources because we have been there too. We know the value of sensory rooms in each unit. We know the value of extra paraprofessionals and extra training. We know the value of all-inclusive playgrounds and events for special education students."

Sold.

I have never liked the phrase, "I have a passion for teaching". You see, as a parent of both a special education child and a regular education child, I have realized that I don't want my kids to have teachers with a *passion for teaching*. I want teachers who have *compassion for people*. I want teachers who feel a strong conviction to help someone learn, regardless of how inconvenient it is. I want teachers who will go out of their comfort zones, throw their pride aside, and deviate from the curriculum that has worked for a hundred kids before if it doesn't work for mine.

If you have this kind of calling and this kind of heart, please consider special education sometime in your career. You never know when you may get an "Isla" of your own in your classroom and become instrumental in a family's story.

There is a quote that is thought to have come from Albert Einstein that says, "There are only two ways to live your life: as though nothing is a miracle, or as though everything is a miracle." I truly believe that, without my Isla Love in my life, I may not have realized the miracle it was to hear June read for the first time. I may not have looked twice at those beautiful red check marks on June's homework, because I would have expected nothing less. I may not have been so overjoyed as Major took his first steps at only nine months or cheered like a fool when he said his first word, "banana," at ten months. And I definitely would not have realized the miracle that a simple conversation can be.

Isla has taught me humility, gratitude, patience, kindness, tolerance, and wonder, and I wouldn't want to know a life without her.

It honestly scares me to think what kind of person I would be today if it weren't for her.

As we prepared to move Isla to yet another school, it was very important for my sanity to shift perspective and realize that our journey will never be over. Isla's story doesn't really have an ending, and I don't want it to end. I still have nights where I am terrorized with fear of what the future might bring for Isla and all of us. I still have to practice incredible patience as Isla changes her mood and mind constantly. I have learned that, to live my best, richest, and happiest life, I need to stop *accepting* Isla and start truly *embracing* her—all of her. Being Isla's mom requires grit, and it requires grit for life.

I am writing this last paragraph on the evening of Isla's tenth birthday. I am filled with gratitude for her life and honored to have been chosen to be her mom. Today, as we sang to her and I watched the candle light from her ten birthday candles bounce off her beautiful hazel eyes, I realized that this girl is everything I'd dreamed of. She is 100% supermodel gorgeous, with legs like Gisele. She has hair like Julia Roberts in *Pretty Woman*, though it's brown and not red. She is a genius in the sense that she has taught herself since birth to cope with an incredibly unique diagnosis that no one could figure out for ten years. She is an athlete who won first place this year in every sport she attempted but one. She has mad talent and can out dance you all night long. We have spent our days and our lives in special programs looking for ways to challenge her and keep her involved in activities and to provide her the most incredible opportunities in life. We have traveled with her to help her become well rounded despite living in a small town. And, oh, Isla does have the biggest heart and the most beautiful spirit. I would like to think that, by sharing her story, she will contribute to the world in some tremendous way.

If she could have, Isla probably would have told me from the beginning that she never needed a light bulb. She has always been a girl on fire.

Letter from the Author

First, let me say thank you for making it all the way through this thing! I hope this book has changed your perspective and left you with some powerful lessons and takeaways, but I wanted to explain that I did not intend this to be a self-help book or a how-to guide. That would be impossible for me to write based on Isla's diagnosis, which is so unique, generally unrecognized, and so specific to her. The tools I might suggest and the advice I might give would differ so much depending on the family, the resources available to them, their geographic location, the specific need they have for their child, and so many more factors.

My initial intent—and the goal I considered with each page and section and anecdote—was simply to tell our family's story to my own children, who were too young to understand it all at the time. However, I do want to selfishly share one small "How to" segment now, while I still have your attention.

How to Support a Family living with a PDA/Autism/Special Needs child

<u>Educate yourself</u>. You cannot—I repeat—you cannot *fully* support a family that has a child with any special need if you don't know anything about it. I honestly feel that to be one of my closest friends and share this life with me and my family, you have to educate yourself on Isla's diagnoses or at least know our story.

Otherwise, there's no way to *fully* understand and support me, my husband, my children, our lives or our decisions.

Be respectful. I don't care if you are young or old, formally educated or not, a doctor or my BFF, the most renowned special education expert or a rookie parent. Please respect my knowledge about PDA/autism in my little girl. Nobody knows her like I do, and it has taken years of researching, studying, reading, trial and error, doctor visits, exams, therapy, ARDs, prayer, and hands-on experience for me to become an Isla expert. I can only imagine this holds true for many other families. It is demeaning and downright degrading when an educator/doctor/therapist, etc. who does not know my daughter at all takes one look and presumes to understand her needs better than I do. This insinuates I am wrong, uninformed, selfish, or clueless. Not cool. And there's nothing more annoying than when people put my little girl in a box based on their one, fictional experience with autism. "Isla is autistic? Gosh I would never have guessed. She seems so high functioning. Have you seen *The Good Doctor*? Isla is going to be a doctor, I just know it." Oh, people, this is why a single story is so problematic.

Don't compare us. It is super important not to compare one family's struggles with another's. I never know how to respond when someone says, "Well, at least Isla doesn't have cancer." Really? I mean really?

First of all I have seen cancer ravage through my family, and I cannot even begin to fathom the fear, desperation, loss, sadness, depression, helplessness, and destruction that a family feels when one of their children has cancer. But still, don't you see the danger in this comparison? How is it helpful to trivialize and minimize someone's struggles, hardships, and challenges this way?

Yes, you are right. Isla doesn't have cancer, and I praise God every day for healthy children. But that doesn't mean we don't matter, or that we're wrong for feeling sad and scared. Trust me. I am sure that most families with special needs children are acutely aware of how much worse it could be. In fact, that reality may help them cope. But please, please don't make us feel like ungrateful complainers.

Love on these families. Never underestimate the needs of a family living with a special needs child. They probably do a very good job hiding the fact that their day-to-day life is extremely challenging, and it's likely they desperately need friends and family who are willing to get gritty with them. Remember my battles with the impossible karate gloves? It was one of my closest friends who said, "Lisa, who cares about the rules? Just put on the gloves before class." She could have said, "Oh yeah, that sucks," or "Eek, I bet that is embarrassing." But no. She got gritty with me and helped me troubleshoot. It's that simple. You don't even have to get dirty to play.

I think I can speak for most parents with special needs children when I say that we don't want your pity. We want your kindness. We don't need your sad puppy dog eyes or your evil eyes or your rolling eyes when our children are not behaving as you expect. We need your encouragement. We don't need negativity or fake friends. We need friends who are genuine and lift us up. So the next time you see or visit a friend or family member who has a child with special needs or see a "special" parent struggling in a store or restaurant, show them compassion. Give them a smile, hug them, and tell them they are doing a great job. If you really have time, show them patience, and allow them to share their story. Everyone has one. And if you are a true go-getter, take time to teach your children the same tolerance and compassion for everyone they meet.

Acknowledgments

<u>"Eileen", "Lorraine", "Michelle", and "Coach Alan"</u>

You rock. You just totally rock. No one else listens to—much less becomes genuinely invested in—my crazy ideas or crazy life. The way you have cheered me on through this whole process sometimes makes me weepy. Your collective hearts are big enough to save the world, one sand dollar kiddo at a time.

<u>Dad and Mom</u>

Your initial reaction to this book was my first indication that I had something special on my hands. Thank you for loving us the way you do.

<u>June</u>

You are the star. You are the unsung hero. You are more than I could have ever dreamed of. You amaze me daily, and you make me so darn proud it hurts.

<u>Major</u>

My strong son. I don't know what I did to deserve to be your momma. You are hands down the wonder of my life.

<u>Greg</u>

On one of the most romantic cards my husband has ever given me he wrote, "You are my game-winning, walk-off homerun." (If you don't understand this, then you aren't a sports fan, which is fine.) Greg, you are my A+. You are my big red check mark and my 100 with a smiley face. (If you don't understand this, then you aren't a nerd, which is fine.) You are our coach, our leader, and our calm in all the storms. There is something so unique and special about a guy who has loved the same girl through all of the seasons of her life and never wavered. I have never taken that for granted.

<u>Isla</u>

Oh Isla the places we have been and the places we will go. This book is my love story for you. You may never be able to read it, but I will do all I can to make sure the world does. Some way, somehow, you will know what an impact you have made and continue to make in so many lives.

To every other person mentioned in this book...you know who you are. Regardless of whether your part was positive or negative, big or small, you too were used for good in Isla's life and mine. Thank you.

About the Author

Dr. Lisa Peña is a Today Show Parenting Team contributor and the founder of The M.o.C.h.A.(TM) Tribe which stands for (M)oms (o)f (C)hildren that (h)ave (A)utism. She is the author behind The M.o.C.h.A. Tribe Diaries which is a website/blog devoted to squashing the idea that autism has a single story. Dr. Peña is a proud coach's wife, a clinical pharmacist, passionate public speaker and a busy mom of three who happily resides in South Padre Island, TX.

For more information, speaking inquiries, questions or to connect with the author please visit:

www.mochatribediaries.com

waitingforthelightbulb@gmail.com

Made in the USA
San Bernardino, CA
08 December 2018